— *The* —
LOUISIANA
FIELD GUIDE

— The —
LOUISIANA
FIELD GUIDE

UNDERSTANDING LIFE IN THE PELICAN STATE

EDITED BY

RYAN ORGERA & WAYNE PARENT

LOUISIANA STATE UNIVERSITY PRESS

BATON ROUGE

Published by Louisiana State University Press
Copyright © 2014 by Louisiana State University Press
All rights reserved
Manufactured in the United States of America
First printing

Designer: Barbara Neely Bourgoyne
Typefaces: Brandon Printed, display; Whitman, text
Printer and binder: Maple Press

LIBRARY OF CONGRESS CATALOGING-IN-PUBLICATION DATA

The Louisiana field guide : understanding life in the Pelican State /
edited by Ryan Orgera and Wayne Parent.

pages cm

Includes bibliographical references and index.

ISBN 978-0-8071-5776-3 (cloth : alkaline paper) — ISBN 978-0-8071-5777-0
(pdf) — ISBN 978-0-8071-5778-7 (epub) — ISBN 978-0-8071-5779-4 (mobi)
1. Louisiana. I. Orgera, Ryan, 1983– II. Parent, Wayne, 1955–
F369.L8845 2014
976.3—dc23

2014005846

The paper in this book meets the guidelines for permanence and
durability of the Committee on Production Guidelines for Book
Longevity of the Council on Library Resources.
∞

For Melli
&
For the Luquette, Parent, Rivière, and Windom families;
thank you for making me part of your "Louisianas."

—RO

For my brothers Dale and Randy:
they're as awesome as the state we love.

—WP

CONTENTS

PREFACE

RYAN ORGERA

As Wayne and I discussed the idea that would become this volume, we
knew we did not want to produce another book about Louisiana that
"pined for yore." Rather, it had to be a timely collection that was both
organic and ordered; creative and succinct; and above all honest. Our
goal remains a pertinent exploration of a multifaceted Louisiana written by local experts who recognize that we have so much to celebrate
and to experience here. *The Louisiana Field Guide* offers portraits of the
state that challenge, reaffirm, and elucidate for locals, newcomers, and
visitors alike.

Our state is one that enjoys a larger-than-life image. Even outside of
its borders, the word *Louisiana* conjures images of thrown beads, king
cakes, hurricanes, corruption, and bayous. Louisiana was the eighteenth
state admitted to the Union, yet despite its long history as part of the
United States, it has retained much of its singularity. Its histories are often framed by French, Spanish, or English colonial struggles; its politics
is peppered with their vestiges; its cultures live and re-create their traditions; and its languages are part of this flux. We have rich and painful
connections to West Africa and to pre-European peoples, and they, too,
create our contemporary Louisiana. Louisianians celebrate the past like
no others. Tradition thrives in every jambalaya pot, on the street signs
of Breaux Bridge, and on the farmland of East Carroll Parish. Louisiana
is a land where we rejoice in our roots in churches, jazz clubs, and Tiger
Stadium. For hundreds of years, we have celebrated Mardi Gras and lit
fires on the levees for Christmas Eve, and at times when celebration

seemed futile or impossible, we have found a way to use our traditions as a means to move forward. Our blithe spirit is not how we mask our travails; it is how we remake and express our histories. Heritage is our grandest asset.

These ways of life unfurl over a land and shore equally singular. Few places have such a bewitching landscape as Louisiana. While we do not boast the mountain vistas of Wyoming or the long, sandy stretches of Florida, we do have spaces and places that inspire a feeling distinctly Louisianian. From the marshes, that pseudo-land between the Gulf of Mexico's waters and more solid soils; to the Atchafalaya Basin, a great carved mass of trees, water, bears, and birds; to the loblolly pinescapes of west and north Louisiana, this state is truly a natural wonder. The often close, small-sky vistas of south Louisiana are marked by ancient, gnarled live oaks that sprouted before the arrival of the first Europeans. In crowded cypress groves, arrow-straight trees filter sunlight amid the profound stillness, interrupted only by a passing heron or the slink of a turtle into our ubiquitous waters. Our landscapes are the products of ancient struggle and process, of primordial geologic and hydrologic movements; they set the stage for a people marked by ancient and concurrent forces.

There is an ineffable quality here, one for which words often fall short to describe the essence of our landscapes, traditions, shared spirit. Our origins, be they Angolan, French, Spanish, or Vietnamese, have rubbed against each other and melded. While we could easily focus on the tragedies that have befallen our state, we have chosen instead in this volume to celebrate how Louisiana expresses itself, be it an expression born from pain or complexity, joy or necessity. The expressions herein pay homage to the curious, the unique, and the unheard in us all. Enjoy this collection, as it represents parts of all of those who truly have known this Pelican State.

ACKNOWLEDGMENTS

This volume is a collaboration, and we appreciate the good work of all the individual authors and the lasting friends we have made in the process. We would also like to acknowledge the efforts of Dustin Howes, whose photos appear in several essays. Dustin's good eye, technical skills, and willingness to meet our needs added joy and real value to this undertaking. Gabe Giffin, who also contributed a photo, worked with us from the beginning, formulating ideas and keeping us enthused. Gabe played an important supportive role throughout. Finally, we would like to thank Andrew Joyner for his contribution of cartography and ideas throughout this process.

— The —
LOUISIANA
FIELD GUIDE

SHAPING LOUISIANA
OUR GEOGRAPHY AND ENVIRONMENT

— ✦ —

THE GEOGRAPHY OF LOUISIANA
KENT MATHEWSON

At a time when some argue that globalization is making the world "flat," through hyper-connectivity and declining cultural diversity, one of geography's main concepts and building blocks—regions—remains a useful way to put people, places, and landscapes in perspective. Topographically speaking, Louisiana may be largely flat, but its diverse peoples, places, and landscapes form a number of regions that are far from featureless. As other essays in this volume make abundantly clear, Louisiana is a place—if not quite a world—apart. Yet, Louisiana shares in larger physical and human geographical patterns that belie complete uniqueness. The state's distinctive geographical traits are best seen and understood within the web of these larger connections. Geography has often been cast as the stage upon which History performs. In the case of Louisiana, its diverse geographies can be seen as the play itself, with history in a supporting role. Geography provides the regional construct to understand differences between places, landscapes, and areas. Louisiana viewed through its regions and their characteristics allows for clear demarcation of its many familiar particularities as well as indications of less recognized similarities with other places or regions.

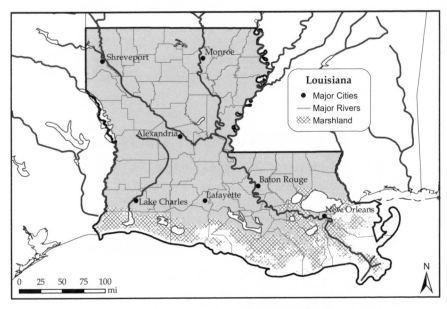

Fig. 1.1. The general geography of Louisiana. *Andrew Joyner*

NATURAL REGIONS

Looking at Louisiana on the continental scale, one can easily envision it as the nation's drain. True, the Mississippi River is Louisiana's most prominent physical feature. It bisects the state, and its delta and mouth both distribute and discharge a continent's worth of water and sediment. But Louisiana and its physical landscapes are much more than just a mighty river and its immense contents. At the state level, looking at the shape of Louisiana, one might easily see a boot. This image is well worn, but not very useful for more than simple locational references: "marsh lands occupy the lower toe part of the boot," or "the sole of the boot is wearing away due to coastal erosion." A more nuanced picture needs to be drawn, one that takes into account not only Louisiana's distinct regional formations, but also something of the processes that brought them into being.

In physical geographic terms, Louisiana's landscapes are relatively recent formations, especially as one travels from north to south. Along its southern margin, today Louisiana is more a work in regress than progress due to sea level rise, subsidence, and silt starvation. Louisiana resides at the base of the Mississippi Embayment, the great floodplain region on either side of the Mississippi River up to the confluences of the Ohio and Missouri Rivers. The origins of this great north/south corridor date to more than 500 million years ago.

By the time humans made their way south into Louisiana, some 10,000 years ago, they encountered varied environments rich in natural resources. These earliest Louisianians were strictly hunters and gatherers, and the bounty of the lands and waters was such that the adoption of agriculture arrived late in Louisiana—after it was well established upriver. The earliest arrivals would have encountered, hunted, and perhaps extirpated the remarkable menagerie of remnant prehistoric megafauna. Giant bison and beavers, mammoths, and other large animals fell to spear-point and fire-drive techniques. But most mammals, birds, reptiles, and fish survived and, combined with wild fruits, nuts, and seeds, provided easily harvested, protein-rich diets.

The first hunter-foragers came to know and inhabit Louisiana's main natural regions. In the north half of the state, the Tertiary hills is the dominant landform region. Below Alexandria, the Tertiary hills give way to more recently emerged Pleistocene terraces. These natural terraces form two disjoined regions of lesser uplands on either side of the Atchafalaya Basin and Mississippi Alluvial Plain. South of these regions are the coastal plains—the Chenier in the west and the Deltaic in the east. The shifting and increasingly ephemeral off-shore barrier islands complete the regional cast, with many post-dating the arrival of people in the uplands. Thus, as one almost imperceptibly rises in elevation going from south to north, the more one descends noticeably in geologic time. From coastal sands, to marshes and relic beach ridges, to terraced prairies and piney woods, to upland forests and alluvial plains, some sixty million years of geomorphic history is exposed and displayed. And over the past ten thousand years, each region has offered its human occupants a varied set of resource opportunities. The original inhabitants may have been mobile upland hunters, but their hunter-gatherer descendants became more sedentary as the aquatic resources of river, bayou, swamp, and marsh encouraged concentrations. When agriculture finally appeared, quite possibly from upriver, the adopters were already largely settled, tending their waterfowl blinds, fish weirs, turtle traps, and shellfish mines. The population had shifted from dispersed seasonal camps to favored waterside sites; from hill to plain, with this regional preference persisting through all subsequent human occupations up to the present.

The two major landform regions, the Uplands and the Lowlands, with their hills and terraces, plains and deltaic formations, also have differentiated collections of soils and vegetation, hydrologic systems, and to some extent climates. Together with landform types, these differing features provide the basis for the state's landscape variations. For example, one of the most distinctive of the Lowland landscapes is the cheniers (French for "place of the oaks"). Occupying the southwestern-most coastal plain, these very recently formed ridges—topped with live oaks and separated by swales that are often inundated—support abundant wildlife. Human occupancy has been mediated by the intermingling of land and water, mostly limiting subsistence activities to hunting and fishing. Ridge and swale alternately serve as refuges for humans and beasts alike. They afford high ground in times of hurricanes, or a first respite for migrating songbirds crossing the Gulf from Central America. The low grounds give aquatic life seasonal opportunities along with varied habitat options. At the opposite side of the state, along the northeast edge, are the Mississippi River loess landscapes. In contrast to the sandy cheniers, the loess land soils are among the richest in the state and were a mainstay of Upland cotton cultivation. These are but two of the more than two dozen eco-regions that constitute Louisiana's varied landscapes.

While each eco-region has its characteristics, Louisiana's climate has a more general occurrence with certain distinctions between the north and south. The north half of the state generally experiences higher maximal temperatures in summer than south Louisiana, often by 5 or more degrees, and correspondingly colder winter temperatures, by the same variance. In the north, rainfall averages some 10 to 15 inches less than in the south; snow flurries, if not snowfall, are usually an annual event, whereas they are a once-in-a-decade rarity "south of I-10." Many tropical and semitropical crops can be grown with care in Louisiana's southern-tier parishes, whereas they are errant experiments elsewhere. Extreme weather events visit Louisiana on a regular basis, but the north-south regional divide is evident here as well. Tropical storms hit Louisiana most years, with major hurricanes wreaking widespread death and destruction about every decade. These named events serve as historical markers in the popular consciousness, segmenting the remembered past into peaks of extreme distress and intervening periods of generalized placidity. The coast generally bears the brunt, though select storm tracks can exact devastation all the way to Louisiana's northern borders and beyond. Louisiana also lies at the base of "Dixie Alley," a funnel-shaped region of heightened tornadic occurrence. Generally less predictable, and more localized, tornados regularly threaten districts but rarely whole regions in Louisiana.

Flooding also occurs locally in the wake of extreme weather events, especially heavy rainstorms. Louisiana's rivers are routinely held at bay by constructed levees, but once every few decades—witness the near levee-topping Mississippi levels of 2011—they break loose and join hurricanes and tornados as potential or actual "natural disasters." Beyond the horizons of historical memory or everyday consciousness lurk other possible major environmental disruptions. Louisiana is not completely immune from earthquake activity. Though Louisiana has not experienced recorded earthquakes comparable to the massive New Madrid (Missouri) earthquake in 1811–1812, it has had lesser events. Perhaps best remembered is the 1930 earthquake that damaged buildings and alarmed citizens in and around Napoleonville. The results of climate change are less speculative. According to many scientists, the barrier islands and much of the southern tier of parishes will disappear beneath rising Gulf waters, with the effects compounded by the subsiding land. In most scenarios, by 2100 Louisiana's climate will be warmer by 3–7 degrees F., and extreme weather events (tornados, hurricanes, and rain storms) will increase in both intensity and frequency.

SETTLEMENT PATTERNS AND REGIONALIZATION

Despite—and in some cases because of—its environmental adversities, past and present, Louisiana has afforded a succession of migrants a stage on which to arrive, set down roots, and usually prosper. Iconic species such as the alligator, snapping turtle and garfish, and the bald cypress tree have inhabited Louisiana's rivers and swamps for millions of years. At the other end of the time range, often revealed as roadkill, the opossum (10,000 years ago), armadillo (c. 1900–1920), and nutria (c. 1930s) are progressively recent settlers arrived from tropical America. New species continue to arrive, often vexing humans and their environs. Kudzu from Asia and water hyacinth from South America decamped after display in nineteenth-century commercial fairs, whereas fire ants, Formosa termites, and Tiger mosquitoes came as commercial stowaways from South America and Asia. Against this backdrop of shifting assemblages of plants and animals—with many species residing in all the state's regions, others securing more local identities—came the first human settlers. This was coincident with the end of the Ice Ages and rapidly changing environments. Hunter-gatherer populations typically grow, if at all, at "glacial" paces. Louisiana's Upland folk were no exception, but those Lowlanders living off aquatic protein sources may have managed healthy

Fig. 1.2. Indian mound/midden at Louisiana State University. *Dustin Howes*

increases. The immense mollusk-shell middens and deposits archaeologists have excavated in coastal zones testify to demographic growth. In the process, these shell gatherers were also literal land builders.

It was Louisiana's first farmers, however, that began to domesticate and transform landscapes in the sedentary ways that would later be appropriated by European immigrants and their African captives for settlement, subsistence, and commodity crop production. Plains and adjacent uplands provided the best lands for both prehistoric and historic settlement and farming. The first farmers are known today from their ceramic remains along with other artifacts. They go by the names of locations where these traits and traces were first unearthed. Beginning about 2000 BCE, some indigenous groups began to cultivate plants, and as time passed, agriculture became more important. By the time the first Europeans visited Louisiana's shores, or made a few forays into the interior in the sixteenth century—such as Hernando de Soto's ill-fated *entrada*—a number of groups were well established, living in villages often with ceremonial structures and extensive agricultural plots. Distinct territories had evolved, with different tribes of linguistically related peoples occupying different regions or parts of the state.

Although Louisiana was part of the Spanish Empire through most of the sixteenth and seventeenth centuries, Spanish interest and occupation were effectively nil. At the end of the 1600s, French explorers coming south from French Canada, the Great Lakes, and the Upper Mississippi region began to lay claim to Louisiana. Almost all of these penetrations were restricted to rivers. By the 1720s, the French had established settlements at Natchitoches (1714) and New Orleans (1718), both favored sites along the state's two main rivers—the Red and the Mississippi. Natchitoches was founded as an interior Uplands defensive outpost fronting the Spanish settlement frontier in east Texas. New Orleans was founded in a defensive position too, but as an inland urban monitor of the Mississippi's entrance. New Orleans immediately became the Lowland metropole. By the end of its first French tenure a half century later, it was among French America's major urban centers along with Quebec City and Cap-Français (now Cap-Haïtien). Lowland Louisiana, via the Mississippi to the north and the Gulf to the south, became

Fig. 1.3. Mississippi River at Baton Rouge. *Dustin Howes*

an active part of the far-flung Atlantic World. West Africa sent enchained labor to plantations in New Orleans's near hinterlands by way of Havana and Cap-Français. European workshops and wineries brought fine and finished goods to the Crescent City's levee. In return, Lowland Louisiana sent indigo, tobacco, and increasingly cane sugar into the Atlantic networks. During the four decades of Spanish tenure (1763–1803) the flows continued, but Seville, Havana, Vera Cruz, and, amazingly, remote Manila became alternate nodes. Toward the end of the eighteenth century the trickle of trade up and down the Mississippi became a rill and later a torrent. At its antebellum apex, New Orleans was the premier city in the American South and second largest port in the United States, and according to some estimates, it was the wealthiest city after New York and Philadelphia.

Settlement patterns from colonial times through the antebellum period reflect in part trade and commercial patterns, though other forces were also at work both reducing the native inhabitants and inducing settlers with other than strictly pecuniary objectives. The sifting and settling of people with differing cultural and ethnic backgrounds were often registered in regional terms. Many of these patterns persist to the present. We will never know precisely how many native peoples lived in Louisiana when the first European arrived, nor their regional groupings. That many died, perhaps more than 50 percent, due to disease introduced during the first two centuries of colonial claims and occupation is certain. After French settlement began in the 1720s, the remaining native peoples largely lost their homelands. Today there are five main groups or tribes: the Coushatta (Koasati), Choctaw, Chitimacha, Houma, and Tunica-Biloxi. The Chitimacha and Houma inhabit marsh, swamp, and bayou areas in the southern tier of parishes. Choctaw groups are dispersed in south and central parts of the state, and the Coushatta and Tunica-Biloxi have small territories in south and central Louisiana, respectively. Only the Chitimacha can claim residence where their ancestors lived at the outset of colonial times. Other Louisiana native peoples have been part of the movement and migration flow that brought subsequent ethnic groups to rest in particular locales and regions.

At the dawn of New World discovery, the Spanish laid claim to the territory now comprising Louisiana with the Treaty of Tordesillas (1494), yet this land remained sight unseen by Europeans until 1519, when Alvarez de Piñeda sailed the coast from east to west. For the next century and a half Louisiana appeared on maps as part of Spanish Florida, but Spanish colonization never materialized. It was left to the French to explore, name, and colonize the area. René-Robert Cavelier, Sieur de LaSalle, a prosperous Canadian fur trader and explorer, claimed and named Louisiana for King Louis XIV in 1682 after descending the Mississippi to its mouth. This act established French claim and control of the Mississippi Valley, a wedge between English colonies to the east and Spanish to the west and east (Florida) until 1763. Accordingly, the flow of colonists over the next century came mostly from France, the French Caribbean, and Canada, and through French-sponsored ventures that brought Alsatian and Swiss Germans to establish farms west and east of New Orleans along the Mississippi—the "German Coast."

Anticipating territorial losses to England with the end of the Seven Years' War and the Treaty of Paris in 1763, France transferred its Louisiana territories to Spain in 1762. Unlike France, Spain recruited few colonists from the homeland or Hispanic America, but it did attract Canary Islanders ("Isleños") and French-speaking Acadians ("Cajuns") to help open up new colonization zones. The Isleños settled in the coastal marshes southeast of New Orleans, where they still maintain concentrations, and on the frontier with British West Florida along Bayou Manchac. The Acadians colonized the largely open levee lands along Bayous Lafourche and Teche, west of the Mississippi. This remains a core area of Cajun culture and settlement, though in the nineteenth century French and Anglo planters often displaced Cajuns from the best lands, prompting them to disperse widely into the marshes, swamps, and prairies of southern Louisiana. With Louisiana part of the global Spanish imperial network, exotic implantations occurred. Filipinos, or "Manila men," jumped ship from time to time and established fishing colonies deep in the coastal marshes, and in small numbers Mexicans from New Spain began what today has become perhaps the largest immigrant stream. They mainly settled between the Sabine River and Natchitoches, where remnants of this Spanish or Mexican heritage continue to be celebrated. During the Spanish period, "Americans," or settlers from the British colonies and then the United States, filtered in from the north and east. These Anglos were outsiders in the Gallic-Hispanic colonial context but became pretenders overnight to cultural and political dominance once the Louisiana Purchase was ratified in 1803. Prior to this, nodes of Anglo concentrations had begun to coalesce in the parishes of West Florida and selected outposts in the northern half of the state.

Under both French and Spanish colonial regimes, and into the first decades of the American period, the largest ethnic groups were not of European origin. In aggregate, native peoples continued to have the largest population of any group until Louisiana statehood in 1812, though they were increasingly marginalized and suffering steady population decline. Even more robust was the African-descended population. Except during the first two decades of colonization, Afro-Louisianians outnumbered the Euro-descended population until after the Civil War. Of this group the largest number were slaves, the majority from the West African Senegambian region, where they had been skilled agriculturalists and artisans, or in some cases literate urban dwellers. In addition, significant numbers of free blacks, or *gens de couleur libres*, emerged, and after the Haitian Revolution (1791–1804) some six thousand free people of color arrived in Louisiana to constitute a caste apart from and between black and white ethnic distinctions. Usually these free people of color were of mixed African and European ancestry. Latin colonial perspectives offered a more nuanced view of racial and ethnic realities than were admitted or permitted by Anglo consciousness. Free Afro-French Creoles were concentrated in certain neighborhoods and wards in New Orleans but were more generally dispersed through the black population in other parts of the state. Discrete populations of Afro-French Creoles formed on either side of the Atchafalaya Basin in Pointe Coupée and St. Landry Parishes. Enslaved Africans and their emancipated descendants (after 1865) were and continue to be concentrated in former plantation areas of the Lowlands and the urban centers of the state. New Orleans remains a black-majority city, though it has lost more than 15 percent of its Afro-descended population since Katrina.

Nineteenth-century Louisiana saw some shifts in its cultural and economic regionalization, but patterns laid down in the colonial period continued to form and inform its landscape evolutions. Antebellum economic development pushed plantation production of commodities for the world market, chiefly sugar and cotton, to new heights. By the 1850s, Louisiana, like Saint-Domingue a century earlier, had become one of the most profitable places on earth. But like its twin in the Caribbean, Louisiana's wealth only selectively rested in place, and then was shattered in rebellion. Both areas became metaphors for differing degrees of poverty and underdevelopment—one a zombified pariah stumbling toward an ever-receding modernity, the other a carnival jester dancing in place while bemusing a disapproving national audience.

Antebellum New Orleans's ethnic geography was also enriched by new infusions of German and Irish immigrants, creating new ethnic neighborhoods. In the post–Civil War period large numbers of Italian immigrants arrived, many of them replacing blacks in the cane and cotton fields. And like blacks, many Italians gravitated to Louisiana's cities once freed from agricultural labor. During America's great Age of Immigration (1880s–1920), Louisiana, mainly through New Orleans, received its share of new workers, though unlike in the North, employment opportunities were more in the primary sector—farm, forest, fishery, and mine rather than in industry. Croatians and Slovenians came to harvest shellfish and, like the Isleños, established communities in the marshes south and east of New Orleans as well as in the city. Immigrants did not arrive solely by sea. Significant numbers of Anglos, especially Scots-Irish Upland southerners, continued the infilling of the northern and Florida parishes that they had begun in the colonial period. Even today, one of the most common generalizations made about Louisiana's regional identity divides the state into the Anglo/Protestant North and the Latin/Catholic South. A small but significant number of midwestern farmers settled on the south-central prairies to raise rice and other grains. Place names such as Iowa, and their distinctive house-type, the "I House," mark this immigration episode. Since the 1960s, when the immigration gates were selectively open again, a few notable ethnic additions and enclaves have developed. In the late 1970s' wake of the Vietnam War, Louisiana became a prime destination for Vietnamese refugees. The Vietnamese have adapted well to south Louisiana, focusing their attention on the harvesting, processing, and wholesale as well as retail sale of seafood. Versailles, the main Vietnamese enclave in New Orleans East, is a superb example of cultural landscape distinctiveness, and the rebuilding of the community after Hurricane Katrina offers an equally good study in cultural cohesiveness and purpose.

The most recent chapter in Louisiana's evolving ethnic settlement geography is in some ways the oldest, save for its original indigenous inhabitants. Migrants from Latin America are making good on the promissory that Spanish cartographic claims made five hundred years ago but that were never really fulfilled. Since banana boats forged links between Honduras and New Orleans more than a century ago, Hondurans have made Louisiana an immigration destination. Over the same period, other Hispanic nationals have made their way to, and often quite successfully in, Louisiana. Most have opted for residence in New Orleans or the southern half of the state. Curiously, the wave of Latino immigrants flooding parts of both the Upper and Deep South in the past two or three decades largely leap-frogged over Louisiana. Katrina changed all that. Louisiana is now a major destination. It is perhaps too early to forecast what geographic changes and configurations this will yield, but it is probably safe to assume that south Louisiana with its Catholic heritage and larger population centers will serve as the main recipient.

— ✦ —

THE TIE THAT BINDS: LOUISIANA'S NATURAL RICHES

A. RAYNIE HARLAN and DAVID P. HARLAN

In Louisiana, our identity as a state hinges largely on the natural setting. The dynamic spectrum of environments, from inland rivers and
floodplains to the coastal marsh, sustains a rich diversity of wildlife and
plants and supports the livelihood of thousands of people who depend
financially on the state's abundant natural resources. The duality in our
relationship with nature is especially apparent in this state. We need its
environments and resources for our survival and well-being; its survival
depends on our responsible stewardship. And our efforts to conserve
the natural beauty and resources of Louisiana have an effect beyond the
state's borders; they are fundamentally intertwined with our need and
sense of duty to share our resources with the larger nation and world.

Enjoying and surviving off of nature, whether it be through hunting and
fishing, bird watching, photography, scientific research, or resource extraction, is and has been for centuries such a large constituent of life for the
people of Louisiana that it is difficult to tease out and define how nature
affects us and how important nature is to us as a community. We become
better citizens when we acknowledge the natural beauty that surrounds us
—it becomes a source of pride. But more than that, nature is in our souls;
it is a part of our framework. It is what makes Louisiana exceptional.

Before the arrival of European colonists, Louisiana was as dynamic
and untamed an environment as could be found anywhere in the United
States. It was a land ruled by water, that relentless force of nature that is
both creative and destructive. Mighty flowing rivers transported much
of the continent's water to the sea freely, and the sea accepted the contribution freely. The rich black earth supported quantities of plants, trees,
birds, reptiles, and mammals, while hundreds of fish and invertebrate
species clotted the dark bayous and turbid waters. The natural richness
of life on the land and in the waters was unfathomable and seemingly
inexhaustible.

The first settlers on this land knew the richness that it possessed. Sated on fish, turtle, deer, bear, and clams, the native peoples thrived. Early pioneers of this vast and bountiful wilderness learned to hunt and fish these waters, backswamps, and marshes. Native flora and fauna enriched the livelihood and culture of our ancestors. Generations of entrepreneurs revealed the countless treasures of this place, and the duality of our identity with nature began to form. Fur, fish, lumber, oil: at one time or another, Louisiana has supplied much of America with each of these natural resources. The Atchafalaya Basin, younger sister to the Mississippi Delta, once dense with 400-year-old bald cypress and Louisiana black bear, has felt the sting of ax and saw, hook and rifle. Many cypress that once towered in the swamp were milled and fitted to an Eastlake shotgun home in New Orleans. Marshes and bayous were severed by oil field canals. Discussing the importance of nature to Louisiana apart from the economic factor is like discussing the importance of religion without including the church.

Louisiana's natural environment provides a connection point to the past, to family traditions that span hundreds of years. It provides the

Fig. 1.4. Waddill Swamp. *Gabe Giffin*

foundation of life for many still today and reminds us that there is something bigger than ourselves. It provides a cathedral where everyone is welcome to worship regardless of political persuasion, race, gender, or education. The voices and wisdom of our ancestors reside in nature and can be invoked at any moment to offer peace and direction and to remind us of what is truly important in our lives.

Bird species, including the whooping crane, Bachman's sparrow, great blue heron, and the swallow tail kite, live and migrate through Louisiana yearly and utilize our natural environments as critical habitat. A significant number of naturalists and bird enthusiasts visit our state to observe these migrations. The brown pelican and the American alligator, which have just recently come back from a population decline, now thrive in Louisiana and serve as state symbols of strength and courage. The successful reintroduction of the Louisiana black bear is testament to the willingness of the Louisiana people to support and place great importance on the unique wildlife of the state. The cypress population has recently gained protection on state lands so that the once-flourishing forests can again stand as totems as they did in past centuries. Louisiana's nutrient-rich waters support unique fish species such as the alligator gar, redfish, Flagfin shiner, Bluehead shiner, the Louisiana pancake batfish, and the Gulf sturgeon. Many of these same species have fought a long battle with us against extirpation, reflecting the duality in our relations with nature that existed in the past and continues to exist today.

The identity, the connections, and the controversies imparted by the natural setting of Louisiana have molded this state into the vigorous and vibrant place that it is today. To define what nature means to the people of Louisiana is to define each individual resident throughout his/her past, present, and future. To the crawfisherman in the Atchafalaya Basin, nature provides a means of self-sufficiency. It provides a link to the lineage of his ancestors and to a tradition that is worn like a badge of honor. To the birder, nature is a source of excitement and competition but also of silence and stillness in the midst of a busy life. To the artist, nature offers inspiration and an ever-changing muse. To the engineer, it presents a challenge but is nevertheless a humbling force in the face of captivity. Nature is the tie that binds.

Fig. 1.5. Turkey Bayou, also known as Cross Bayou. *Raynie Harlan*

FURTHER READING

General Geography

Yodis, Elaine G., and Craig E. Colten. *Geography of Louisiana*. New York: McGraw-Hill, 2007.

Physical Geography

Kniffen, Fred B., and Sam B. Hilliard. *Louisiana: Its Land and People*. Baton Rouge: LSU Press, 1988.

Native Peoples

Kniffen, Fred B., Hiram F. Gregory, and George A. Stokes. *The Historic Indian Tribes of Louisiana: From 1542 to the Present*. Baton Rouge: LSU Press, 1987.

Settlement Geography

Newton, Milton B., Jr. *Louisiana: A Geographical Portrait*. Baton Rouge: Geoforensics, 1987.

Political Geography

Parent, Wayne. *Inside the Carnival: Unmasking Louisiana Politics*. Baton Rouge: LSU Press, 2004.

Historical Geography

Colten, Craig E., ed. *Transforming New Orleans and Its Environs: Centuries of Change*. Pittsburgh: University of Pittsburgh Press, 2000.

Goins, Charles Robert, and John Michael Caldwell. *Historical Atlas of Louisiana*. Norman: University of Oklahoma Press, 1995.

Historical Cartography

Lemmon, Alfred E., John T. Magill, and Jason R. Wiese, eds. *Charting Louisiana: Five Hundred Years of Maps*. New Orleans: Historic New Orleans Collection, 2003.

Historical Geography of New Orleans

Campanella, Richard. *Bienville's Dilemma: A Historical Geography of New Orleans*. Lafayette, LA: University of Louisiana at Lafayette, 2008.

Lewis, Peirce F. *New Orleans: The Making of an Urban Landscape*. Santa Fe, NM: Center for American Places, 2003.

LOUISIANA HISTORY

ALECIA P. LONG

It feels rather foolhardy to attempt a summary of Louisiana history in such a short space, but even a cursory look at the personalities and events that populated the colony's, the territory's, and then the state's history suggests a certain amount of bravado and recklessness might be appropriate to the task.

Groups of hunters, traders, and people of vision inhabited the area that became Louisiana long before Europeans arrived. Three thousand years before Spanish conquistadors appeared, Native Americans constructed an impressive compound on the banks of a relict course of the Mississippi River. They chose a spot for their settlement that protected them and their massive building project from annual floods. That site also allowed them to put their pirogues in the water at the foot of the nearby bluffs, allowing them to travel as far as the Ozarks and modern-day Illinois along continuous water routes. Today that site, located in East Carroll Parish, is called Poverty Point. When it was completed around 1500 BC, it was the largest and most complex compound of earthworks anywhere in North America. That is what I mean by people of vision.

On the eve of European arrival, there were about 70,000 Native Americans in the vicinity of modern Louisiana. Their first contacts with their would-be colonizers exposed them to diseases against which they had no resistance. Epidemic illness slashed their numbers in half by the time the French first attempted to settle the wild and watery environs that hugged the Gulf Coast.

René-Robert Cavelier, Sieur de LaSalle, had sufficient courage and ambition to offset his legendary surliness. Above all else, LaSalle wanted wealth and glory and, upon receiving permission from Louis XIV, sought to achieve these twinned goals through exploration of the great river that Father Jacques Marquette and Louis Joliet had located a decade earlier. Warnings about hostile Indians kept Marquette and Joliet from descending the river to its mouth. LaSalle pushed those warnings aside and, with the critical help of Indian guides, relocated the Mississippi and sailed to its mouth in the winter and spring of 1682. On April 9, somewhere in modern-day Plaquemines Parish, LaSalle made a hurried but vast claim and named it for his king and patron:

I, René-Robert Cavelier de La Salle, by virtue of His Majesty's commission, which I hold in my hands, and which may be seen by all whom it may concern, have taken and do now take, in the name of His Majesty and of his successors to the crown, possession of the country of Louisiana, the seas, harbours, ports, bays, adjacent straits, and all the nations, peoples, provinces, cities, towns, villages, mines, minerals, fisheries, streams and rivers, within the extent of the said Louisiana.

Even today, the claim is astounding in its breadth. But audacity was a key ingredient in LaSalle's early successes. After pushing himself and his men back up the river and to New France, LaSalle returned to Louis XIV's court, where he received permission to make a return trip with the goal of establishing permanent settlements. His second voyage would end not in glory but in ignominious defeat. Somehow—probably due to faulty navigation—LaSalle and his party missed the mouth of the Mississippi and wound up in Texas. Undeterred, LaSalle put up a makeshift settlement called Fort St. Louis and then, with a small group of men, began an overland trek to try to relocate the Mississippi. Privation combined with his well-known imperiousness led to a mutiny on the part of his men, who unceremoniously killed their leader somewhere in the Texas countryside on March 19, 1687. His dreams died with him, and it would take another dozen years before France would again attempt to settle its nascent claim.

In 1698 two ambitious brothers with roots in French Canada led the second settlement attempt. Pierre and Jean-Baptiste Le Moyne—known most commonly as the Sieurs Iberville and Bienville—sailed for Louisiana from LaRochelle, France, in the fall of 1698 and arrived in early 1699. The most durable of their early Louisiana settlements were actually in the modern-day states of Mississippi and Alabama. There, on the unpredictable coastline, several dozen men and boys began the arduous task of creating viable settlements on the marshy lowlands Iberville originally selected. Had it not been for local Native Americans, and Bienville's skill at finding ways to ingratiate himself with the local tribes, the first ragtag colonists probably would not have survived the early years. Iberville returned to France three times in the colony's infancy and, during his third return, was redirected to fight for France against the British in the Caribbean. He died there of mosquito-borne illness, and his younger brother, Bienville, became the de facto leader of the struggling colony.

While other men were dispatched from France to take control of the colonial enterprise, death, disease, and administrative infighting stymied development and left Bienville the only viable leader on the ground for much of the first two decades of the eighteenth century. Between 1712 and 1729 various profit-driven administrative schemes were tried—all of them directed from France by men who had no desire to go to Louisiana but ardently desired to make it a profitable concern.

The most infamous of these company men was John Law, a Scotsman who charmed and schemed his way into the favor of the French regent, the Duke d'Orléans. Law set up a gigantic pyramid scheme designed to attract investment in France's colonial holdings. Like the recent sub-par mortgage meltdown, the group of Law-inspired companies ultimately collapsed under the weight of Law's dubious promises and their flimsy financial underpinnings. Like a disgraced modern-day CEO, Law left France incognito and the Louisiana economy in ever more difficult financial straits.

Still, there were men and women, thousands of whom were forced migrants from the prisons of France and the slave jails of the West African coast, who kept the Louisiana experiment afloat throughout the 1720s. Near the end of that decade a greedy, foolhardy attempt to eject the Natchez from some of their richest lands ended in a surreptitious and skillful Native American uprising. Not surprisingly, the Natchez objected to being ordered out of their largest remaining villages so that two colonial officials could set up a massive tobacco plantation. On the morning of November 29, 1729, the Natchez executed their well-laid plans. The Indians infiltrated the nearby French fort and, within a few hours, killed 200 colonists and captured another 350. The so-called Natchez Massacre—one might also consider it a revolt—was a stunning but also short-term victory for the tribe. Within a year and with the help of Choctaw allies, the French overwhelmed the Natchez. By 1731 the last 500 members of the tribe had been rounded up and sold as slaves to the Caribbean. The French traded them for Africans, who they believed would be more compliant.

The French may have defeated the Natchez, but neglect from the homeland and ongoing conflicts with various native groups continued to thwart economic development. France, Spain, and England were at nearly constant warfare in these years. French and British enmity and competing geographic claims sparked open warfare on the North American continent in the 1750s. Known as the Seven Years' War *and* the French and Indian War, the conflict ended in the early 1760s. The final terms reached in the 1763 Treaty of Paris virtually eliminated France's colonial empire in North America. The Spanish, who knew Louisiana was a losing economic proposition, conceded to take the colony, in large part to keep it out of English hands, and to use it as a buffer zone to protect their still lucrative colonial holdings in Mexico from Anglo encroachment.

The Spanish did not, however, rush to take effective control of Louisiana. In fact, the Crown did not even send its first governor to the colony until 1766, and his brief tenure was a disaster. Antonio de Ulloa was an intelligent, refined man of science, but not a man of diplomatic skill. He was also allotted so few troops that he could undertake no serious military operation. With fewer than one hundred men at his disposal, he declined to take official possession of New Orleans and let the French flag continue to fly. The Louisiana colonists, who regarded themselves as French, were simultaneously used to and in some instances had come to prefer imperial neglect. They were suspicious that the Spanish might interfere in the make-do economic system they had cobbled together over the previous decades. In October 1768, led by a group of wealthy French Creole elites, a rowdy, intoxicated group of colonists ejected Ulloa from

New Orleans and symbolically rejected Spanish domination of Louisiana in what has come to be known as the 1768 Revolt.

Any elation or liberty the colonists acquired was short lived. The Spanish were not amused and the next year sent an Irish-born Spanish general named Alejandro O'Reilly, who sailed up the Mississippi and landed at New Orleans—this time with a force that rivaled the population of the city itself. O'Reilly executed or imprisoned the leaders of the 1768 Revolt, dismissed the French Creole–dominated Superior Council, and set up a Spanish colonial governing body. Only later would folks in Louisiana come to think of the Cabildo as just a building. Between 1769 and 1803 the Cabildo was the central governing body of the colony. O'Reilly's sojourn was brief but very effective. He firmly established Spanish control and sailed back to Spain, leaving behind a succession of less well known but generally pragmatic leaders who guided Louisiana in the final years of the eighteenth century.

Although the Spanish are sometimes considered the least significant of Louisiana's three colonial masters, it was during this period that the colony achieved the support and enlightened—even *laissez faire*—leadership it needed to achieve stability and begin to grow and prosper. The Spanish were particularly aggressive at seeking migrants to inhabit the colony. In fact, the largest numbers of Acadian settlers were brought to Louisiana during the Spanish period. These beleaguered refugees grew into one of the state's most characteristic and vibrant cultural groups, and they enhanced the colony's very durable French cultural identification, but it was the Spanish who facilitated their arrival and supported them economically in their lean early years. After 1787, the Spanish were even willing to accept English-speaking Anglos who wanted to move westward into the Louisiana backcountry, so long as they would swear loyalty to the Spanish Crown and the Catholic church.

In the early nineteenth century, France's ambitious post-Revolutionary leader, Napoleon Bonaparte, schemed and intimidated Spain into returning Louisiana to him. Napoleon dreamed of reestablishing French control of the once lucrative but unstable colony of Saint-Domingue. In order to make the island's plantation economy profitable again, Napoleon would have to betray the ideals of liberty, equality, and fraternity promised by the French Revolution and reestablish slavery on the island, which had been taken over by former slaves after a decade-long revolution of their own. The small leader's vast plans foundered when 80 percent of his army fell victim to disease on the island. After the failure of the Saint-Domingue expedition, Napoleon's need for Louisiana as a supply depot evaporated. Never one to waste a crisis, Napoleon surprised American envoys Robert Livingston and James Monroe by offering to sell all of Louisiana to the United States for a negotiated price of 80 million francs, about $15 million.

The American envoys who had been sent by Thomas Jefferson only to purchase New Orleans—and with it permanent access to the mouth of the Mississippi—took a chance and acted in a way that went far beyond their mandate and anything the U.S. Constitution anticipated or allowed. Who needed a Constitution anyway when offered the deal of a lifetime? Fully aware of this wrinkle, Thomas Jefferson replied in a letter to James Madison, "The less we say about the Constitutional difficulties the better."

Not everyone in the United States thought the acquisition of Louisiana was a good idea. Some believed the people of Louisiana could never become the kind of virtuous citizens needed to make a democracy work. Others felt it was simply impossible for a single government to oversee such a vast area effectively. Jefferson, who knew time was of the essence and passage of the treaty tenuous, pushed for quick approval. The U.S. Senate confirmed the Louisiana Purchase Treaty on October 20 and French envoy Pierre Clément de Laussat transferred Louisiana to the United States three months later, on December 20, 1803, at New Orleans.

Although the Louisiana Purchase Treaty promised the inhabitants of the colony *cum* territory a swift road to statehood, it did not happen for nine years. That fact alone fostered tension between the inhabitants of the Territory of Orleans and its third and final colonial master. The first appointed American leader was poorly equipped at the start for the daunting job ahead. William Charles Cole Claiborne was Jefferson's fourth choice (his first three candidates, all better known than Claiborne, had turned him down flat). As historian John Kukla rightly opines, the only things Claiborne had working against him were "his youth, inexperience, and total ignorance of the language" spoken by the overwhelming majority of the people he was designated to lead. Complicating matters further, Claiborne lost his wife and daughter to fever in the first year of his tenure. After that, he did what most other savvy colonial governors had done—he married into the established Creole power structure. His marriages to Clarissa Duralde (who died in 1809) and thereafter to Suzette Bosque tightened his connections to local elites. Apparently, Claiborne grew into his responsibilities and grew on the inhabitants over time. He was so well regarded at the time of statehood in 1812 that he became the state's first elected governor.

Their linguistic difference with most of the rest of the nation was only one reason Louisianians were viewed with such great suspicion and skepticism in the early nineteenth century. The complex racial makeup of the populace, especially its highly visible population of free people of color, gave the rest of the nation pause. Many Americans openly doubted the loyalty of the new state's exotic people and believed, when push came to shove, they might prefer to return to France or Spain. Mutual suspicion began to dissolve in the aftermath of the extraordinary American victory at the Battle of New Orleans in January 1815. The War of 1812 began as a grudge match between Britain and the United States, and the military engagements of its first two years were concentrated on the East Coast. Yet the war would conclude in a spectacular fashion near New Orleans. Although peace negotiations were underway at the time, both sides decided to negotiate from positions of strength. Thus, plans for the British to invade the Gulf Coast continued to unfold. In December 1814, several thousand battle-tested British troops were ferried ashore and marched through miles of mud and muck until they reached the plains of Chalmette. Had they continued marching into New Orleans on Christmas Eve of that year, a distance of less than four miles, the history of the city and the nation might look quite different. As it was, the British decision to stay put, combined with Major General Andrew Jackson's well-known and, in this case, fortuitous belligerence, set the tone for the next two weeks of skirmishing and position-fortifying. Several small engagements gave Jackson time to augment and outfit his army, which was largely held together by loyalty to or fear of Jackson. Either inclination was fine with him, and he declared martial law in New Orleans to make sure all of the city's inhabitants knew it. Jackson's troops were a badly supplied and motley lot. The well-equipped British soldiers called Jackson's diverse, undersupplied men "the dirty shirts"—and the charges were not just insulting but true. Yet the heroism and good fortune of Jackson's multicultural, multilingual force led to one of the nation's most iconic military victories.

Things should not have gone as well as they did for Jackson and his men on the morning of January 8, 1815, but bad luck plagued the British and doomed their complex battle plan. The class politics of the British attack strategy—putting Irishmen and African-descended Jamaican troops in the front as cannon fodder—did not work out so well. The Irish and Jamaicans, it seemed, did not think January 8 was a good day to die, and they hung back, throwing the battle plan into chaos. As the fog began to lift over the battlefield, the British forces were in disarray but also in range of the American forces' cannon and smaller firearms. More than three hundred troops and the majority of the British commanders in the field were wiped out in under an hour. Jackson reported fewer than ten men killed during the same period. The American forces' triumph over the British was both astounding and stupendous. That unlikely victory also propelled the lanky, cranky Tennessean into the national spotlight and ultimately into the White House.

Louisiana followed Jackson's trajectory into national politics. The state's conservative 1812 Constitution enfranchised a very small number of voters, who generally tended to their own cotton and sugar and ignored all else. But when John Quincy Adams and the East Coast elite cheated Jackson and the common man out of the presidency in 1824, voters in Louisiana got interested in national politics for the first time. Although the interest of the state and its people in the federal government and its affairs has ebbed and flowed in the ensuing two centuries, by 1828 Louisiana had unquestionably become woven into the national fabric. Unfortunately, its simultaneously strengthening identity as a southern slaveholding state would lead it to sever its national connection in 1861.

The fortunes of Louisiana's political and commercial interests were driven by the currents of the Mississippi but also increasingly interconnected with the manufacturing economies clustered in the northern states and in industrializing parts of Great Britain. So long as cotton, sugar, and produce came down the Mississippi for deposit, trade, or distribution, and slaves could be driven by foot or via water into the nation's largest cluster of slave markets at New Orleans, and from there back into the fields and households of the wealthy or aspiring, Louisiana's commercial and plantation elite were more or less sanguine and satisfied. There were, after all, undeniable material advantages to being integrated into the international banking and commerce economies so long as the individual, patriarchal prerogatives of slaveholders were not challenged.

The perception and reality of threats against the institution of slavery split the nation apart, and though its economic interests might rationally have dictated another course, Louisiana dove off the cliff of uncertainty with its Confederate sister states in January 1861. The defense of slavery was understandable in economic terms. After all, land was the only asset that exceeded the value of slaves in the first half of the nineteenth century. Yet the cruel history of slavery and the soul murder of millions of human beings did not garner the South much in the way of positive karma or good luck over the course of the long, bloody four years that followed. Although some people could never accept it (and some still cannot get past it), the South lost the Civil War. In the wake of that defeat slavery ended; and, in fits, starts, and despite awful acts of violence, Louisiana slowly became American once again.

The state suffered great physical damage during the war, yet many of its inhabitants seemed not to lose their taste for violence or killing as a form of political expression. Over the next three decades, competing political factions bent on either destroying or dominating each other engaged in outrageous acts of murder—whether the hundreds of individual lynchings or the single deadliest instance of Reconstruction violence, which occurred in 1873 at the Grant Parish Courthouse in Colfax, where white Democrats killed at least 150 black Republicans in a pitched battle for political control of the parish. The process of Reconstruction was particularly nasty in Louisiana, and by the mid-1870s, violence and killing had replaced voting as the most common political acts a citizen was likely to engage in (or fall victim to). Racial animosity sucked up whatever oxygen was left in the body politic, and a nasty brand of self-avowed white supremacists, known as the Bourbon Democrats, dominated the state's government, such as it was, until the early twentieth century.

Even as the Progressive movement swept the nation in those decades, Louisiana reformers remained committed to making whatever changes they deemed necessary at the state and local levels. An interesting example of this can be seen in the women's suffrage advocate Kate Gordon, who fought long and hard for women's voting rights but lamented the passage of the Nineteenth Amendment to the U.S. Constitution. She feared a federal amendment guaranteeing women the right to vote would also enfranchise African American women and thus challenge the de facto disfranchisement of African Americans by the state's 1898 constitution. Reformers and good government advocates represented some improvement over the violent depravity that characterized the Bourbon era, but it would be three forces of nature that would combine to change the course of history and the locus of power in Louisiana in the twentieth century.

The discovery of oil in 1901 and its subsequent extraction from the ground would create new job opportunities for the people of the state. Those jobs would draw workers away from agriculture and into occupations that, though dangerous, could provide a family with prospects for opportunity and education that had never existed before. The oil econ-

Fig. 2.1. Louisiana's first oil well. *Louisiana Conservation Review*, *Courtesy of LSU Libraries*

omy would also draw new citizens, regular and corporate, who brought new points of view and new kinds of power grasping to the state's political life.

Like the oil companies, the Mississippi River, though still a central provider of the state's economic well-being, proved it was never under anyone's effective control. Although the Army Corps of Engineers worked diligently to control the river, the "levees-only" policy it adopted in the late nineteenth century actually exacerbated the potential for annual spring flooding. In its 1926 annual report, the Corps made the following rosy assessment of its efforts: "It may be stated that in a general way the improvement is providing a safe and adequate channel for navigation . . . And is now in condition to prevent the destructive effects of floods." Yet, in early 1927, as one Delta dweller observed, "It started raining and it never did stop." By the time 1927 was over, more than 160,000 homes had been flooded and more than 325,000 people were living in temporary Red Cross camps while they waited for the water to recede. Louisiana,

Fig. 2.2. Flood of 1927. *Slide Collection of the U.S. Army Corps of Engineers, New Orleans District, Louisiana Digital Library, Baton Rouge, La.*

Mississippi, and Arkansas took the brunt of the damage. The loss and destruction of homes and farms was so widespread that even rural people—who were generally suspicious of government—were willing, even anxious, to accept help from the federal government in the face of such devastating losses of life, land, and the ability to make a living.

The aftermath of the Great Flood of 1927 created a political sea change, and in no way was this more obvious than in the election to governor of the third force of nature that changed the state in the early twentieth century. Huey Pierce Long hailed from upcountry Winn Parish but had big-time ambitions—ultimately, to be president of the United States. Along the way he pulled Louisiana into the twentieth century, especially through building overpriced but badly needed infrastructure, including more than 7,500 miles of roads constructed variously of concrete, asphalt, gravel, and no small amount of graft.

Despite the positive benefits he provided individuals and the state, Long also dragged Louisiana's reputation back into the mud with his occasionally outrageous behavior, his voracious longing for the spotlight, and his unabashed and probably pathological desire to have power over everyone and everything in his ever-growing orbit. Once Long entered the U.S. Senate in 1932 (while still maintaining absolute power over politics in Louisiana), he began to push his Share Our Wealth agenda nationally. His ideas, though often inchoate, certainly pushed Franklin Roosevelt—who saw Long as a political threat—in the direction of greater social service provision, especially for the elderly. Long went further, arguing openly for wealth redistribution. Long's Share Our Wealth program and clubs argued, "None shall be too big, none shall be too poor." His proposal to impose 100 percent taxation rates on any income over $8 million a year made his mostly wealthy critics howl. But, in the context of the Great Depression, people were willing to consider unorthodox political proposals—empty bellies and virtually no prospects led people in directions that were not even subtly Socialist.

On September 8, 1935, Long was shot, allegedly by a skilled young surgeon named Carl Austin Weiss, who, puzzlingly, did not actually have a gun in his hand or vicinity in evidence photos of the shooting's aftermath. He did, however, have at least sixty projectiles in his body. Long

Fig. 2.3. Huey Long statue, Louisiana capitol grounds. *Dustin Howes*

had at least one projectile that surgeons removed in the hours after the shooting, but the Kingfish bled to death internally and died just before dawn on September 10. His last words are reputed to have been, "Don't let me die. I've got so much to do." The official story of the assassination—which bodyguards and cronies had more than a week to rehearse before being called before a friendly investigative committee—was that Weiss shot Long, presumably over perceived racial insults to his family. This conclusion, conveniently, made the Kingfish a martyr.

His martyrdom, whether authentic or manufactured by a cabal of jumpy bodyguards and self-interested political lackeys, fueled continuing support for Longism in the state. Huey's immediate predecessors were so greedy and out of control that the federal government was able to make cases against them and—in the little bit of breathing room and freedom of opinion that returned in the wake of Huey's demise—Louisiana juries were actually willing to convict members of the Long machine. The trials of 1939, often referred to as the Louisiana Scandals or the Louisiana Hayride, seared the state's corruption into the national imagination in ways we all continue to endure. That series of events also inspired the great American literary classic, Robert Penn Warren's *All the King's Men*.

Despite the scandals and the knowledge that the Long machine—though arguably populist—was always on the take, the people of the state had an incredibly durable appetite for the kinds of hokey, carnivalesque roadshows that Huey's younger and even more unhinged brother, Earl, used to keep himself and the Long machine in power and in the governor's office every other four years, as the state constitution then allowed. Unlike Huey, whose deep ambition kept him mostly on an even mental keel, Earl was potable, quotable, flammable, and often had his fly down to boot. Crude doesn't begin to describe Earl's strangely appealing persona. But perhaps laughing was as good as crying for people whose only opportunities and educational enhancements had been provided under the leadership of the Longs. The brothers were a strange admixture, but their influence on Louisiana in the twentieth century, and maybe even the reaction against it in the early twenty-first, are proof positive of how profoundly those two troubled, talented brothers changed the state.

When Earl Long had a mental breakdown in 1960, the nation's attention was drawn to Louisiana, once again for reasons that were more freak show than admiring. Earl expired in a hospital bed while smoking, but there was no reason to fear bland normality or honest government would dominate Louisiana politics for long. For one thing, the civil rights movement was at its apex, and though Louisiana politicians tried by fair means and foul to keep social segregation and political exclusion in place, it would be another southerner who would, in the segregationist's view, betray the cause of white supremacy. President Lyndon Baines Johnson, who as a young man had been inspired by Huey Long, surprised everyone, maybe even himself, by becoming the chief executive who signed both the Civil Rights Act in 1964 and the Voting Rights Act in 1965. These landmark pieces of legislation challenged the segregationist status quo in the state, as well as the rest of the country, and profoundly changed the political equation in the decades to follow. As African Americans returned to the voting rolls, often under federal supervision, a slow shift rightward began to take hold among the state's voters. Many Democrats felt betrayed, or at least aggrieved, by the successes of the civil rights movement. Slowly, almost imperceptibly at first, the Republican Party began to make inroads in Louisiana politics for the first time since Reconstruction.

In the meantime, there was a new wily fox, this one of the silver variety, waiting in the wings to reap the rewards—political and monetary—of the state's newly diversified electorate and the federal largesse meant to resolve the state's enduring problems related to poverty. Edwin Edwards was the state's next great flawed messiah. His domination of the state's political apparatus, like that of the Longs before him, ended in an ignominious crash. While Huey was shot and Earl politicked himself to death, Edwin unabashedly flaunted his fast and loose style of financial management along with his girl and gambling indiscretions. For three decades, he seemed unable to be convicted, even as those close to him were often caught and sometimes incarcerated. Even now, his first biographer has gone to great lengths to claim that his trials and ultimate conviction were as much examples of unfortunate federal overreach as they were of any solid evidence of substantive wrongdoing. A longer look over the state's history in the twentieth century, and of Edwards' career specifically, suggests such argument is characterized by special pleading. Nor is such an argument particularly edifying in a state where the poverty of political choices and the anemia of the democratic process still plague the body politic. When a Nazi-Klansman can nearly win the governor's office, and can only be beaten by a man who everyone admits is a lovable rogue and crook, there is, to state it modestly, significant room for meaningful democratic advancement.

As Louisiana entered the twenty-first century, it had overcome an oil glut and returned to a respectable level of employment, but its negative social indicators remained high. Nature, too, served up hard-to-digest reminders that she would always be in the driver's seat. Hurricanes Katrina, Rita, Gustav, and Ike hammered different parts of the state and projected poverty, tragedy, and stomach-turning government ineptitude out into the stratosphere. British Petroleum's pursuit of oil and profit brought the state and the Gulf of Mexico the Deepwater Horizon oil spill in the spring and summer of 2010. As the reappearance of oil on our coastline after Hurricane Isaac attests, the aftermath of that environmental catastrophe will be with us, in some form or the other, for decades to come.

The enduring puzzle of Louisiana's history, for this historian at least, is how a state with such an impoverished democratic tradition has, at the same time, been the site of so much rich and unique cultural creativity. Perhaps a retreat into private life, and into the sensual joys of a good meal, a cool drink, a hot dance, or an astounding schedule of nearly nonstop annual festivals, makes sense. Perhaps that culture of joy and sensuality has been the tradeoff and salve for such continually disappointing politics.

Those who have understood our state best and have created and conveyed its gifts and charms in artistic or literary terms knew and know that Louisiana's beauty and natural abundance are fragile and ever changing. In Louisiana, nature, like beauty, is not an abstraction. The state of nature, in Hobbesian terms at least, is always on full-blown display. Our state and her urban crown jewel, New Orleans, remain the most violent places in the nation. In some sense we have gone from being an eighteenth-century rogue colony to becoming a twenty-first-century gangster's paradise. Whether it is a stubborn social problem or poverty-borne pathology, violence—both state sanctioned and extralegal—remains at the heart of the state's reputation and its reality.

Still, in the shadow of all those problems (or maybe as a reflection of them), culture leaks through and bubbles up like the oil and gas deposits scattered around the state. If there is anything that keeps Louisiana appealing amid all this, it is the pleasantly predictable generosity of its people, the love of food and drink, and the willingness always to share these simple but dependable delights with others. The sharpness of the smells and the range of colors in the evening sky may help others understand why, even as our coastline dwindles, our determination to hold on to what makes this place so special and unique hardens. For me, living in Louisiana is a lot like driving through the sugar parishes in the fall, when one is overwhelmed by the heavy smells of sugar processing. On those crisp afternoons, the air is redolent with the fragrance of cane being crushed—the results of back-breaking toil combined with the promise of incomparable sweetness.

The dark parts of Louisiana's history often threaten to engulf the thinking and teaching of professional historians, and they have a distressingly deep pool from which to draw. But, as I think, and write, and teach about Louisiana, I strive to remind my students—many of them the next generation of leaders and followers—that despite a dismal record of political manipulation, the state's people seem, generation to generation, to inherit hardiness, resilience, and a genius for optimism.

Louisiana's history is full of engrossing episodes and colorful, memorable characters. It is my hope and belief that the tragedies and comedies of Louisiana politics do not overwhelm the creativity, charm, and durability of its common people. Despite plague, pestilence, storm, and the abuses of the powerful, the people of Louisiana continue to preserve and perpetuate their distinctive cultures in the face of increasingly heavy natural and national odds. The historian Lawrence Powell begins his recent study of New Orleans by quoting the philosopher Friedrich Nietzsche, who opined that "the secret for harvesting from existence the greatest fruitfulness and the greatest enjoyment is—to live dangerously." As we sail into the twenty-first century on this old, lovely, leaky boat called Louisiana, most people in the state know intuitively and experientially exactly what Nietzsche meant.

FURTHER READING

Dawdy, Shannon. *Building the Devil's Empire: French Colonial New Orleans.* Chicago: University of Chicago Press, 2009.

Fairclough, Adam. *Race and Democracy: The Civil Rights Struggle in Louisiana, 1915–1972.* Athens: University of Georgia Press, 1999.

Hair, William Ivy. *The Kingfish and His Realm: The Life and Times of Huey P. Long.* Baton Rouge: LSU Press, 1996.

Johnson, Walter. *Soul by Soul: Life inside the Antebellum Slave Market.* Cambridge: Harvard University Press, 1999.

Keith, LeeAnna. *The Colfax Massacre: The Untold Story of Black Power, White Terror, and the Death of Reconstruction.* New York: Oxford University Press, 2009.

Kukla, Jon. *A Wilderness So Immense: The Louisiana Purchase and the Destiny of America.* New York: Alfred A. Knopf, 2003.

Long, Alecia P. *The Great Southern Babylon: Sex, Race, and Respectability in New Orleans, 1865–1920.* Baton Rouge: LSU Press, 2004.

Mitchell, Reid. *All on a Mardi Gras Day: Episodes in the History of New Orleans Carnival.* Cambridge: Harvard University Press, 1995.

Northup, Solomon. *Twelve Years a Slave.* Edited by Sue Eakin and Joseph Logsdon. Baton Rouge: LSU Press, 1968.

Powell, Lawrence N. *The Accidental City: Improvising New Orleans.* Cambridge: Harvard University Press, 2012.

Usner, Daniel H., Jr. *Indians, Settlers, and Slaves in a Frontier Exchange Economy: The Lower Mississippi Valley before 1783.* Chapel Hill: University of North Carolina Press, 1992.

LOUISIANA CULTURES
A CREOLE MOSAIC

JOYCE MARIE JACKSON

Louisiana was populated with numerous Native American groups long before European exploration began in the area. The French and Spanish conquests during the sixteenth and seventeenth centuries and the forced migration of Africans produced a new cultural landscape. This mosaic canvas of Indian, African, French, and Spanish influences during this period is the foundation for the state's cultural richness. What led so many to leave their homes and come to this region, exchanging the familiar for the unknown? For Africans, there was no choice. For some Europeans, it was a pull to the New World, for others, it was a push from the Old. Economics, politics, and religion all played a part, and the answers are as varied as the groups themselves. It is best to begin with a story, a narrative about how this state emerged. The story is rather involved—in fact, one that I split into several sections but one that has a lot to tell in terms of the scope and depth of human diversity in Louisiana.

Creative blending of cultural aesthetics and repertoires has occurred in other places in our country but in few places to the acknowledged extent and with the public vitality of the traditional cultures in Louisiana. Distinctive architecture ranges from shotgun houses and creole cottages to spacious and decadent plantation homes. The cuisine tempts the appetite with gumbo, jambalaya, andouille and boudin sausage, seafood po-boys, *cochon de lait* (roast suckling pig), crawfish bisque and étouffée, café au lait and beignets, coffee-and-chicory, and bread pudding. The rhythms of jazz, blues, zydeco, Cajun music, gospel, country and western, rock and roll, and hip hop provide a musical kaleidoscope to satisfy the ear. To hear the variety of musical styles, to see the wide-ranging arts and architectural traditions, to taste the renowned cuisine, and to celebrate at one of the myriad festivals around the state should all lead one to reflect on the social and environmental conditions that birthed this culture.

THE POWER OF THREE

There were three significant cultures during the colonization and early development of Louisiana—Native Americans, Africans, and Europeans (French and Spanish). I want to start this discussion with the first families—Native Americans. Native Americans are too often relegated to caricature, and we frequently overlook their rich and diverse histories, as well as how their cultures have helped to shape ours.

For many millennia before the arrival of Europeans, Native Americans inhabited Louisiana, and it is home to the earliest mound complex in North America, dating to the Archaic period (8000 BCE–2000 BCE). The Watson Brake site near Monroe is thought to be almost two millennia older than Poverty Point, the largest and most well known site in the state, near present-day Epps. According to Jon L. Gibson, Poverty Point is thought to have been the first complex tribal culture in North America because it may have hit its zenith around 1500 BCE and lasted until approximately 700 BCE.

A large number of present-day place names in Louisiana are transliterations of those used in many Native American languages, including Atchafalaya, Avoyelles, Caddo, Houma, Natchitoches, Tangipahoa, and Tchoupitoulas. However, place names were probably the least of what was gained from the indigenous people during the exploration and settlement of Louisiana. Daniel Usner Jr. refers to the evolution and composition of a regional economy that connected the Indian villages across the lower Mississippi valley with European settlers and African slaves along the Gulf Coast and lower banks of the Mississippi as the "frontier exchange." Gwendolyn Midlo Hall gives us a vivid account of the Europeans' reliance on Indians during the French period (1699–1763): "The Indians of Louisiana taught the white colonists a great deal about the flora and fauna, the topography of the land, the building of boats, the navigation of the rich network of treacherous waterways that allowed communications among French settlements, hunting, fishing, warfare, agriculture, techniques of building houses, clothing and dress, preparation and preservation of food, and herbal medicine."[1]

So the Indians taught the economy of the swamp and the cultivation of indigenous crops to the new arrivals. French and Canadian soldiers and settlers lived with Indian tribes in the early years of colonization in order to survive famines, to learn their language, to seek protection, and to marry. Consequently, many of the early French settlements of lower Louisiana began in Indian villages, and the French officers relied heavily on their Indian warriors for protection. Unfortunately, later on the Indian and European communities underwent a reversal of roles. European settlements that once attached themselves to Indian villages to survive were now helping to support the Indian villages. The Indian-European contact impacted every aspect of tribal life and cost the tribes dearly.

Indians also formed an alliance with Africans, who had been in Louisiana since the early 1700s. There were three primary origins of Africans in the region. Of the first group, twelve enslaved Africans were captured as plunder by the French army in the Spanish War of Succession in 1710. Others entered the colony directly through the French colonial transatlantic slave trading system. The years 1717–1743 saw the importation of slaves to Louisiana from the western interior and coastal areas of Africa. Most of these came directly from the Senegambia region of French West Africa. The second primary group of Africans came via the French West Indies, namely Saint-Domingue or Haiti, during and after the Haitian Revolution (1791–1804). In this group there were those who came on a volunteer basis, the *gens de couleur libres* (free people of color), and for others it was a forced migration with plantation owners—their masters. The third group of Africans came in later from the Atlantic seaboard, by way of the British North American trade routes.

Of the Europeans, the French explorers first came through Canada down the Mississippi Valley in order to prevent England and Spain from gaining control of the mouth of the Mississippi River. Later the French colonists came directly from France, Nova Scotia (Acadians), and Saint-Domingue. The earlier population consisted of colonial administrators, officials, soldiers, landowners, and businessmen, as well as others on the lower social and economic ladder, including prisoners, derelicts, prostitutes, and the like. There was a continuous flow from France throughout the nineteenth century.

Although Spain was the political ruler and colonizer of the Louisiana Territory from 1763 to 1801, no substantial number of Spanish immigrants came to the region except colonial administrators. Therefore, the Spanish cultural influences were largely absorbed by the dominant French culture. Later, Hispanics arrived from Spain, the Canary Islands (Isleños), and the Caribbean Rim.

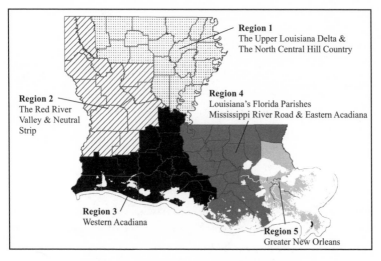

Fig. 3.1. Cultural Regions of Louisiana. *Andrew Joyner*

FIVE REGIONS OF THE STATE

We can divide Louisiana into five regions based on cultural and geographic factors (fig. 3.1). These are not rigid but fluid boundaries, as several of the regions as well as their parishes and culture groups overlap. However, the regions are defined by similar physical and cultural features, namely, 1) shared climate and landforms; and 2) similar ethnic heritage, language, religion, occupations, cuisine, music, and/or recreation. All the regions have aspects that distinguish them from the rest of the state. Each region has several names, and the most prominent ones are listed here.

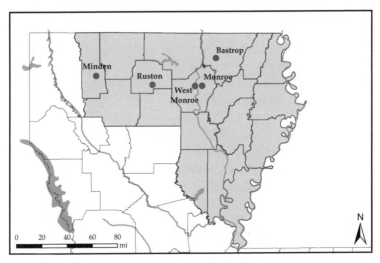

Fig. 3.2. The Upper Louisiana Delta and the North-Central Hill Country.
Andrew Joyner

Region 1: Upper Louisiana Delta/Upland South/North-Central Hill Country/Sportsman's Paradise

The first Spanish explorers under Hernando de Soto, in 1540, found American Indians, people from the Caddoan and Muskogean language families, living mainly in the northern section of the Lowland areas (fig. 3.2). So we have Indian and Spanish influence in the northern region of the state much sooner than the French. In 1714, French colonists under the leadership of Louis Juchereau de St. Denis established the first permanent settlement in Louisiana at Natchitoches. Located on the Red River, characterized by rich soil, and the nexus of importation of enslaved Africans from the French West Indies in 1716 and French West Africa in 1720, Natchitoches proved integral to the cotton and sugar plantation system in the region. This Cane River area was highly influenced by French Creole planters and by an enclave of *gens de couleur libres*.

This enclave of *gens de couleur libres* was from the Isle Brevelle colony founded by freed slaves. The colony's well-educated members of mixed ethnic origins (Indian, African, French, and Spanish) held themselves apart from the other Americans, black and white, who lived in the less fertile piney woods around the plantations. Some of these Creoles of color owned plantations. The French Creole heritage is still prominent with this group today, setting them apart as somewhat unique from the rest of north Louisiana.

Culturally, north Louisiana is described by geographer H. F. "Pete" Gregory as a patchwork quilt, each piece remaining intact, coexisting with the others. Each strip of this quilt, northwest, north-central, and northeast, has many separate colors and textured pieces representing distinctive communities. Today, the north-central region has Indians that are mainly descended from the Koasati and Choctaw tribes that migrated to the area after Europeans began settlement. The Koasati settled in Elton in Allen Parish, the Choctaw migrated from Mississippi, and the Jena band settled in LaSalle Parish. They all continue to speak their languages, Koasati maintain coiled pinestraw basketry and racquet games, and the Jena still practice deerhide tanning. Many Indians in this area still maintain rural occupations of farming, trapping, and fishing.

The strong lure to this area was economical and fertile land that could produce the agricultural and financial staple of the antebellum South—cotton. People who settled in the Upland South region came from Georgia, Alabama, Mississippi, Tennessee, and the Carolinas. They had small farms and a strong Protestant work ethic. The Lowland South settlers were descendants of Englishmen and Scots from other parts south and the Atlantic seaboard. They established cotton plantations near the Mississippi, Red, and Ouachita Rivers and thus were dependent on a large slave population. Although many ethnic groups were represented, in northeast and north-central Louisiana the predominant groups were British American (especially Anglo-Scotch-Irish and Anglo-Celtic) and African American. However, with their strong Protestant ethic, it was the Scotch-Irish who gave the region its distinctive social, moral, and religious face. Further, there are Italians, Hungarians, Czechs, Greeks, and others throughout northern Louisiana, but those of Scotch-Irish descent continue to be the main shapers of the regional culture. In this relatively

Fig. 3.3. Easter Rock ritual at True Light Baptist Church, Winnsboro, Louisiana.
J. Nash Porter

isolated, mostly rural area and with the over-all Anglo tone of the region, the cultural groups overlap less than in south Louisiana. The twin cities of Monroe and West Monroe situated on the Ouachita River are prime examples of the juxtaposition of north Louisiana's predominant cultures: Lowland and Upland South. Monroe, located on the east bank with its rich delta soil, had large plantations, whereas West Monroe had smaller farms with higher lands and piney woods.

The prevailing Protestant heritage is reflected in religious ritual, including all-day singings and "dinners on the ground" for both white and black congregations. Gospel is the preferred sacred music of both black and white congregations, but is performed in a very different style by each group. The Dr. Watts long-meter or lining-out songs are still popular in the more rural churches, and river baptisms, a significant sacred rite of passage, were still commonly practiced in both congregations until the fifties. Now you find them occasionally in a few black churches. In addition, the shape-note or sacred harp tradition is still practiced, as evident at the annual singing conventions for blacks and whites in the Monroe area. In this tradition, a system of four shapes to designate the musical symbols *fa, sol, la,* and *mi* is employed as an effective way of teaching people to read music. This system was an outgrowth of the New England singing school movement and the Great Awakening. A unique ritual still surviving in a black Baptist rural plantation church in Winnsboro is the Easter Rock (fig. 3.3). Women of several churches coordinate this ritual dating from before the Civil War in which annually, on the eve of Easter, they celebrate simultaneously the death and resurrection of Christ. It is clearly a vestige of the antebellum circular "ring shout" that was performed in clandestine settings by enslaved Africans. During an earlier time the ritual was performed in several parishes, including Concordia, Franklin, and Catahoula.

In the early twentieth century, the secular music scene was just as varied as the sacred. Old-time country, bluegrass, and later rockabilly are prevailing music traditions in the northern region of the state. Many people would gather for the still-vibrant Dixie Jamboree country music show in Ruston and the now-defunct *Louisiana Hayride* radio show in Shreveport. These venues and the artists who performed there were famous even outside of Louisiana, for people would flock to them from other states, especially in the Ark-La-Tex region.

Commercial country music began in 1922 when a Texan named Alexander "Eck" Robertson and Oklahoman Henry C. Gilliland finished their gig playing for the Confederate Soldiers' Reunion in Richmond, Virginia, and decided to take a trip to New York. Armed with their fiddles, they journeyed to the Victor Talking Machine Company, where they recorded six sides for Victor. (These were not the very first recordings. There were several cylinder recordings from the turn of the century, and some 78s that predated the 1922 recordings.) Although these recordings are noteworthy, the later recordings of James Charles Rodgers, deemed "Father of Country Music," were more significant for Louisiana musicians. Rodgers had a short tenure in the industry (1927–1933) but was prolific, recording 111 sides in six years. His repertoire ranged from popular songs, sentimental ballads, folksongs, and vaudeville songs to blues and blues-style songs. In combining the blues theme with the yodel, he was innovative. His repertoire and singing style influenced a number of new young country singers, including Gene Autry and Louisiana's own Jimmie Davis, a two-term governor (1944–1948 and 1960–1964) and a 2008 inductee into the Louisiana Music Hall of Fame. Davis began his singing career as an imitator of Jimmie Rodgers. Davis's most famous song, "You Are My Sunshine," was recorded by 350 artists, sold millions of records, and was translated into thirty languages. It was designated one of Louisiana's two state songs. Many years later, another Louisiana native son, Van Williams, guitarist and vocalist, has shown a preference for the blend of diverse elements found in Rodgers's music.

Other north Louisiana artists such as Ferriday's Jerry Lee Lewis and Mickey Gilley combined the region's rock and roll with the Mississippi Delta blues and developed the popular rockabilly genre. Juke joints and honky-tonks sprinkled the rural and small-town landscapes where the Mississippi Delta blues and rhythm and blues (discussed more later) were performed by blacks, including the legendary Huddie "Leadbelly" Ledbetter. Hailing from Morningsport in Caddo Parish near Shreveport, Leadbelly was noted for the gift of lyrical composition and for singing his way out of prison in Angola, Louisiana, and Parchment, Texas. Folklorists John and Alan Lomax recorded him in the 1930s for the Library of Congress.

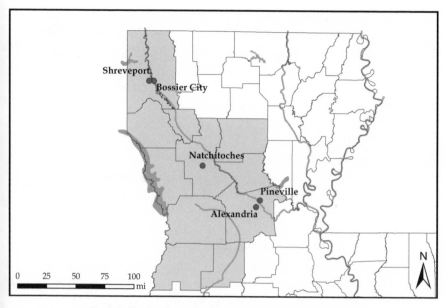

Fig. 3.4. The Red River Valley and Neutral Strip. *Andrew Joyner*

Region 2: Louisiana Red River Valley/Neutral Strip/the Crossroads

It is very hard to define a demarcation line between some of the regions. There is some overlap, but basically the Red River Valley includes Shreveport/Bossier City, Alexandria, and Natchitoches, spanning the state from Shreveport to the Sabine River from the Zwolle area through Beauregard Parish (fig. 3.4). These areas are all Lowland South, tied to the plantations lining the Red River. The region is largely rural, with a strong forestry product industry in addition to concentrations in oil and gas. This region is home to several groups of Native Americans, including the Tunica-Biloxi, Koasati, and Jena Choctaw, all of whom are federally recognized.

This strip of land located in the west-central part of the state was not included in the 1803 Louisiana Purchase because it was considered "No Man's Land," the "Neutral Strip," the "Neutral Zone," or the "Free State." In 1806 it was officially referred to as the "Neutral Ground" by Gen.

James Wilkinson of the United States and Lt. Col. Simón de Herrera of Spain in an agreement between those two countries. Because they could not agree on who would claim the area, they both declared it neutral ground to prevent an armed battle or full war breaking out. The region's boundaries were never defined except for a general statement that the Sabine River was to the west and the Arroyo Hondo (Calcasieu River) was to the east, the area near Natchitoches to the north and the Gulf of Mexico to the south. This area was roughly 5,000 miles and was characterized by what is known as an "outlaw culture."

In order to understand why and how this part of the state gained an outlaw persona, we have to explore a bit of its history. After the Louisiana Purchase, this region served as a buffer zone between Spanish and American lands. It became a demilitarized zone, basically outside of the law, thereby serving as a refuge for those of a criminal nature. Many capitalized on the opportunity, including squatters, deserters from both countries' armies, and escaped slaves. Thieves and conmen took advantage of the commerce along the El Camino Real, the royal highway that connected Mexico City to Los Adaes, a Spanish mission near present-day Robeline (fig. 3.5). John Murrell, the land pirate, was known to have worked the area. According to Mark Twain in *Life on the Mississippi* (1883), "the once celebrated Murel's Gang . . . was a colossal combination of robbers, horse-thieves, negro-stealers, and counterfeiters, engaged in business along the river." Twain goes on to compare Murrell to Jesse James in the same book.

Another infamous land pirate working the Neutral Zone was Jean Lafitte. During this era the privateer was well known for marketing enslaved people and other contraband. He smuggled them into the United States by way of the Calcasieu and Sabine Rivers. Owing to the ban on the transatlantic slave trade in 1808, slave trading within the South escalated, and Lafitte realized large net profits from the sale and trade of Africans into Louisiana.

Clandestine activities like these destabilized the region for over a decade. The two governments were compelled to deploy military expeditions to expel the outlaws and criminals who were making legal travel and trade in the region dangerous and unprofitable. There was so much illegal activity in the Zone that John Quincy Adams called it the "back-

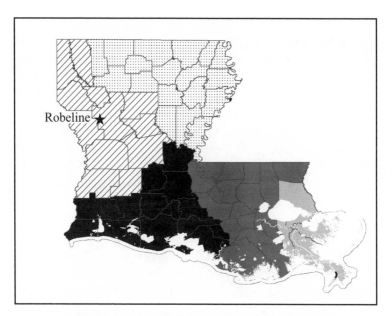

Fig. 3.5. Location of Robeline, Louisiana. *Andrew Joyner*

door to the U.S."[2] In 1821, the United States was finally granted ownership of the region by the Adams-Onis Treaty, which clearly and elabo-
rately defined its boundaries.

Communities began to flower as soon as 1822, taking advantage of
timber, cotton, and other resources. Spanish speakers of Choctaw-An-
glo descent lived in the old No Man's Land to the west of Natchitoches
on the Texas/Louisiana border. Spanish officials encouraged Indians to
move there; homesteaders, runaway slaves, and persons of mixed heritage joined them. In most of the literature, this region has never been
defined by a particular culture. Nevertheless, the mixed-heritage people
referred to as "Redbones" and "Sabines" have a strong presence and an
important historical role in the region.

Who are the Redbones? Any attempt to identify the origins of Louisiana Redbones is complicated because of the complexity of the study
of triracial people, the murkiness of colonial genealogical studies, and
the conflicting opinions of scholars as well as Redbone descendants.
Some descendants never accepted the term "Redbone" as an ethnonym,

or proper reference to themselves. Some simply consider themselves Americans of unknown origin, while some have claimed Moorish and Turkish as well as Native American ancestry. Joey Dillard, a black English scholar, says that the term likely came from the West Indies, where the term "Red Ibo," pronounced "Reddy Bone," referred to a mixture of races. In 1932, Webster Talma Crawford wrote a study of the Redbones that was not published until 1993. In it he gives his theory of the origins of this people: "Their name, 'Redbones,' serves as a convenient label for a people who combine in themselves the blood of the wasted tribes, the early colonists or forest rovers, the runaway slaves and the stray seamen of Mediterranean stock from coasting vessels in the West Indies or Brazilian Trade . . . for it had been said that Hannibal was a 'Redbone' . . . and we may call those People most properly, 'Moors.'"[3] This theory perhaps sheds light on the origins of this group before coming to Louisiana.

In surveying more of the literature, I find that most scholars and descendants generally believe that the original Louisiana Redbones migrated from the Eastern Seaboard—North Carolina, South Carolina, and Virginia—to Louisiana in the late 1700s and early 1800s. Their identity is based on their appearance in the 1810 census as "the other free people" (initially about twelve families). Therefore, they were considered to be different from those known as free people of color although they were not white. Some of the Redbone names that appear in the census are the same ones that appear in Paul Heinegg's book *Free African Americans of North Carolina, Virginia, and South Carolina from the Colonial Period to about 1820*. The debate will continue over biracial, triracial, and quadriracial identity, some pointing to African American and others to a predominantly Native American or white identity. Their origin was also believed to be Indian and Portuguese or Melungeon, but the former group was not known and the latter was not definitive.[4] The anthropologically accepted theory, which I consider highly simplified, is that early Spanish explorers, colonial officials, and settlers intermarried with various Native American groups. The most critical factor is how Redbones were perceived by "white" society and placed, in most instances, in a minority status. Most who have restored this group agree that the Redbone moniker was not used much on the Eastern Seaboard, but only after the post-revolutionary Louisiana migration.

In the pre–Civil War era, triracial people were classified as free persons of color. This classification has led many researchers to identify triracials as freed slaves, which is erroneous. After the Reconstruction period, those triracials who appeared to have European features passed for white, and those who exhibited black features were classified as black and forced to blend into the African American community based on the "one-drop" rule. However, during the antebellum era, free people of mixed race could have up to one eighth or one fourth (one grandparent) African ancestry (depending on the state) and be legally white. The one-drop rule was not adopted as law until the twentieth century (first in Tennessee in 1910). These measures did much to destroy many triracial communities, but some still exist and occupy lands that their ancestors settled generations ago.

Importantly, "one must examine social, economic, political, and cultural configurations and not merely the ethnic mixture itself in order to explain the emergence of separate mixed-blood (mixed ethnic) groups."[5] Darlene Wilson has made observations of Melungeon ethnicity, relevant also to Redbone ethnicity: "The complexity of upcountry Southern social relations among mixed-ancestry people cannot adequately be rendered in simple either/or models nor by admonishing us to consider them as simply tri-racial isolates. . . . Every family line will be differently constructed and one should be wary of over generalization."[6]

Redbones now embrace their heritage, with some actively doing genealogy studies, and the term is more readily accepted than in the past. Marriage outside the group is more common than in the past. There is a strong matrilineal tendency among this group, with women using their maiden name after marriage and children carrying the mother's surname. Most Redbones are Baptist, and many religious leaders in the southwestern and central regions of Louisiana are from their community. Also of interest is that many in the group still practice traditional healing practices.

Even with the stabilization of the Neutral Zone that occurred with the signing of the Adams-Onis Treaty in 1821, the region continued to have a bad reputation for generations. During the Civil War, the former No Man's Land became a haven for deserters and jayhawkers. At the beginning of World War II, the zone was an area where the military practiced maneuvers. Later, Fort Polk was built in the town of Leesville.

In terms of cultural activities in the region, the community of Florien in Sabine Parish celebrates the Neutral Strip with its annual Florien Free State Festival. The festival features comedy skits between the Free State Gang and the Law, syrup-making, street dances, and a variety of food. Redbones notwithstanding, in essence this region is defined not so much by a specific culture as by an attitude of being different from the rest of the state.

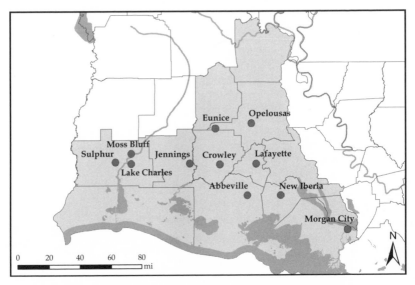

Fig. 3.6. Western Acadiana. *Andrew Joyner*

Region 3: Western Acadiana/Cajun Country

The western Acadiana parishes are mostly rural and located from west of the Atchafalaya Swamp to the Texas border to the coastline of the Gulf of Mexico and up to Avoyelles Parish—essentially a triangular region (fig. 3.6). Within the region, the culture is further divided into prairie Cajun (agriculture and livestock) and wetlands Cajun (fishing and trapping). The main urban areas are Lafayette, Lake Charles, New Iberia, Houma-Thibodaux, and Morgan City. The Louisiana Prairie, Bayou Teche, coastal marshes, and parts of the Atchafalaya Swamp are also in this area.

Acadiana as a whole includes twenty-two parishes. Four of the parishes—St. Charles, St. James, St. John the Baptist, and Ascension—are also considered River Road parishes (see Region 4). Culturally, Acadiana is not a monolithic, homogenous Francophone area as most people think; it is a complex synthesis of Indian, French, African, Spanish, and German influences. H. F. "Pete" Gregory's strip quilt is an apt analogy, with a bit more blending taking place.

Acadiana is home to several American Indian groups, including Chitimacha, Tunica-Biloxi, Attakapas, and Koasati. Some Indians have retained their own unique cultures and languages, despite European contact. For instance, the Chitimacha and Koasati have maintained greater separation from Cajun culture as evidenced by their native language retention and basketry traditions. On the other hand, the Houmas and some other Louisiana Indian groups have blended with the European groups to a large extent, including the adoption of the French language.

The earliest Germans came in 1722 from the Rhine River region and settled on the *côte des Allemands,* or German Coast, the present-day parishes of St. John the Baptist and St. Charles. They easily assimilated with the French, engaged in agriculture, and provided much of the produce for New Orleans. When a second wave of Germanic immigrants came to Louisiana fleeing political strife and religious persecution, they became for a time the largest immigrant group in Louisiana. Some German-Catholic immigrants settled in Robert's Cove, near Rayne in Acadia Parish, and maintain a St. Nicholas celebration and Germanfest today at St. Leo's Catholic Church. Some popular attractions are German singing, folk dancing, and foodways. Other than these celebrations, the Germans are not so readily identified today because of their gradual assimilation into Louisiana French culture, including their names and food. Anti-German legislation initiated during World War I spurred on this assimilation, causing a decline in the language and other customs as well as intermarriages between Germans and their Cajun and Anglo neighbors.[7]

Of course the largest and most influential cultural group to inhabit Acadiana is the Cajuns, those descendants of French Acadians who were expelled from Nova Scotia by the British during the French and Indian War in 1755 and began arriving in Louisiana in the 1760s. These small farmers developed the First Acadian Coast settlement, which was in Ascension Parish in 1764 and was listed in 1805 as Acadia, part of the

Second Acadian Coast. The parish seat was Donaldsonville, which in January 1830 became the capital of Louisiana for two years. St. James Parish is adjacent to Ascension and thus continued the expansion of the Acadian Coast with more immigrants from Nova Scotia. Collectively, the areas were originally known as the *Comté d'Acadie.*

Not everyone who is culturally Cajun descended from the Acadian exiles, and not everybody who lives in Acadiana is culturally Acadian or speaks Cajun French. An excellent example are the Spanish colonists who became the political rulers of the Louisiana Territory from 1763 to 1801. Most of the Spanish arrivals in the area were colonial administrators, businessmen, and planters, so the Spanish immigrants and their influences were small in numbers, thus easily assimilated into French culture. A small number of Hispanics did arrive from Spain, the Caribbean Rim, and the Canary Islands.

The Canary Islanders, or Isleños, who settled in St. Bernard Parish (Region 5), were contemporaries with the Acadians arriving in the 1770s, but they were largely independent of Cajun cultural influences. They were originally sent to Louisiana by Charles III of Spain to protect the territory, especially New Orleans, during the Spanish era and his regime. So the Isleños that came were soldiers, farmers, fishermen, and trappers comfortable with rugged terrain. Some were and continue to be singers of complex narrative songs called *décimas,* whose lyrics can recount the exploits of knights from the Middle Ages or the issues focusing on fishermen in today's coastal town of Delacroix.

Among the other cultures that are largely independent of Cajun influences are Croatian fishermen from the Dalmatian coast of Yugoslavia, who settled in coastal Plaquemines Parish (Region 5), and started the oyster industry, which is still strong and controlled by them today. Italians arrived on post–Civil War plantations during the same era as sharecroppers to replace enslaved Africans. In addition, there are some English-speaking communities in the Atchafalaya Basin and the Morgan City area. These enclaves relocated to the levees when they were rebuilt for flood control and others came from the Carolinas' coastal fishing areas and became shrimpers.

A sizable Creole population came to this area from Saint-Domingue during the Haitian Revolution. Some settled in the urban and cosmopolitan area of New Orleans, and others in the rural and urban areas of Acadiana. This group of Creoles, also French speaking, lived on the southwest prairie and near the southeast bayous. They were free people of color and landowners who lived in close proximity to Cajuns. Although they were ethnically distinct, they had a shared identity in terms of occupations, cuisine, Catholicism, Mardi Gras, language, and musical genres.

There are two predominant musical genres in Acadiana. The first is Cajun dance music, identified by the influence of French folksongs and country and western music. The song styles are found in ballads, waltzes, and two-steps with an emphasis on the melody and use of fiddle and accordion. The second type is the Creole or Afro-French music known as zydeco. This genre is influenced by French folksongs, blues, and rhythm and blues. The repertoire of songs also comes from ballads, waltzes, and two-steps, with an African/Caribbean emphasis on percussive rhythms. The dominant instruments are accordion and *frottoir* (metal washboard). Both genres were revitalized in the 1980s. Dewey Balfa, the Cajun fiddler born near Mamou, launched school workshops focusing on Cajun music in that decade. The "Zydeco King," Clifton Chenier from Opelousas, received both a Grammy and a National Endowment for the Arts Heritage Award in 1983, inspiring a new cadre of zydeco and Cajun musicians to preserve and perform the music.

Another musical form, *chansons de Mardi Gras* (Mardi Gras songs), accompanies the *courir de Mardi Gras,* or "Fat Tuesday Run." The rural Mardi Gras ritual is associated with pre-Christian Celtic Europe and with fertility and renewal. It also has origins in medieval France and is similar to traditional European customs such as mumming and wassailing, evident at Christmas, New Year's, and Epiphany. Various Acadian communities such as Church Point, Mamou, Basile, Eunice, and Elton actively celebrate the tradition every year. Deralde is known for the Creole version of the same ritual. Sometimes these participants don "white face" to portray the other for a day. Mardi Gras is the final day before the Lenten season begins. The participants wear masks, colorful costumes, and capuchins (pointed hats), and they dance, drink alcohol, beg for money and food, chase chickens, use whips, and sing *chansons de Mardi Gras.* This is one of a number of cultural traditions that has contributed to the infectious "la joie de vivre" that is the motto in this region of the state.

Surprisingly to most, Acadiana at one time also had a strong jazz community. By the 1920s, New Iberia was a hotbed of jazz musicians. The area supported a musical awareness similar to that of New Orleans, but on a smaller scale. Harold Evans and the Black Eagles Band were in demand. In addition, names like Harold Portier of Parks, and Gustave Fontenette, founder of the Banner Orchestra, which was the largest and best "reading" orchestra in the area, dominated the region. Renowned trumpet player William Gary "Bunk" Johnson actually left New Orleans to play with the Banner in New Iberia, and Lawrence Duhé and Evans Thomas of Crowley also played with the Banner. By the end of the 1930s, the Banner Orchestra was one of the most celebrated jazz bands in the state. "When the band was really hot you had to book the job almost a year in advance," reminisced Harold Portier in 1998, the year before he passed as the last of the great jazzmen from this region. Unfortunately, the bands and most of these musicians were never recorded. The bulk of music traffic centered on New Orleans, which was far away, and record producers had no interest in going off the beaten track to discover new talent.

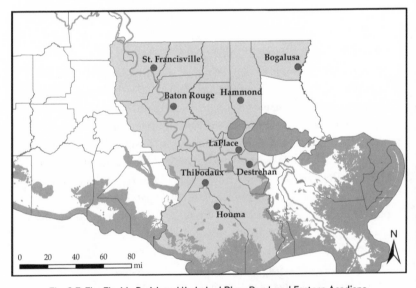

Fig. 3.7. The Florida Parishes, Mississippi River Road, and Eastern Acadiana.
Andrew Joyner

Region 4: Louisiana's Florida Parishes, Mississippi River Road,
and Eastern Acadiana

Louisiana's Florida Parishes constitute the "toe of the boot" with bound-aries south of the Mississippi border, east of the Mississippi River and Bayou Manchac, and west of Lake Pontchartrain (fig. 3.7). During the colonial era, this region was part of the Spanish Territory of West Flor-ida, thus the designation Florida Parishes. However, neither French nor Spanish culture had entered this area during the colonial period. The region consists of a Tidewater planter enclave in the most fertile parts of West Feliciana, surrounded by predominantly Upland South yeoman farmer settlements in the less productive piney woods areas of East Fe-liciana. The topography and soil composition of the Felicianas dictated this particular settlement pattern. This area consisting of British and African American cultures is also populated with a significant number of Italians and Hungarians living in the capital city of Baton Rouge, small towns, rural areas, and in the piney woods. The heart of the piney woods is St. Helena Parish, the northern half of Tangipahoa Parish, and Washington Parish. Most of this area was rolling hills, small farmsteads, and towns sparsely populated until the turn of the century, when the national lumber companies changed the landscape and lifestyle of the re-gion by cutting down large masses of timber and constructing railroads. Another distinct cultural area in this region is the Mississippi River Road area, also referred to as Plantation Country, which covers the parishes from St. Francisville to north of New Orleans and includes French and Lowland South plantation culture, having more plantations than any other area in the South. The urban center of Baton Rouge is a part of this area as well. Common symbols of these two distinct cultural regions from the past as well as today are old plantation homes, sugarcane fields, live oak trees, and Spanish moss.

The most obvious Indian influence on the region is in place names such as Bogalusa, Manchac, Tangipahoa, and Tunica. The name Is-trouma (from the Choctaw for "red stick," *isti huma*) provided the name of the capital city, Baton Rouge. It referred to a red pole, once a tribal boundary marker, raised on the bluff of the river to separate the Houma from the Bayougoula to the southwest.[8]

In the early 1700s Europeans first began to describe the tribes in the area and their languages. The majority can be traced to the Muskogean languages: Acolapissa, Tangipahoa, Houma, or Choctaw. The Muskogee villages were either on the Mississippi River, along the Pearl River, or on the shores of Lake Pontchartrain. These tribes were often targeted for military and political purposes. Fred Kniffen, Pete Gregory, and George Stokes assert that "from the name Acolapissa, Choctaw or Mobillian jargon for 'those who see and hear,' it might be inferred that the members of this border tribe served as outposts against possible enemy incursions from the west."[9] The Tunica, who replaced the Houma, made material gain by becoming middlemen in the salt and livestock trade with Caddo and Latino populations in Texas and northwest Louisiana. According to Gregory, "They were also a mercenary tribe, serving first for the French in the Natchez war and later augmenting the Spanish troops under Bernardo de Gálvez in 1779 at the Battle of Baton Rouge, during the American Revolutionary War."[10]

During the American period, the Choctaw were abused, ridiculed, and killed, so they allied themselves with the French Creoles, some living on the grounds of the plantations. The French Creoles incorporated the Choctaw into their poetry, art, and literature. They loved the Choctaw game of stickball, which they called *Raquett*, and even formed their own teams.

By the 1930s there were a small number of Choctaw in Bayou Lacombe, living in shotgun houses that had been abandoned by the sawmills in the midst of pine stumps. Most had to fall back on old skills and traditions like subsistence farming, hide tanning, basketry, hunting, trapping, beadwork, and silversmithing. In the 1960s, the Indian Angels were formed in Baton Rouge. This non-Indian group strived to help preserve Indian culture by organizing pan-Indian pow-wows, and also lobbied the U.S. government on their behalf. The petrochemical plants lining the banks of the Mississippi River in Baton Rouge and Baker have caused not only the Choctaw and other Louisiana Indian groups, but also Indian groups from other states (Apache, Sioux, Creek), to migrate to the capital city for jobs. Trying desperately to regain their heritage and celebrate a shared identity, the Choctaw have formed a "new tribe," the Louisiana Band of Choctaw, a group with cultural, economic, and political agendas.

The Felicianas were the two parishes where large cotton plantations loomed near the Mississippi River before the Civil War. In addition to the Red River and Mississippi Delta regions, the Felicianas were one of Louisiana's "Black Belt" areas. African Americans made up over 60 percent of the population due to the institution of slavery in the antebellum period. After emancipation, many former slaves and their descendants remained in the area to work crops of cotton and later corn and sweet potatoes. The wage/contract system of labor was the most popular for the new freedmen and women but only lasted through the 1870s due to crop failures. Sharecropping, sharetenantry, renting, and other variations then developed. There was also the crop lien system, which generated a large body of folklore based on the dishonesties of the system. These systems finally began to change during the 1950s and '60s with the advent of tractors and the civil rights movement.

For the first time since Reconstruction, major changes began to take place in the economic and social relationships of the cultures in this area and others. Many blacks broke their associations with plantations, the balance of political power was altered, and public schools were integrated. Economically, blacks made gains as successful carpenters and other craftsmen, paper mill workers, schoolteachers, club owners, and nuclear power plant workers. Although some still worked on plantations and farms and rented houses and land lining the Mississippi River, many moved to Baton Rouge to work at the refineries on the river. A black exodus from rural areas of the region can clearly be seen in each census of the last five to six decades. Blacks from Zachary, Slaughter, St. Francisville, and Baker helped to populate Baton Rouge. According to Edna Jordan Smith, a teacher and public librarian, a large black community in South Baton Rouge was "basically built by Black Felicianians."

Music plays a pervasive role for blacks in the Florida Parishes. From gospel music sung in church every Sunday morning to blues played in honky-tonks, clubs, and at backyard barbecues, all genres common to the area came directly from the folk tradition. The genre created by anonymous black musicians from plantations, farms, and small towns came to be called the "blues" because of its serious and personal treatment of the human condition. But of course there were joyful and lascivious lyrics as well. Many bluesmen sang about their life experiences, and the rhetori-

Fig. 3.8. Tabby Thomas performing at the Baton Rouge Blues Festival.
J. Nash Porter

cal "I" was a projection of the singer and his audience. Certain qualities of timbre and vocal and instrumental techniques are associated with this manner of expression, and flattened, shaded, and slurred notes that produced particular sounds are recognized as part of its musical vocabulary.

But why did the blues genre thrive in the Florida Parishes? It is a rich region of traditional black culture. The answers are found in physical as well as environmental factors. The region was quite isolated, rural and agricultural. There were a significant number of exclusively black villages, just as there were many exclusively white villages. Also during the timber era and the longstanding tradition of turpentine and lumber camps, many black males worked the "barrel houses," singing and playing after work and moving around the circuit from one village to another. The levee system lining the River Road contributed to the segregation of the labor force. There was no comparable concentration of segregated labor force anywhere else in the state. In addition, this region is in close proximity to Mississippi, a traditional stronghold of the blues also due to the state's plantation economy.

Baton Rouge is considered a blues city, and has prided itself for many years on producing an annual blues festival, featuring both the "front porch" variety and large concert blues bands. Frequent past performers were Silas Hogan, Arthur "Guitar" Kelley, Lightnin' Slim, Henry Gray, Raful Neal and his family, and Tabby Thomas and his family (fig. 3.8). The younger blues generation, including Kenny Neal, Chris Thomas, and Larry Garner, keeps the tradition thriving in Baton Rouge and elsewhere.

Italian immigrants came to the Florida Parishes as an alternative labor force, replacing newly emancipated blacks. Most were farmers from southern Italy and Sicily escaping poor economic conditions. They entered through New Orleans, where some settled, but the majority moved on to work the sugarcane plantations lining the Mississippi River. Some eventually purchased land, became truck farmers, and began farming strawberries, especially in Tangipahoa Parish (Independence and Hammond).

Some of the old-country traditions persisted with the second generation, such as arranged marriages, friends or family members serving as midwives, and an array of traditional medical remedies handed down through the years. Singing, dancing, and playing music were by far the most important leisure pastimes. A brass band was formed in the Independence area as early as 1880. Under the leadership of Sam Marretta, by the 1920s the band played traditional Italian music for almost all community occasions, including weddings, receptions, and feast day celebrations for the saints (i.e. St. Joseph, St. Expedito, St. John, and Our Lady of Perpetual Help). Most Louisiana Sicilians had a strong devotion to the saints, some keeping statues or altars in their homes and some even building chapels dedicated to specific saints. On feast days, the brass band would travel from one altar to the next, playing and eating at each. Once a year in April, the community would produce a festival to help preserve and express their traditional folklore and identity, featuring traditional music, dance, and cuisine.

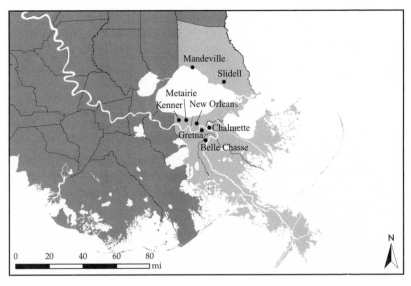

Fig. 3.9. Greater New Orleans. *Andrew Joyner*

Region 5: The Greater New Orleans Area

When you mention Louisiana to people outside of the state or country, they will probably say, "Oh yes, I have been to New Orleans" for Mardi Gras, Jazz Fest, or a vacation. Louisiana's identity is inextricably linked to the Crescent City (fig. 3.9). New Orleans is unique in U.S. history as a city with French, Spanish, African, and English heritage and is better described as the Creole capital of the state. The city merits this designation because of its Mediterranean-African roots and plantation heritage and economy, which make it more akin to the societies of the French and Spanish West Indies than to the American South. The city itself emerged from a small enclave that for almost a century had been neglected by both France and Spain. New Orleans before the Louisiana Purchase was already the capital of a vast empire and had the mighty Mississippi River at its heart, but before this, it was never more than a village, a pawn of the politics of a war-torn Europe. When it became part of the United States, it grew into a metropolis as the center of the lucrative cotton trade and one of the wealthiest cities in America. It was the nation's largest port before the Civil War as cotton was floated downriver and beyond to the Gulf and then to American and British fabric mills. To visitors and even people from other parts of Louisiana, the city seemed more European and cosmopolitan than American and southern, and it attracted the attention not only of the nation but of the world.

Life in the small colonial village of New Orleans, bordered by a swamp and practically isolated from the rest of the world, was already creolized. The layering of African, French, Spanish, and American influences along with the first layer of indigenous people during the sixteenth and seventeenth centuries formed the foundation of the city's culturally rich landscape.

Before the founding of New Orleans, Native Americans had already created a portage between the headwaters of Bayou St. John and the Mississippi River for a route from the river to Lake Pontchartrain. This became a strategic trade route for the Indians as well as the French. Bienville forged alliances with the Choctaw to help protect them from slave catchers and their Indian allies from South Carolina, but forming a rapport was also a precondition for their own survival. For instance, during frequent famines, French soldiers were sent to live with Indians so they would not starve. Soldiers also lived in Indian villages to learn their languages in order to act as interpreters. They also married Indian women. Indeed it is not surprising that French troops sought refuge among the Indians when deserting, and so did enslaved Africans when attempting to escape slavery.

The Chitimacha who lived near New Orleans had an estimated population of four thousand during the early period of colonization. They relied on the economy of the swamp and of the tidal wetlands in and around New Orleans and taught the techniques of cultivating corn, squash, potatoes, tobacco, and other indigenous crops to the French. By this time their villages were composed of sturdy, wooden houses, and their crafts were well developed.[11]

The largest, most culturally complex Indian nation in the state was and is the Houma. They adapted themselves to the lower coast not far from New Orleans around the late 1780s and have become astute boat-wrights with excellent shrimping and fishing skills. They are considered some of the best fishermen in south Louisiana. In addition, their eighteenth-century contact with the French and their isolation from others has limited language exchanges, making them among the most traditional speakers of the Acadian dialect in the state. French language and music dominates the Houma communities.

In the 1700s, the Indians had a standard of living that compared to the average European's. They were competent farmers and had access to rich plant foods and sources of fish and game, although they had no animals to serve as beast of burden. Most of the Louisiana Indians lived in permanent or semipermanent villages, unlike the western plains Indians who lived in nomad-like tepee dwellings. Groups who lived in close proximity to New Orleans, such as the Chitimacha, made their dwellings from palmetto fronds layered over a pole framework. During this period they had a largely Stone Age technology. Their main tools were the ax and adz. Both were made from stone and were used to build canoes and other wooden objects.

With the help of the Indians, the New Orleans colony survived, but the French settlers were in a constant state of insecurity in a world where they were too few to do without the Indians and yet too weak to control them. Although there was intertribal fighting before and after the Europeans, it was war, the threat of war, and/or enslavement that forced the tribes to relocate several times. In addition, assimilation into other Indian groups or into black and white populations led to the extinction of the language and culture of a vast number of lesser tribes. The Chitimacha fought a long war with the French, and it is believed by some that New Orleans is built on Chitimacha land. The Choctaw gave up their ancestral land, and through an imposed treaty, the majority of the group was relocated to the Indian Territory in Oklahoma. The vanished Indian nations left their mark in many ways. Then as now, sensibilities and performance practices were expressed in dance, music, storytelling, and culinary and decorative arts. Numerous place names in the greater New Orleans region, such as Tchoupitoulas, also attest to their former presence.

French Louisiana was a chaotic world in which France's major concern was to prevent England from gaining control of the mouth of the Mississippi River. After establishing a beachhead at Biloxi in 1699 on what is now the Mississippi coast of the Gulf of Mexico, the next strategic move by Jean-Baptiste Le Moyne, Sieur de Bienville, was to incorporate New Orleans as a city in 1718. In 1722 the city replaced Biloxi as the seat of government for French Louisiana.

New Orleans was a great world port and had worldwide trade ties. It was second to New York as a U.S. immigration point of entry during the nineteenth century. However, this reputation began developing during the eighteenth century when the first French arrived. The main streams to colonize initially were French Canadians, most natives of Quebec who had previously penetrated the Mississippi Valley from the Great Lakes of Michigan to the Gulf of Mexico. Some were from Canadian nobility, ruling elites and landowners. Both Pierre Le Moyne, Sieur d'Iberville, the founder of the Louisiana colony, and his brother, Jean-Baptist Le Moyne, Sieur de Bienville, the founder of New Orleans, were French Canadians. Their profiteering and malfeasance led the way for other counterparts to have a stronghold in New Orleans. These included pirates from the Caribbean, who enriched themselves through smuggling, seizing ships, goods, and slaves, and raiding settlements; and Canadian *coureurs du bois* (runner of woods), who engaged in the fur trade without permission from French authorities and were also experienced in trading and living with Indians.

Of the French who came directly from France to help colonize New Orleans, many were the rejects of society: prisoners, prostitutes, vagrants, smugglers, and soldiers condemned to the galleys for desertion. Many of these people were resistant and challenged the brutal and exploitative social structure of pre-Revolutionary France. Others migrated directly from the region of Acadia (now Nova Scotia and New Brunswick, Canada) to become the Acadian refugees discussed earlier. They were forced to leave French Canada after the British won the Seven Years' War. It was also during this time (1762) that the Treaty of Fontainebleau ceded Louisiana to Spain. Some of the Acadians settled in New Orleans and married into other French families, but the majority moved to the rural and agricultural areas of southwest Louisiana.

The third group of French speakers to colonize the area, also refugees displaced by war, were the residents of Saint-Domingue. The Haitian cultural legacy is evident first with the population expansion during and after the Revolution. These refugees began migrating to New Orleans during the 1790s. This migrational trickle to New Orleans turned into a flowing stream by 1808–1809 when they also started coming from Cuba. After Napoleon invaded Spain in 1808, the Spanish government ordered the expulsion of all French colonists from Cuba, so in less than five years the Saint-Domingan refugees had to undergo their second uprooting, and this group's next and permanent stop was also New Orleans. By this time, the displaced residents of Saint-Domingue were doubling the population of New Orleans. In 1791, before the refugees, New Orleans had 4,446 inhabitants. In 1797, the population had increased to 8,056, and in 1809 the numbers were roughly 13,810. This migration solidified the three-tiered society structure—consisting of whites, free people of color, and enslaved blacks—that is so unique to Louisiana. It was also this migration of refugees that solidified the Haitian French cultural legacy that is still prominent in the Crescent City today. Emigrants from Saint-Domingue coming into the New Orleans region constituted the largest single migration into the Louisiana Territory since its colonization. In spite of the fact that the Louisiana Purchase (1803) was occurring during the refugee flow, the Saint-Domingans were the major contributing factor to the resilience of French Creole culture in New Orleans for over the next two hundred years.

Because of the demography and history, this region afforded Haitians the opportunity to obtain success without assimilating into the dominant culture. Whites moved into positions of political power, educational authority, and economic influence. Free blacks also found a certain amount of freedom and privilege not afforded to them in other regions. The enslaved continued with similar tasks as before since the territory had the same climate and topography as the sugarcane-growing areas of Saint-Domingue. However, some were able to cultivate their own crops and sell them at the marketplace known as Congo Square.

Some major aspects of the Haitians' influence on the New Orleans region were architecture (shotgun houses), French-language newspapers, French language, sugarcane cultivation, French continental and Creole cuisine, classical and folk music, dances (calinda, bamboula), religion (Vodun), and traditional healing practices. Haitians also introduced Freemasonry and French opera along with the expansion of comedy and theatrical performances to the city of New Orleans.

Had it not been for the influx of refugees from the Haitian Revolution, French Creole culture would not have developed as it did in New Orleans. So, although most people refer to New Orleans as a French city, indeed, in reality it is a Haitian Creole French or French West Indian city. There is no doubt that the Haitian community played a significant role in implanting new elements, altering current practices, and blurring racial boundaries in matters of culture, religion, law, and language. After this third group of French and Haitian Creole language speakers migrated to the greater New Orleans region, there was a continuous flow of immigrants from France throughout the nineteenth century, with a substantial flux just before the Civil War.

The first enslaved Africans were brought to New Orleans directly from Africa and were there with the French from the first days of its founding (1718). By as early as 1721 seven slave ships had arrived from Africa, and by that time Africans constituted almost one half of the total population of the city.[12] Labor was a chronic problem in the colony, and slavery and subsidized colonization were the primary solutions. The first groups came from the Senegambia area, the Windward Coast of West Africa, and the Bight of Benin. Later groups came through the entrepôt of the French West Indies—Haiti and Martinique. Some were still brought in illegally after 1808, when the international slave trade was proscribed. Others came in with farmers from southeast areas such as Kentucky looking for new farmland, while others were sold downriver from Upper South states like Virginia and the Carolinas that had depleted acreage of tobacco lands. The early uniqueness of their ethnicities and their definite cultural and social patterns became blurred to a certain extent after many years of being in the colony, but the cultural impact was much more than a result of timing and large population numbers. They gained an identity, a kind of African, diasporic, creolized cultural blend due to their common positions as enslaved people and *gens de couleur libres.* They have a certain creolized coexistence (slave and free), so I view them as a collective cultural community instead of separating them by groups when we speak of culture. In addition, Africans and people of African descent who came (forcefully or willingly) into this territory gained a certain identity because of the character of New Orleans and southern Louisiana and the society that emerged from it, a three-tiered multiethnic society.

As a result of this creolized identity, unique place-based street traditions emerged out of a cultural epicenter referred to as Congo Square. In the 1800s this square was like a scene from an African village with the added cultural presence of the Indians of the area, who utilized the square initially to barter and sell their produce to the colonials and to celebrate their corn feasts. Located at the back of the original city of New Orleans—today's French Quarter—the square was in the Faubourg Tremé, where the majority of Creoles lived and where, before the Civil War, blacks owned 80 percent of the property. This is the area where blacks, then and now, strolled down the streets, as writers, dancers, and musicians flourished and strutted the second-line parades with the rest of the community. These parades accompanied the black social aid and pleasure clubs on each of their Sunday anniversaries, the jazz funerals as they celebrated death, and the Mardi Gras Indians as they celebrated life. The Mardi Gras Indian street ritual is practiced exclusively by blacks, who drew on Amerindian, African, and West Indian rhythms and motifs to create a folk ritual unique to New Orleans. Intricately beaded suits with an array of colorful feathers and plumes are a hallmark of the black Indians (fig. 3.10). The tribes—or gangs, as they are sometimes called— move through the community in an informal competition with a call- and-response creolized song chant, punctuated by drums, tambourines,

Fig. 3.10. Gang Flag Irving "Honey" Banister of the Creole Wild West,
New Orleans Mardi Gras Indians. *J. Nash Porter*

bottles, and other makeshift instruments. The black Indians' street rituals reflect respect and homage to the American Indian and to the African ancestral legacy. The above cultural street traditions practiced by blacks in New Orleans are all informed by the cultural, linguistic, and aesthetic historical memory of West and Central Africa, and by Native American and circum-Caribbean synthesis. All of this contributes to the cultural uniqueness of New Orleans.

The earliest Germans arrived in 1722 and settled upriver from New Orleans. Many of these Germans from the Rhine River region assimilated with the French, Acadians, and Creoles, so that even their names began to be pronounced and spelled in a French way. Some moved from the rural areas to the cities. Many settled in the Florida Parishes, like the Baton Rouge area, with place names showing their influence (Kleinpeter, Essen, Dutchtown). Large numbers from the rural areas as well as those who came directly from Europe arrived in New Orleans during the first four decades due to the tobacco industry. The second wave of German immigrants came into the territory between 1840 and 1860, fleeing political strife. Many settled in the Eighth and Ninth Wards in downtown New Orleans and in a few of the uptown suburbs, forming their own churches, schools, social clubs, lodges, theaters, and newspapers. For a time they were the largest European immigrant group in Louisiana, but the group has not retained any visible identity.

The Irish also came into New Orleans during the earliest days of the colony owing to their allegiance with France and Spain against the English. However, the largest immigrant population of Irish people came to New Orleans during the 1800s fleeing famine in their home country. Most remained in New Orleans and were manual laborers who eventually moved into the building trades, saloon business, and law enforcement. The Irish Channel neighborhood of New Orleans gained its name from the large population of Irish people living there in the past, but Irish residential character and identity have disappeared except for nostalgic moments like the annual St. Patrick's Day parade and the drinking of green beer.

Italians became prominent in New Orleans during the Spanish period because a number of them were members of the military service. The next wave consisted of seamen and ship owners, and some were believed to be associates of Jean Lafitte, bearing such names as Chigizola and Beluchi. Many settled in the Vieux Carré with its focal point of the Italian church built a century before by Don Andrés Almonester as a chapel for the Ursuline nuns. After World War I, new Italian arrivals settled in the downtown or "Mediterranean" part of the city, establishing themselves in the grocery and restaurant business and sharing their traditions of classical and popular music. Even today, Italians in New Orleans preserve ethnic folklore including the cult of St. Rosalie, where the statue of the saint is carried in a procession. Also, the celebration of St. Joseph's altars takes place on March 19, featuring elaborate home and community altars stocked with Italian ritual foods accompanied by a children's pageant after which the food is given to the poor in the community.

The French, Africans, Spanish, Germans, Irish, and Italians compose the largest ethnic groups to arrive in New Orleans. Numerous smaller immigrant groups arrived in colonial times and at later times in history that are also important to the character and identity of New Orleans today. Among these are the Jews, Greeks, Yugoslavians, Lebanese, Chinese, Filipinos, Japanese, East Indians, Vietnamese, and Croatians.

Hurricanes Katrina and Rita led to a recent wave of Latin immigrants drawn by the rebuilding trades. These groups from Central America include Hondurans, Belizeans, and Garinagu, people of African descent who speak the Garifuna language.

All these cultures came to the New Orleans region with definite social and cultural patterns, but they gained a more complex identity through their stay there. This implies a creolization due to their coexistence (chosen or forced), as well as the distinctive character of the place and the society that emerged from it. New Orleans has its own cultural identity like no other city. Some call it creolization, and some call it the New Orleans assimilation. Regardless of what it is called, most people recognize it whether they are locals or visitors. It is the factor that continues to bring visitors back. It is the factor that holds most residents to the city even when a category-five hurricane is heading its way—and even after that hurricane has ravished the city, people still want to come back, rebuild, and live.

NOTES

1. Usner, *Indians, Settlers & Slaves in a Frontier Exchange Economy*, 6; Hall, *Africans in Colonial Louisiana*, 14–15.

2. Marler, *The Neutral Zone*.

3. Crawford, *The Cherry Winche Country*.

4. Dr. Brent Kennedy, the leading Melungeon researcher, believes the Melungeons are a mix of some of the eastern Indian tribes that were forced westward by European diseases, remnants of a pre-Jamestown Spanish colony in South Carolina, and Portuguese/ Turkish peoples who were rescued from slavery in South America and put ashore on Roanoke Island by Francis Drake in the late 1500s. See Kennedy's book *The Melungeons*.

5. Gildemeister, "Local Complexities of Race in the Rural South," 9.

6. Wilson, "A Response to Heinige," 292, 293.

7. Sexton, *Cajuns, Germans and Les Americains*.

8. Gregory, "Indians and Folklife in the Florida Parishes of Louisiana."

9. Kniffen, Gregory, and Stokes, *The Historic Indian Tribes of Louisiana*, 50.

10. Gregory, "Indians and Folklife in the Florida Parishes."

11. Cummins, "Toward Unknown Destinies: Native Peoples and European Explorations," 7.

12. Hall, *Africans in Colonial Louisiana*, 58.

BIBLIOGRAPHY AND FURTHER READING

Blassingame, John. *Black New Orleans, 1860–1880*. Chicago: University of Chicago Press, 1992.

Crawford, Webster Talma. *The Cherry Winche Country: History of the Redbone*. Brandon, Miss: Dogwood Press, 1993.

Cummins, Light Townsend. "Toward Unknown Destinies: Native Peoples and European Explorations." In *Louisiana: A History*, ed. Bennett H. Wall. 2nd. ed. Arlington Heights, Ill.: Forum Press, 1990.

Dessens, Nathalie. *From Saint-Domingue to New Orleans: Migration and Influences*. Gainesville: University Press of Florida, 2007.

Evans, Freddi Williams. *Congo Square: African Roots in New Orleans*. Lafayette, La.: University of Louisiana at Lafayette Press, 2011.

Gibson, Jon L. *The Ancient Mounds of Poverty Point: Place of Rings*. Gainesville: University Press of Florida, 2001.

Gildemeister, Enrique E. "Local Complexities of Race in the Rural South: Racially Mixed People in South Carolina." Thesis, State University of New York College at Purchase, 1977.

Gregory, H. F. "Indians and Folklife in the Florida Parishes of Louisiana." In *Folklife in the Florida Parishes*. Baton Rouge: Louisiana Folklife Program, Office of Cultural Development, 1989.

Hall, Gwendolyn Midlo. *Africans in Colonial Louisiana: The Development of Afro-Creole Culture in the Eighteenth Century*. Baton Rouge: LSU Press, 1992.

Heinegg, Paul. *Free African Americans of North Carolina, Virginia, and South Carolina from the Colonial Period to about 1820*. 5th ed. Baltimore, Md.: Clearfield, 2005.

Jackson, Joyce Marie. "Rockin' and Rushin' for Christ: Hidden Transcripts in Diasporic Ritual Performance." In *Caribbean and Southern: Transnational Perspectives on the U.S. South*, ed. Helen A. Regis. Athens: University of Georgia Press, 2006.

———. "Cultural Continuity: Masking Traditions of the Black Mardi Gras Indians and the Yoruba Egungun." In *Orisa: Yoruba Gods and Spiritual Identity in Africa and the Diaspora*, ed. Toyin Falola and Ann Genova. Trenton, N.J.: African World Press, 2005.

Kennedy, N. Brent, with Robyn Vaughan Kennedy. *The Melungeons: The Resurrection of a Proud People*. 2nd ed. Macon, Ga.: Mercer University Press, 1997.

Kniffen, Fred B., Hiram F. Gregory, and George A. Stokes. *The Historic Indian Tribes of Louisiana: From 1542 to the Present*. Baton Rouge: LSU Press, 1987.

Koster, Rick. *Louisiana Music: A Journey from R&B to Zydeco, Jazz to Country, Blues to Gospel, Cajun Music to Swamp Pop to Carnival Music and Beyond*. Cambridge, Mass.: De Capo Press, 2002.

Marler, Don C. *The Neutral Zone: Backdoor to the United States*. Brandon, Miss.: Dogwood Press, 1996.

Merrill, Ellen C. *Germans of Louisiana*. Gretna, La.: Pelican Press, 2005.

Sexton, Rocky L. *Cajuns, Germans, and Les Americains: A Historical Anthropology of Cultural and Demographic Transformations in Southwest Louisiana, 1880 to Present*. Iowa City: University of Iowa, 1996.

Spitzer, Nicholas R., ed. *Louisiana Folklife: A Guide to the State*. Baton Rouge: Louisiana Folklife Program, Office of Cultural Development, 1985.

Trout, Robert O. "The People of the North Central Louisiana Hill Country." Ph.D. dissertation, Louisiana State University, 1955.

Usner, Daniel H., Jr. *Indians, Settlers & Slaves in a Frontier Exchange Economy: The Lower Mississippi Valley Before 1783*. Chapel Hill: University of North Carolina Press, 1992.

Wilson, Darlene. "A Response to Heinige." *Appalachian Journal* 25.3 (Spring 1998): 292–293.

www.louisianafolklife.org.

LOVE VINE AND LIVED RELIGION IN LOUISIANA

MICHAEL PASQUIER

Robert Penn Warren begins his Pulitzer Prize–winning novel *All the King's Men* with death. He takes you, the reader, down a rural highway in a car that loses control, hits the shoulder, and crashes into something that ends your life. Two men in a cotton field see the smoke of the accident, let slip the words "Lawd God," and return to the hoe and blade with little more than a thought of your well-being. Several days later, employees of the Highway Department visit the scene of your demise and mark the spot with a metal sign on which is painted a skull and crossbones. Warren ends the passage with a simple statement—"Later on love vine will climb up it, out of the weeds"—thus concealing from the world a terrible event wrought with religious significance. After all, where there is death, there is religion.

All the King's Men is best known as a novel inspired by the life and death of Huey Pierce Long, the fortieth governor of Louisiana who was shot in the state capitol building on September 8, 1935. He died two days later at the age of forty-two. According to some reports, his last words were, "God, don't let me die. I have so much to do." An estimated 200,000 mourners converged on the grounds of the state capitol to attend the funeral of a high school dropout from Winnfield, Louisiana, who would go on to serve as a U.S. senator and who would consider challenging Franklin Delano Roosevelt for the office of U.S. president. Today, Long's body remains buried under a statue bearing his likeness at the center of the state capitol garden. His memory is protected from love vine.

Both of these episodes—the fictional death of an unnamed reader and the actual death of a political icon—raise questions about what we see and do not see, what we know and do not know, what we forget and what we remember about religious life in Louisiana. They shift our attention from the center of public life to the periphery of everyday life. They move between a landmark site like the state capitol to an obscure marker on the side of a lonely highway. And they demand an extension of the definition of "religion" beyond matters of theological belief and church affiliation by including such things as the words we use to call upon deities ("Lawd God," "God, don't let me die") and the ways we memorialize life and death (roadside shrines, statues). In short, these two episodes expose the embeddedness of religion throughout the cultural landscape of a state with deep religious roots in places often overlooked by professional historians and lay observers alike.

By reflecting on the manner in which we look for religion in Louisiana, we can enliven the stale and oversimplified distinction between Protestant north Louisiana and Catholic south Louisiana. We can scrutinize the findings of the 2008 American Religious Identification Survey, which identified 31 percent of Louisiana residents as Catholic, 57 percent as Protestant, 1 percent as "Other" (Jewish, Muslim, Buddhist, Hindu), and 8 percent as "None" (agnostic, atheist). And we can discover how religion is lived in Louisiana, how it is practiced and imagined over the course of everyday life at particular times and places. Within these unconventional parameters for studying Louisiana's past and present, our search for what we might call "lived religion" concentrates on four seemingly insignificant objects: a pile of dirt, a box of photographs, a tattered book, and a one-room structure. The result is a history of religion liberated from love vine, protected from erasure, but hardly scratching the surface of what we can know about religion in Louisiana.

THE TUNICA TREASURE

In 1968, Leonard Charrier discovered the site of a Tunica Indian village and cemetery in West Feliciana Parish. He was not a professional archaeologist. He was a guard at the Louisiana State Penitentiary with an interest in treasure hunting. Jeffrey Brain, a Harvard archaeologist who would lead a formal excavation of the site in 1972, described the discovery as "the sort of archaeological find that comes along once a generation . . . perhaps even once a century or once a country." The relics dated to the mid-1700s, a period of intense trade between the Tunica and the French. After a decade of legal maneuvering, the Louisiana Supreme Court finally ordered that the collection of over 200,000 objects (pottery, ceramics, glassware, metals, beads) be returned to the Tunica-Biloxi tribe in Marksville, Louisiana, where they remain to this day and which laid the foundation for federal legislation known as the Native American Graves Protection and Reparation Act of 1990.

The Tunica maintained an uncommonly close alliance with the French during the eighteenth century, which explains the unprecedented size of the collection. Because of their unique relationship, the Tunica allowed a Roman Catholic priest named Albert Davion to operate as a missionary in Tunica villages from 1699 to 1720, the longest residency of any missionary among an Indian group in French colonial Louisiana. Given the prolonged interaction, it is reasonable to assume that the Tunica accepted the religious teachings of their ordained guest. The archaeological and ethnographic record, however, proves otherwise. Of the hundreds of thousands of objects removed from the burial ground, archaeologists uncovered only a handful of signs of Christian practice: remnants of five crucifixes, a Jesuit ring, and an assortment of beads that may or may not have been attached to rosaries. Moreover, of the limited written sources that mention the Tunica religion, almost all of them question the authenticity of their Christian faith, describing even the few baptized Tunicas as "bear[ing] no mark of being a Christian but the name, a medal, and a rosary."

But what did it mean to be authentically Christian in eighteenth-century Louisiana? For a Jesuit, it meant the strict observance of Roman Catholic teaching. That being said, to privilege the perspective of a French missionary over that of a Tunica Indian is to disregard the mutability of religious beliefs and practices in the volatile world of colonial Louisiana. Indeed, the Tunica frustrated Jesuits precisely because of their willingness to incorporate features of Christianity into what was already a highly formalized religious system of their own. It is no accident, then, that Harvard archaeologists unearthed the skeleton of an adult male that was buried under a mound of dirt with a gun, 20 bullets, 2 gun flints, a pair of scissors, a knife, a broken mirror, 68 white beads, 14 copper bracelets, and, perhaps most interesting of all, a perforated breast plate in the shape of a medallion that was used by the French as a skimmer for cooking. What was intended to be a culinary utensil had become a sacred object to be worn around the neck in anticipation of the afterlife.

Archaeological discoveries like this one demonstrate how almost anything can be made into something religiously meaningful. They also shed light on the fact that there are winners and losers in history books, and it is the winners that usually decide what details to include and how to interpret those details. Were it not for the illegal exhumation of a burial mound by a local treasure hunter, we would not know how resilient the Tunica were to the theological prodding of a Catholic priest and how successful they were at adapting their traditional religious practices to a changing world. Hundreds of Indian mounds dot Louisiana's landscape, some (on the grounds of the LSU campus in Baton Rouge) more prominent than others (hidden under brush and forest along the Mississippi River). Poverty Point, located in West Carroll Parish, is by far the most famous. Finished around 1500 BC, it is a physical reminder of the long history of people developing religious beliefs and practices in what would become the state of Louisiana.

THE STORYVILLE PORTRAITS

Ernest Bellocq was born in New Orleans in 1873. He worked as a commercial photographer. He died in 1949. During his lifetime, he was an incredibly ordinary man. He left no written materials and very few photographs for archivists to store and historians to ponder. Then, in 1966, a photographer named Lee Friedlander acquired 89 glass plates of never-before-seen pictures taken by Bellocq during the 1910s. New York's Museum of Modern Art exhibited the photographs and published a book about them in 1970. They came to be known as the "Storyville Portraits" because of their depiction of women who worked in the legalized red-light district of New Orleans called Storyville. According to the photographer Nan Goldin, the "portraits transcend the portrayal of the prostitute as an object" by including both clothed and nude women who appear relaxed and sometimes even playfully aware of the camera. Goldin compliments Bellocq for "never betray[ing] his respectful and nonjudgmental position in his portrayal of the women," though she avoids any discussion of the portraits' religious implications.[1]

Religion, quite understandably, isn't the first thing that comes to mind when viewing Bellocq's photographs and when reflecting on the prostitutes of Storyville. But religion was often on the mind of Bellocq, a person who attended the Jesuit College of the Immaculate Conception (now Jesuit High School) as an adolescent and who regularly photographed Catholic churches and schoolchildren as an adult. Several of these photographs still exist, one of which features a group of Catholic

Fig. 4.1. Priest and students of the College of the Immaculate Conception, New Orleans, ca. 1905, photo by Ernest J. Bellocq. *Courtesy of the New Orleans Province Archives, Society of Jesus, Loyola University Monroe Library*

boys seated around their ordained teacher and dressed in military uni-
forms indicating their membership in the Jesuit College Cadet Corps
(fig. 4.1). Moreover, Bellocq's brother, Leo, was a Jesuit priest who entered a seminary in rural Grand Coteau, Louisiana, at the age of nine-
teen, took his final vows in 1913, and worked as a teacher at Jesuit High
School until his death in 1952. Leo left behind no personal papers that
might help us determine what he thought of Ernest's activities in Storyville. Today, it is rumored among Jesuits that, after Leo died, a stash
of his brother's photographs was found in a box under his bed and later
destroyed.

Ernest and Leo Bellocq were two among thousands of men with experiences of Storyville. Indeed, what little we know about the Bellocq
brothers is a consequence of our interest in the women of Storyville.
And still we are left with more questions than answers, not only about
the religious lives of the Bellocqs, but also about the identities of the
prostitutes depicted in the portraits. Yet from this shallow pool of visual
evidence we can see how the line between the sacred and the profane
is not always bright, quite like the porous paved boundaries separating
Storyville from the rest of New Orleans and the camera resting between
the eye of the photographer and his subject. We can also notice details,
however minute, that reveal more about a person than their body shape
and job description. One of Bellocq's portraits, in particular, reinforces
this point. It is of a woman standing in front of a mirror, her left hand
tucked under her chin, and on her finger is a wedding ring.

Bellocq's photograph of a nude woman wearing a wedding ring in
a brothel is as important to our understanding of religion in Louisiana
as his photograph of schoolboys surrounding a priest on the steps of a
church. They both tell us something about our tendency to want to separate things into clearly defined "sacred" and "profane" categories. In so
doing, we avoid the humanity of those in the photographs, the thoughts
and feelings and experiences of those faces frozen in time and place.
We also take at face value what we see and read into the photographs,
instead of contemplating all that might have happened in the lives of the
subjects before they were photographed, the details of the photographic
moment, and where their lives went afterwards. In other words, Ernest
Bellocq wasn't just a photographer of prostitutes. He was also a Catholic.

Leo Bellocq wasn't just a priest and teacher to Catholic schoolboys. He was also a male resident of the Crescent City. And the women in the photos weren't just prostitutes. They were also mothers and daughters who most likely came from Christian families and who probably identified themselves as Christians.

THE KINGFISH BIBLE

In 1982, Louisiana State University history professor David Culbert sat down with Don Devol to talk about his old boss, Huey Long. Devol was the personal secretary of Long at the time of his assassination in 1935. He was the person responsible for packing up the U.S. senator's office in Washington, D.C. One item that didn't get sent back to Louisiana was a ragged book containing hundreds of Long's pencil marks and scribbles. Devol donated the book to Louisiana State University in the 1980s,

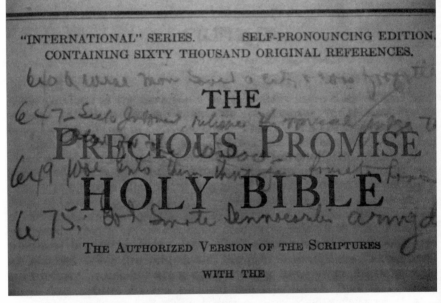

Fig. 4.2. Title page of Huey P. Long's personal Bible, showing Long's handwritten notations. *H. Donald DeVol Papers, Mss. 3653, Louisiana and Lower Mississippi Valley Collections, LSU Libraries, Baton Rouge, La.*

where it is kept in a rarely opened box alongside thousands of other boxes in the stacks of Hill Memorial Library. The book is a bible, *The Precious Promise Holy Bible* to be exact (fig. 4.2). During the interview, Culbert expressed surprise at the thoroughly used state of the bible because of Long's reputation as an infrequent churchgoer with a knack for peppering his political speeches with biblical references. "But from the degree [to] which that Bible was used," Culbert said, "it made me decide that Huey really was paying it some attention." Devol agreed with Culbert's estimation, adding that Long "used to say that the Bible was the greatest instrument going," and that "he really knew that Bible from cover to cover."[2]

Reading someone's personal bible is like peering into someone's personal thoughts about religion. The parade of underlined passages, asterisked words, and marginal notations reveal a man immersed in the scriptural tradition of Protestantism. In the Old Testament, Long concentrated on the legal passages of the Torah, especially those that discuss poverty and the responsibility to care for the poor. "For the poor shall never cease out of the land," he underlines in chapter 15 of Deuteronomy, "therefore I command thee, saying, Thou shalt open thine hand wide unto thy brother, to thy poor, and to thy needy, in thy land." He did the same in the New Testament when he marked a line in chapter 25 of Matthew, wherein it is written, "Verily I say unto you, Inasmuch as ye have done it unto one of the least of these my brethren, ye have done it unto me." In contrast to this merciful tone, Long underlined another passage in chapter 10 of Matthew: "Think not that I am come to send peace on earth: I came not to send peace, but a sword." Verses such as these fit neatly into the populist and sometimes martial rhetoric that went along with Long's "Share Our Wealth" movement, so it is hardly surprising to find them highlighted in his bible.

Equally interesting are points where Long seems to contemplate his own personal salvation and his role as a kind of warrior-prophet fighting on behalf of ordinary people. Reading chapter 16 of Matthew, Long asked himself, "For what is a man profited, if he shall gain the whole world, and lose his own soul?" For someone with such incredible secular power and irreverent character, it's possible that this existential question was not easy for Long to answer. By reading in between the lines and at the margins of his personal bible, we're left wondering how Long reconciled his worldly political ambition with the Christian message of otherworldly salvation. If anything, Long was a man who wanted to be remembered on this earth. It was an anxiety that he expressed at the top of the title page of his bible, where he summarized a passage in Ecclesiastes in the following revelatory terms: "a wise man saved a city and was forgotten." Imagine the similarly telling scribbles in the personal bibles of living and deceased residents of Louisiana, just waiting to be explored.

THE BAYOU CHURCH

J. B. Barnes is a resident of Lockport, Louisiana, where he has lived and worked on the grounds of a sugarcane plantation for over fifty years. During that time, on practically every Sunday, he has traveled down a highway along Bayou Lafourche to another plantation in Larose, Louisiana, where there sits a one-room church surrounded by sugarcane fields and a shuttered paper mill. He is the oldest deacon and second-oldest member of a 22-person congregation that represents four generations of African American Baptists. White owners of the plantation built the church for their black resident-workers in the 1930s. Two of the current deacons have been members of the congregation for their entire lives. Both of them were born on the plantation. And both of their sons are now deacons at the same church (fig. 4.3).

The generational depth of this tiny congregation is not uncommon in the many black Baptist churches that dot the rural roadways of Louisiana. Their rectangular frames, unspectacular steeples, and white walls are a fixture of Louisiana's bucolic landscape. Yet despite their omnipresence—or perhaps because of it—it's likely that over half of Louisiana's total population has never set foot inside a black Baptist church and never contemplated what religion is like for its members. In many ways, the following words spoken by Martin Luther King, Jr., in 1963, are as true today as they were then, and are as true for Louisiana as they are for most other states: "At 11:00 on Sunday morning when we stand and sing and Christ has no east or west, we stand at the most segregated hour in this nation."

Fig. 4.3. Israelite Baptist Church, Lockport Louisiana. *Michael Pasquier*

Visiting Barnes at his house is an education in the racial and religious history of Louisiana. Situated on a nineteenth-century sugarcane plantation, Barnes's home rests behind the "big house," cattycorner to the overseer's house, and in front of a row of dilapidated field houses built for African American workers in the early twentieth century and still rented by poor residents today. Barnes has lived at this site for over half of a century. But when asked the question "What does 'home' mean to you?" he chose not to reflect on the past or the present. Instead, he sang a song that signified hope for a future in heaven, away from Louisiana, and without a trace of his memory on earth. He sang:

> I've got a home over the mountain
> I've got a home over the mountain
> And I must get there on time.
> You know I started on this journey
> Seems like a long time ago.
> You know I thought it would be easy
> Lord I did not know.
> That's why I'm holding, holding my portion
> Until it's safe for me to climb.
> I've got a home over the mountain
> And I must get there on time.

As common as a church is to our understanding of religion, J. B. Barnes's church on a bayou in Lafourche Parish is not exactly like any other church in Louisiana. To understand one church doesn't mean that we can understand all churches. To believe otherwise is to do the work of love vine, to obstruct pathways for knowing about Barnes's expectation of salvation by listening to him sing a song that he learned in church. The same might be said of an Indian mound, a photograph of a prostitute, or a senator's bible. In other words, religion as it is lived in Louisiana isn't always obvious to us, and it has a lot to do with love vine.

NOTES

1. Nan Goldin, "Bellocq Epoque," *ArtForum International* 35 (May 1997).

2. Don Devol Oral History Interview, Mss. 4700.0009, Louisiana and Lower Mississippi Valley Collections, LSU Libraries, Baton Rouge, La.

SUGGESTED READING

Bennett, James. *Religion and the Rise of Jim Crow in New Orleans.* Princeton: Princeton University Press, 2005.

Clark, Emily. *Masterless Mistresses: The New Orleans Ursulines and the Development of a New World Society, 1727–1834.* Chapel Hill: University of North Carolina Press, 2007.

Long, Carolyn Morrow. *A New Orleans Voudou Priestess: The Legend and Reality of Marie Laveau.* Gainesville: University Press of Florida, 2007.

Nolan, Charles E., ed. *Religion in Louisiana.* Lafayette: Center for Louisiana Studies, University of Louisiana at Lafayette, 2004.

O'Neil, Charles Edwards. *Church and State in French Colonial Louisiana: Policy and Politics to 1732.* New Haven: Yale University Press, 1966.

Pasquier, Michael. *Gods of the Mississippi.* Bloomington: Indiana University Press, 2013.

———. *Fathers on the Frontier: French Missionaries and the Roman Catholic Priesthood in the United States, 1789–1870.* New York: Oxford University Press, 2010.

THE MANY LANGUAGES OF LOUISIANA

— ✦ —

LOUISIANE/LOUZYANN/LUISIANA/ LOUISIANA

RYAN ORGERA

The richness of Louisiana lies in the colorful manner language and cultures unfold across the state. Many of our languages are part of larger linguistic systems and groups, but like our food, people, and politics, we are often singular in our speech. Sometimes the origins of our expressions are evident, and other times the banality of entrenched usage overshadows the truly tortured oceans, roads, and ages that words have traveled. Louisiana's languages, be they English, French, Vietnamese, or Coushatta, depict how we understand our corner of the planet. Each of our tongues is interconnected; we share words back and forth, and each language is all the richer for it.

The words we use in English, in Louisiana, the words that make our speech distinct to others, are almost universally of an origin other than the British Isles. For instance, we understand the word "zydeco," but we may not know that it comes from a Creole pronunciation of *les haricots* (snapbeans); or that "alligator" is a mangled version of *el lagarato* (Spanish for lizard); or even that the words "okra," "gumbo," "yam," "banjo," and "voodoo" all hail from the African continent. When we go fishing and catch a "choupique" or a "sac à lait" we are using Louisiana French in English. Even the New Orleans tradition of daiquiris is named for an ore-mining beach town in eastern Cuba, which in turn derives its name from the native Taíno language. Even the name of our ubiquitous mosquito (or "maringoin" in parts of south Louisiana), like "daiquiri," comes from Spanish (for "little fly"). After all, Louisiana and much of the United States were at one time part of a Spanish empire.

Often overshadowed by larger groups, the Isleños of Louisiana are descendants of Canary Islanders (an archipelago administered by Spain off the western coast of Morocco). They first arrived here in 1778 as guards against possible English invasion of Spanish Louisiana. Amazingly, much like the Cajuns, they were able to maintain their language for more than two centuries. In part, the success of Louisiana's local languages was, and to a lesser extent is, due to the remoteness of the communities. Often geographic features such as bayous, rivers, lakes, or hills, coupled with limited or infrequent mobility, account for the largest rifts in linguistic evolutions, or here they account for multigenerational language retention. The largest concentration of Isleños is in St. Bernard Parish; however, Hurricane Katrina displaced many of them throughout south Louisiana. In March, the Isleños, along with thousands of other Louisianians and even once the King and Queen of Spain, celebrate their culture during their annual *Fiesta*. The Isleño dialect is regrettably endangered and is currently spoken by a largely elderly population.

So many languages have existed and faded in Louisiana. For instance, the Sicilian and Italian languages would have been a relatively common reverberation in the streets of New Orleans in the nineteenth century; talk of *la zuccarata* (the sugar harvest) would have sounded familiar to passersby as *immigranti* headed to sugar parishes. In the more distant past would have been the prevalence of various West African and Bantu tongues of enslaved peoples in Louisiana. And, perhaps most faded and largely assimilated into tongue-twisting quotidian speech: Native American languages. The Atchafalaya Basin, Tchoupitoulas Street, Ouachita Parish, and the mightiest of all our rivers, the Mississippi, all derive their names from indigenous American languages. Yet of all our non-English languages, none seem to have endeared themselves to the daily imagery of life *en Louisiane* like French.

Fig. 5.1. Historical marker in French. *Dustin Howes*

— ✦ —

LES CADIENS

AARON C. EMMITTE

Cajun French is a dialect of French that is still spoken throughout much of south Louisiana. In recent years, as academic interest in this dialect continues to grow, it is sometimes referred to as Louisiana French. This term serves to more readily include those speakers of French who are not of Acadian descent, such as the Houma Indians, as well as those whose families immigrated to Louisiana directly from Europe or other Francophone areas around the world.

Currently, the majority of Cajun French speakers live in the twenty-two parishes collectively known as Acadiana or the Acadian Triangle. This geographical region stretches from Cameron Parish in the southwest corner of the state, to Lafourche Parish in the southeast, and Avoyelles Parish in the north. Although there are Cajun French speakers living outside of this area, as well as Cajun communities in both Texas and Mississippi, Acadiana serves as the epicenter of Cajun culture. Within Louisiana, there exists to date little accurate data to determine the precise number of Cajun French speakers still living. This inexactitude is due to the unclear and often confusing nature of the language-oriented questions on the U.S. Census. However, most academics and historians agree that there are 100,000–150,000 Cajun French speakers in Louisiana. This number is in a constant state of decline, however, as Cajun French is primarily spoken by older generations and has not often been passed on to children. But a resurgence of interest among younger Cajuns in this heritage language has helped serve as a catalyst for the "Cajun Renaissance" currently taking place throughout the region.

The history of the Cajuns and Cajun French is well documented. Speakers of what is today referred to as Cajun French are descendants

Fig. 5.2. The twenty-two Cajun parishes of Louisiana. *Andrew Joyner*

of the Acadians from Nova Scotia who were expelled by the British in the mid-eighteenth century in what is known as *Le Grand Dérangement* (the Great Upheaval). Because of this expulsion, roughly 3,000 Acadians eventually made their way to Spanish-controlled Louisiana over the course of the second half of the eighteenth century. There they settled along the marshes and prairies of south Louisiana, forming close-knit, isolated communities. Even today, one can see these communities throughout south Louisiana, as many Cajuns continue to live in the same areas settled by the expelled Acadians over two hundred years ago—a tribute to the resilient and proud nature of the Cajun people and to the ongoing fight to preserve this unique language, culture, and heritage.

The ever-growing interest in Cajun French over the past fifty years has generated several avenues by which younger Cajuns can learn the language. Thanks to the preservation efforts of CODOFIL (Council for the Development of French in Louisiana), which was created by the state in the 1960s, there are currently more than 26 French immersion programs in 9 parishes where one can witness children as young as five or six learning and speaking French. This number is on the rise due to Act 679 of 2010, guaranteeing at least one public immersion school in each of the twenty-two parishes of Acadiana. In addition to these state-funded schools, there are several private bilingual schools throughout Louisiana. Louisiana State University, the University of Louisiana at Lafayette, and Tulane University also offer courses in Cajun French. Each of these education efforts is a testament to Louisiana's ongoing commitment to language preservation.

Despite the unfortunate assumption by some that Cajun French is not a "real" variety of French that can be easily understood by speakers of other dialects, this in fact could not be farther from the truth. Differences certainly exist between Cajun French and other varieties spoken in the Francophone world (much like the differences found in varieties of English around the United States and the UK), but these differences rarely prevent other Francophones from understanding Cajun French. In fact, there are countless accounts of French tourists who came to Louisiana and were surprised and impressed by the French that they heard spoken in the state. In turn, when speaking with almost any Cajun, one will most likely hear a story of success at communicating with a Francophone tourist who suddenly needed help—whether it be directions to the French Quarter or help at a local bank.

Although one cannot deny the overall decline of Cajun French since the earlier half of the nineteenth century, the resilient nature of the Cajun people, as well as Louisiana's ardent appreciation of Cajun culture, has slowed this lamentable process. Just drive along any rural highway in Acadiana until you find yourself at a local dance hall or grocery store, and your ears are sure to be filled with the sound of Cajuns speaking French. And while there are perhaps only a handful of monolingual Cajun French speakers alive today, the ever-growing interest of younger Cajuns in the language as well as the continued popularity of Cajun music ensure that the language will live on in some capacity for many generations to come. For, as any Cajun will tell you: in the face of adversity, *lâche pas la patate!* (Don't give up!)

— ✦ —

CREOLE FRENCH IN LOUISIANA/ KREYÒL ANDAN LA LOUZYANN

THOMAS A. KLINGLER

Louisiana Creole is a French-based creole language that shares many features with the other French creoles of the world, and in particular with Haitian Creole. It is an endangered language that is spoken primarily by elderly Louisianians and is no longer being passed on to younger generations. While no reliable statistics exist, recent fieldwork suggests that only a few thousand fluent speakers remain, mostly concentrated in several areas of south Louisiana. The largest numbers today are spread along Bayou Teche from Prairie Laurent in the north to St. Martinville in the south, but pockets of speakers remain in what used to be the main Creole-speaking corridor along the Mississippi, in the parishes of Pointe Coupée, St. James, St. John the Baptist, and St. Charles; a very few speakers may also still be found along the north shore of Lake Pontchartrain in St. Tammany Parish, downriver from New Orleans in Plaquemines

Parish, and far to the north along the Cane River in Natchitoches Parish. The language is not linked in an exclusive way to any single ethnic group, as it is spoken by whites as well as by African Americans and Creoles of color. It displays considerable geographical and ethnic variation, with most white speakers employing a greater number of French-like pronunciations and grammatical forms.

Determining who speaks Creole is complicated by the labels speakers use to refer to their language variety. There is a close association of ethnic labels with language labels, such that people who refer to themselves as Creole—primarily African Americans and Creoles of color—tend also to apply the same name to the variety of French that they speak. In some cases that variety is what can linguistically be defined as Louisiana Creole, but often it is in fact closer to the "Cajun" French spoken by those who also typically identify themselves as Cajuns.

The origins of Louisiana Creole are not fully understood. Because of its affinity with Haitian Creole, coupled with the documented migration to Louisiana of more than 10,000 slaves and free persons from the former French colony of Saint-Domingue (modern-day Haiti) in the first decade of the nineteenth century, it is sometimes claimed that the language was imported to Louisiana from Saint-Domingue and is thus an offshoot of Haitian Creole. This claim is thrown into doubt, however, by archival evidence showing that a creole language existed in Louisiana well before the influx of former residents of Saint-Domingue. The possibility therefore cannot be excluded that Louisiana Creole is indigenous to the region, having arisen on site through linguistic contact between French colonists and African slaves.

Creole shares most of its lexicon with Louisiana French (commonly known as Cajun), but the two varieties can most clearly be distinguished on the level of grammatical structure, in particular in the pronoun and verb systems. The following examples of English cue sentences translated into Creole and French, gathered through fieldwork among native speakers, illustrate a few key differences between the two varieties. A French-based spelling has been used to represent the Creole sentences so as not to make the differences between them and their Louisiana French equivalents appear greater than they in fact are.

English cue sentence	Louisiana French	Louisiana Creole
1. I have five dollars.	*J'ai cinq piastres.*	*Mo gain cinq piastres.*
2. He threw me the ball.	*Il m'a 'voyé la pelote.*	*Li 'voyé mon la pelote.*
3. He's rich.	*Il est riche.*	*Li riche.*

Notable differences include the subject pronouns *j'* (< *je*) for the first-person singular and *il* for the third-person singular in French versus *mo* and *li,* respectively, in Creole; the Creole verb *gain* instead of French *ai* (*avoir*) for 'have'; the placement of the first-person singular indirect object pronoun *m'* before the verb in French versus the placement of Creole *mon* after the verb (sentence 2); and, in sentence 3, the absence of the copula *est* ('is') in Creole.

In areas where French and Creole speakers live in close contact, one often encounters a mixing of features typical of the two varieties. This is the case in St. Landry Parish, for example, where one speaker translated sentence 2 as *Il a 'voyé mon la pelote,* where the subject pronoun and the formation of the past tense (*a* + *'voyé*) are typical of French, but the indirect object pronoun *mon* is more typical of Creole in its form as well as in its placement after, rather than before, the verb.

— ✦ —

CAJUN VERNACULAR ENGLISH

SYLVIE DUBOIS

Cajuns live all along the Gulf Coast from Texas to Mississippi but are primarily concentrated in the small rural towns of southern Louisiana. In Louisiana they joined many other French dialect–speaking populations as well as other people who had a language other than French as their first. Even after the Louisiana Purchase, when English became the de facto official language, Cajuns living in rural communities continued to speak only French. They lived, as many continue to live today, in small towns in close-knit extended families; they maintained their coherence as a separate ethnic group until the turn of the twentieth century, when they began to assimilate into the Anglo-American dominant culture. Today, their economic status has improved and the Cajun Renaissance has ignited a pride in Cajun ancestry and in their contribution to the unique character of Louisiana. While most Louisianians do not speak French, much of the English spoken in the state is inflected and peppered with French.

Cajun Vernacular English (CVE) is spoken by French/English bilinguals and, to some extent, English monolinguals living in French-dominant rural areas of south Louisiana. This vernacular has changed dramatically over three generations against a complex and dynamic social and linguistic background. Although the state government mandated English as the sole language of education in 1929, English was not used extensively within the Cajun communities and in the family setting. Moreover, English was not thoroughly learned since many attended school irregularly or left school early. For quite a while English may have been the language of the classroom, but Cajun French was the language of the playground. It is this generation, people who are eighty years or older today, who are the original speakers of CVE.

The post–World War II generation reaped the financial and social benefits of several far-reaching changes, notably the expansion of educational networks, the modernization of the road system, the mechanization of agriculture, and the development of the oil industry. These changes disrupted the socioeconomic order on which the small francophone communities rested and thus accelerated their assimilation into American Anglophone culture. Those who, for ethnic or linguistic reasons, did not assimilate—i.e., those who maintained bilingualism—became definitively marginalized. Their francophone culture was discredited, their variety of French was devalued, their variety of English was ridiculed. The children of the original CVE speakers, who had grown up speaking French within their families, began to learn English better than their parents, attended school more regularly and for longer, and became financially more secure.

What stopped this cultural change from completely taking over is popularly called the Cajun Renaissance. In many ethnic groups, it is often the third generation in the language change/replacement process who feel the loss of culture the most. The old have not lost it, the middle-aged have consciously rejected it, and it is the young who suffer a sense of loss. Today, things Cajun have risen to an unprecedented status among Cajuns as well as outsiders. Cajun music, Cajun food, children's books about Cajun life, serious Cajun literature—all backed up by state government support for its formerly French-speaking citizens—are to be found everywhere. Tourists come from near and far to participate in Cajun festivities. Bilingualism, however, has suffered a tremendous loss. The dilemma for Cajuns is that they no longer have the linguistic distinctiveness they once had; those who want to mark their Cajun identity linguistically have only English as a vehicle. The young have begun to use some aspects of the CVE of their grandparents, the variety of English that had been widely rejected by the middle-aged at the same time that they were rejecting French.

Although some of the features that are characteristic of CVE are also well-known variables in southern American English, the origins of this dialect lie within the Cajun community and cannot be attributed solely to interference from French or to the spread of these features from the surrounding English dialects. Some of the Cajun variants that began in the accented speech of the oldest of the speakers in our sample have either been passed on to the next generation of speakers or have been recycled as markers of social identity by the youngest speakers.

Two fundamental phonological principles are at the heart of CVE. The first is the dropping of final consonants. This occurs in both long and short words. This phonological rule has a consequence: important contextual final consonants (like -ed denoting past tense or -s marking plurality) are deleted at the ends of words, as in *retire* (retired) or *cow* (cows). The second phonological principle is the reduction of elongated vowels that is so commonly associated with other varieties of southern English, as in *fahr* (fire).

Other distinctive features are associated with CVE. CVE speakers do not aspirate (producing an audible puff of breath) [p, t, k] at the beginning of a word, as in: "plant," "table," and "car." By not aspirating [p] in the word *pat,* it has the effect of sounding like *bat* for American English speakers. The word *hair* pronounced without [h] sounds like *air.* CVE speakers also substitute the consonants [t, d] for [th, dh]. The paradigm 'dis, dat, dese, dose' (this, that, these, those) is well known in Louisiana to describe how Cajuns talk. The letter *r* at the end of words is often dropped, such as the pronunciation *lettuh* (letter). CVE speakers also use what is known as a rolled [r] in words that begin with [tr, dr, fr], for example *tree*. They also delete the letter [l] in words such as *celery, jewelry,* and *help,* producing *cerey, jewery, hep.*

Cajun men and women have changed their ways of speaking over three generations because they belong to a cultural enclave that for several generations has been forced to change in the direction of a more dominant Anglo-American culture. The last twist of the CVE story is the gender differentiation in the usage of several CVE features in the younger generation. Young men recycle the CVE forms used by their grandparents' generation, while young women generally use the standard southern features introduced by the middle-aged speakers. This gendered pattern can be attributed to the fact that the Cajun Renaissance largely affects the sphere of traditional male activities such as boating, fishing, and hunting, and the display of Cajun culture associated with tourism (e.g. few women participate in the traditional *courir de Mardi Gras* or take tourists on trips up the bayou). Music is traditionally an essential part of the Cajun male culture; even Cajun cuisine is publicly displayed as part of the male domain. A higher percentage of Cajun men than women are involved in Cajun advocacy organizations or report listening to Cajun radio programs. Young women have not moved to recycle the CVE features because they have fewer reasons than young men to associate themselves linguistically to the current understanding of a Cajun identity, which is largely masculine.

The birth of CVE occurred less than a hundred years ago; in that time it developed into a quite distinctive vernacular, came very close to dying, and was reborn. In fact, without its rebirth in recent times, we may well have failed to notice the birth at all. We would have said it was just the way people speak who learn English as a second language. Like so many varieties of accented English, it is not expected to be passed on to subsequent generations. The story of the fate of the languages of the Cajun people mirrors their history, and the comings and goings of CVE are intimately connected to the social and economic buffeting of the Cajun community since the turn of the twentieth century. The way Cajuns speak stems from their dialect's unique journey through time. Power rivalry between several social groups in constant concurrence shaped their linguistic history, which is a story about linguistic persistence.

SELECTED READINGS

Dubois, Sylvie, and Barbara M. Horvath. "When the Music Changes, You Change Too: Gender and Language Change in Cajun English." *Language Variation and Change* 11.3 (1999): 287–313.

———. "Sounding Cajun: The Rhetorical Use of Dialect in Speech and Writing." *American Speech* 77.3 (2000): 264–87.

———. "Verbal Morphology in Cajun Vernacular English: A Comparison with Other Varieties of Southern English." *Journal of English Language and Linguistics* 31.1 (2003): 1–26.

———. "Cajun Vernacular English: Phonology." In *A Handbook of Varieties of English*. Vol. 1, *Phonology*, edited by E. W. Schneider et al. Berlin: Mouton de Gruyter, 2005. 407–16.

Klingler, Thomas A. "Louisiana Creole: The Multiple Geneses Hypothesis Reconsidered." *Journal of Pidgin and Creole Languages* 15.1 (2000): 1–35.

———. *"If I Could Turn My Tongue Like That": The Creole Language of Pointe Coupee Parish, Louisiana*. Baton Rouge: LSU Press, 2003.

Neumann, Ingrid. *Le créole de Breaux Bridge, Louisiane: description grammaticale, textes, vocabulaire*. Hamburg: Buske, 1985.

Neumann-Holzschuh, Ingrid. *Textes anciens en créole louisianais*. Hamburg: Buske, 1987.

Valdman, Albert, Thomas A. Klingler, Margaret M. Marshall, and Kevin J. Rottet. *Dictionary of Louisiana Creole*. Bloomington: Indiana University Press, 1998.

Valdman, Albert, Kevin J. Rottet, et al. *Dictionary of Louisiana French: As Spoken in Cajun, Creole, and American Indian Communities*. Jackson, MS: University Press of Mississippi, 2010.

LITERARY CARNIVAL AND THE DREAM STATE

KAREN WILLIAMS

Through all the Dream State's *sturm und drang,* Louisiana literature continues to thrive. Although Louisiana can no longer boast the richest city in North America (as New Orleans was in 1840), our literature continues to shine a light on regional color and transmute it into an aesthetic of universal significance, one that is varied, but not motley; local, but not parochial. From John Kennedy Toole's vivid portrait of New Orleans's Irish Channel residents and French Quarter bars to Walker Percy's existentialist visions of carnival krewes and moviegoers; from Kate Chopin's pictures of Grand Isle as an exotic resort for wealthy Creoles to Ernest Gaines's exploration of race, food, and culture in his painstakingly real glimpses of Louisiana life—Louisiana literature encapsulates the varied regions, seeming contradictions, and clashing cultures that make up the state.

LOUISIANA FOLKLORE

Louisiana is of course ripe with folktales that detail the resilience of its inhabitants. Unfortunately we need to broadcast more clearly our unique stories. Some remain simply local treasures, while others have been usurped by later writers, Yankees, or even Walt Disney. Creole, Cajun, African, Anglo, and Isleño cultures (as well as others) contributed their own traditions. For example, the Isleños, immigrants from the Canary Islands who settled south of New Orleans, are known for their *décimas*, songs written traditionally in ten-line stanzas, which often satirize local residents or events. Originating in sixteenth-century Spain, the form was brought to Louisiana in the 1780s. Typical titles include "Wila the Mule," "The Giant Trout," "Mosquitoes and High Water," with updated songs such as "Welfare Work" and "The Crab Fisherman's Lament." Irvan Perez, a renowned *décima* singer who lost his home in 2005 to Hurricane Katrina and who died of a heart attack in 2008, recorded an especially rousing number about trying to move an old mule by boat. The mule is excitable and uncooperative, and the boat is in danger of capsizing. The men frantically prod and beat the old mule until he's still. When they reach shore, the mule is dead. A little different from the traditional idea of beating a dead horse but with an equally important lesson, this proverb comes directly from experiences in the Louisiana wetlands.

Like the *décimas*, the tales of Br'er Rabbit found a home in south Louisiana. Widely popularized by Joel Chandler Harris in 1880 and by Walt Disney in his 1946 *Song of the South,* Br'er Rabbit tales were being celebrated in the early 1800s at Laura Plantation near Vacherie and were collected by a young neighbor, Alcée Fortier, in the 1870s. Fortier went on to publish his Louisiana folktales at about the same time as Harris. Originally West African tales of trickster figures like the hare, in the American South the stories centered more and more on the rabbit. In French Louisiana the character became Compair Lapin, who was able to outsmart any fool or any circumstance. Folklorists recognize in the resourceful rabbit the indomitable spirit of slaves who managed to survive with wit, sagacity, and a bit of scornful humor directed toward slaveowners. Perhaps the most widely known tale involves the tar baby, concocted by Br'er Fox, who finally thinks he has the erstwhile rabbit trapped. Readers have to be careful to hear the whole story, however. While Br'er Rabbit does become ensnared with the tar baby and falls into Br'er Fox's custody, he escapes with his famous plea: "Please, Br'er Fox, do whatever you want with me, but don't throw me into that briar patch."

The Acadians, dispersed from Novia Scotia or *Acadie,* also have a rich variety of tales dealing with the Louisiana landscape. Early tales reveal newcomers' apprehensions about entering a new territory. Struggles with climate, clashes with other cultures, and uneasy Americanization abound in the early literature. Cajuns were particularly impressed by a native insect that seemed to be waiting for their fresh supply of human blood, perhaps foretelling Anne Rice's later vampire tales set in Louisiana. Often in the Cajun tales, however, it is other ethnicities that are not able to cope with life's irritations. In her collection of folktales, J. J. Reneaux recounts the story of three Irishmen who come "down the bayou" in hope of making a living from the warmer climate and the rich soil. Darkness falls, and they are completely lost in a watery wasteland, beset by bloodsuckers that they cannot see. They can run nowhere to elude the swarming pests. So they do the only thing possible: wait until morning and head out, vowing to return to Ireland and not complain about eating another potato.

Besides having to confront new monsters, the Cajun settlers also brought with them from France and then from Nova Scotia a creature who would become a new-world counterpart to a European beast. The werewolf transformed into the loup garou, used by parents to lure their children into good behavior: "If you're not good, the loup garou will get you!" In many Cajun tales the beast is in human form during the day, but a wolf at night, especially during the full moon. Some tales mark the loup garou as someone who has sold his soul to the devil. In Louisiana culture there is an interesting variation in the making of new werewolves. Instead of being bitten by a wolf, the one affected has drawn the blood of the animal, which turns the animal into a human. Then, if the blood drawer can be silent for a period, such as 101 days, all will be well. But if he blabs, they both revert to werewolves. Besides not being as bloodthirsty as the typical werewolf, the loup garou sometimes becomes a helpful, but shadowy, presence to a particular individual. Loulan Pitre, father of filmmaker Glen Pitre, details the story of oyster cleaners laying off work for a much-needed rest. The next morning, they find the oysters have been cleaned. After several days, one man decides to stay at night to glimpse the benefactor—none other than the loup garou!

Of course any canon of folklore should include stories of princesses, beautiful maidens, rival females; and it should also focus on the hearth or the kitchen as the heart of the culture. In Louisiana, however, the magic beans or stone soup is not merely the appetizer to the main course of the story. The food gains ultimate, almost sacramental importance. Reneaux recounts the story of a beautiful shiny-faced Cajun girl named La Graisse who manages to win the love of a prince. But his female cook is jealous and afraid of losing her job, so she commands La Graisse to see what it's like to slave over a burning stove. The kitchen gets hotter and hotter, and La Graisse begins to melt. A warning bird goes to retrieve the prince, but when he arrives, it is too late. He tries to scoop up his love, but she keeps slipping out of his grasp. Now she haunts the kitchen in a thin film of grease; cooks may try to wipe her away, but she remains.

CATEGORIES OF CARNIVAL

Its numerous celebrations and festivals set Louisiana apart as a state, and it is a state that often looks at the world through the lens of carnival. Carnival is characterized by eccentricity, by free and familiar contact, by startling combinations, and by an insistent emphasis on the body. Carnival is a world acknowledging shifts and change as the norm. A king may become a servant, a pauper may become rich; somewhere inside a wizened hag is a beautiful young girl and vice versa. In carnival there is a mixing of high and low; misalliances such as beauty and ugliness existing together; luxuriant growth in the midst of rampant decay; and a focus on food and the body, both literally and symbolically.

A quick or a thorough survey of Louisiana literature reveals the proliferation of carnival. Of course New Orleans bursts with carnival, but it is not confined to the Crescent City. A popular contemporary play, *Steel Magnolias*, made into a film starring Julia Roberts in 1989, focuses on the northwest Louisiana town of Natchitoches, oldest permanent settlement in the Louisiana Territory. Writing a tribute to his sister and mother, Robert Harling provides a hysterically funny story of his sister's struggle with and ultimate defeat by diabetes. Combining laughter and grief in this way is a long-established carnival motif, as evidenced in the great French Renaissance writer François Rabelais. One of the earliest European carnival stories involves the monsters Gargantua and Pantagruel; Gargantua experiences simultaneously the height of joy and the depth of sorrow at the birth of his son Pantagruel, as the mother dies during the difficult labor. Likewise, in *Steel Magnolias*, M'Lynn and daughter Shelby fight and love each other through each stage of Shelby's childhood and young adulthood, the mother at first lamenting her daughter's pregnancy, which will surely tax her fragile system. Yet M'Lynn loves her grandchild unreservedly, paying attention to Shelby's declaration: "I would rather have thirty minutes of wonderful than a lifetime of nothing special."

Eccentric characters of various status and wealth interact in that mecca of feminine power the local beauty shop, owned by the kindly Truvy. Customers include the wealthy but crass Ouiser Boudreaux; the more reformed, but wicked wit Clairee; and of course the mother/daughter pair of M'Lynn and Shelby. Added to the mix is a young, destitute, abandoned wife who goes through equal stages of Pentecostal fervor and much-needed periods of secular exuberance. All of these women gather to gossip, judge, laugh, and love one another in the midst of frequent bickering and occasional tragedy.

The image of southern belle is both upheld and satirized by the characters. For her wedding, Shelby insists on turning the church into a repository for every shade of pink, a nauseatingly feminine rendition reminiscent of Pepto-Bismol. The elegant bridal cake is nicely juxtaposed with a red velvet groom's cake in the shape of an armadillo, complete with rodent tail and whiskers, that bleeds when cut. The wedding feast is also highlighted by feuding with neighbors (shots are fired). There is a reminder that death and disease may overtake the happiest occasions in the ominous arrival of Ouiser's mange-ridden dog and in Shelby's diabetic seizure the very morning of the wedding.

The saddest and funniest scene of the film occurs at the grave site of Shelby only a few years later, where the women have gathered to comfort the longsuffering but usually upbeat and determined M'Lynn. Annabelle, in her religious mode, tries to assure M'Lynn that God is in control and has taken Shelby home. In her grief, M'Lynn discards this comfort and states her anger: "I just want to hit somebody." Quickly Clairee grabs hold of Ouiser and tells her to punch away. From uncontrollable tears, everyone except for Ouiser erupts into uncontrollable laughter.

Even the north Louisiana city of Monroe, far removed from New Orleans not only in geography but in religious practices, attitudes, and general culture, becomes a nexus of carnival through the eyes of John

Dufresne, who sojourned there during a stint of teaching at what was then called Northeast Louisiana University. In *Louisiana Power and Light*, he chronicles the history of the hapless Fontana clan, "the most executed family in the history of Louisiana," who stumbled through the wilds of Chauvin Bottom and viewed the flood of 1927 as vengeance of the Lord for the sins of Monroe, refusing any offers of food or shelter. Dufresne paints Monroe as a town built on stories. Small enough for everyone to know everybody's else's business, it is a place where intricate relationships of love and business result in betrayals, divorces, even assassination attempts. He joyously mixes together a Pakistani motel operator sent to America as a divine savior for his family, a local politician who continues to serve after being shot and rendered mentally incompetent, an intellectual who holds the best carp tournament in the area in his swimming pool, and the last remaining Fontana, who was raised by nuns and wooed away from the priesthood by a young runaway who had traveled to New Orleans and witnessed Ignatius Reilly (John Kennedy Toole's fictional masterpiece of grotesque gluttony) selling hot dogs. Comedy prevails through horrendous betrayals, numerous birth defects, and horrifying deaths. Yes—I said comedy. Billy Wayne Fontana's ancestors include Napoleon Fontana, who ingeniously designed an armadillo evening bag whose handle was the animal's own tail. Unfortunately contracting leprosy from his products, Napoleon returned home "with four of his toes wrapped in a knotted calico neckerchief." Syphilitic women and mental defectives somehow manage to propagate, rendering names such as Positive Wasserman Fontana. The community is hopeful that the clan will die out with Billy Wayne, especially after his wife is unable to conceive; but he remarries and has two children, one with a heart defect and one with flippers for legs. Both sons die fantastic deaths, and Billy Wayne martyrs himself by retreating into the woods. Believing himself an "abomination," he makes himself "a crown of nettle":

> The nettle, of course, itched, stung, blotted his skin no doubt, and within hours swelled his eyes shut. So there he was, the final Fontana, stumbling through his ancestral home, blind as his daddy, eyes without light, trying to exorcise his tenacious demons or atone for this original sin he carried in his genes, when he fell into a nest of cottonmouths. We found him in

the morning, bloated with swamp water and venom, and covered with snakes. (chap. 13)

Through the ordeals of Billy Wayne, Monroe emerges as a place of gossip, friendship, kindness, brutality, vengeance, and forgiveness. On the surface, Monroe is the plain southern Protestant town devoid of New Orleans vices, Cajun exuberance, and plantation country manners and presumptions. But as Dufresne points out, north Louisiana was once host to a civilization of continental importance, a Native American settlement of trade, science, and agricultural innovations, with a storytelling tradition as old as the land itself.

MIXING OF CULTURES

The mix of reality, magic, high and low, and contrasting ideologies is a prime focus of Robert Olen Butler's collection of short stories, *A Good Scent from a Strange Mountain*. Butler presents Vietnamese immigrants who interpret Louisiana through Eastern eyes, seeing the Superdome as a giant mandarin hat, both welcoming and confounding them. In "Fairy Tale," New Orleans provides refuge for an abandoned young woman who wants to be both a practicing Catholic and a bar girl, but who ultimately finds herself the heroine of a fairytale about an exotic transplant (a nutria, representing herself) and a sunburnt duck, a Cajun veteran who falls in love with her after professing his love for her country. Butler sets his stories in Louisiana from Lake Charles to New Orleans, imagining the lives of North and South Vietnamese, old and young, male and female, Buddhist and Catholic. In "Love," a man who had been a spy, an important courier for the Americans, finds himself aground in Gretna without his former power. The man who used to be able to command fire from heaven is surrounded by a Vietnamese community who no longer respects him. In addition, his beautiful wife attracts attention from unworthy Vietnamese men. In a new land, this small, unimposing man must find a new way to exert power. He visits a voodoo doctor, who sends him on various tasks to secure his wife's love and defeat her lover. He must fill a hog bladder with items including blood and she-goat droppings, which he retrieves from the Audubon Zoo petting area, confusing the group of schoolchildren watching his every move. Next he must throw the sack across the man's house, but it lands in a tree that the dignified man must then climb, only to see his wife and her lover run out to discover him. Luckily, the voodoo works as he falls from the tree to the dismay of his wife, who accompanies him to the hospital and can never again doubt her husband's love.

The stories use ghosts, tales of ancestor worship, and enigmatic parrots to blur the distinctions between myth and reality. Louisiana serves in the tales as a foreign place that is yet somehow familiar to the Vietnamese citizens who feel betwixt and between worlds—a common aspect of carnival culture. Louisiana both welcomes and repels, invites and excludes. Like other immigrants before them, the Vietnamese have made their indelible mark on the Louisiana landscape, even creating their own enclave named Versailles in New Orleans East. The area was heavily damaged by Hurricane Katrina but one of the first to be rebuilt because of strong community ties and the fervor of its residents to recreate their gardens, markets, and worship centers.

CARNIVAL FIGURES

Louisiana has rich literature in all regions—northern, central, and southern. As one might expect, however, the highest concentration of literature comes from artists living in or writing about New Orleans. Carnival ideas prevail from early writings by George Washington Cable and Kate Chopin to modern writers like Anne Rice, Walker Percy, and John Kennedy Toole, and extend to the body of literature written as a response to Hurricane Katrina.

As early as the 1880s, Cable recognized the romance of New Orleans, noting the tensions between the "Americans" and the white Creoles of French descent, whose dialect he detailed. In *The Grandissimes*, Cable writes of an elite French Creole family surprised by the American purchase of the city in 1803. He also chronicles the tale of Bras Coupé as an indictment against slavery. A powerful Jaloff prince in Africa, Bras Coupé was captured and brought to New Orleans as a slave. All who see him witness a man of force and dignity. He is slave but king still. Unable to adapt, he breaks his bonds and retreats to the swamps surrounding

New Orleans. He is captured upon returning to claim his wife. Branded, ears shorn, and hamstrings cut, he is left to die but emits no moan, at the end declaring that he is going to paradise—"To Africa."

The juxtaposition of opposites such as the slave/king and the eccentricity of New Orleans characters, both distinctive elements of Louisiana carnival, are paramount in this early novel, and are manifested a hundredfold in Toole's modern-day novel of New Orleans, *A Confederacy of Dunces*. Published posthumously in 1980 after Toole's mother demanded Walker Percy's attention, the novel brims with carnival-like figures: Mancuso, a bumbling undercover policeman; Irene, an overbearing, alcohol-guzzling mother; several bona fide hags of surprising vitality; a Nazi-like bar operator who uses her body as well-oiled machine; a wannabe stripper; a gang of homosexuals threatening to wage peace through degeneracy; a legion of black factory workers reluctantly demanding better conditions; Jones, a black hipster one step ahead of vagrancy; and George, a teenage conman selling pornography to the schoolboy market—all propelled to greater and greater idiocy by one Ignatius J. Reilly, buffoon extraordinaire. Ignatius is no typical buffoon, however. Possessing an advanced degree in medieval studies, he abhors the popular culture of the 1960s while simultaneously guzzling donuts, hot dogs, soda pop, and contemporary TV shows and films, which he watches to express his displeasure. Harkening back to those gigantic figures Gargantua and Pantagruel, Ignatius becomes the grotesque gourmand whose impressive bulk continues to transgress its boundaries. Who can forget the blue and yellowed eyes, the Vaselined mustache, the pachyderm hips? From start to finish the reader is inundated with images of Ignatius's body and bodily functions. The opening sentence lets us know we are in for a grotesque treat: "A green hunting cap squeezed the top of the fleshy balloon of a head. The green earflaps, full of large ears and uncut hair and the fine bristles that grew in the ears themselves, stuck out on either side like turn signals indicating two directions at once." Operating according to the rhythms of his pyloric valve, Ignatius combines in himself astuteness and stupidity, a professed concern for the soul with an obsession for feeding and enlarging his intimidating girth. As in carnival, conflict, both verbal and physical, infiltrates the scenes. Ignatius engages in one hilarious assault after another, tapping the effete Dorian Greene with a plastic scimitar, hurling the end of the hot dog wagon directly at George's crotch, and finding his throat between Mr. Clyde's corroded hot dog tongs after he eats up all the profits. The insistence on the body prevails in every scene, and it is quite fitting that Ignatius becomes both the purveyor and consumer of hot dogs since sausages, tripe, and wieners are traditional carnival fare both for their phallic manifestations and for the idea of eating something that was once part of the stomach or even bowels, as casings were often made from intestines. Carnival mixes together the eater with the eaten, the disgusting with the delicious, camaraderie with discord, as free and familiar contact and marketplace manners rule.

Of course, New Orleans's literary canon includes genres besides fiction. Poetry, song, and drama are especially prominent. The songs of the Mardi Gras Indians provide a third carnival figure joining Cable's slave/king and Toole's grotesque gourmand: the beautiful big chief extolled in the lyrics of the Indians, various groups of working-class blacks that have sewed their own sequined suits and paraded in their neighborhoods on Mardi Gras day. The chief is the dominant figure of pride and power: "He won't bow down, down on the ground." His suit is the prettiest, his crown the grandest, his singing the best. As you might expect, rival gangs argue that their chief is superior, with many songs making reference to meeting the boys on the battlefield and settling scores on Mardi Gras day, a once common occurrence. A number of the songs also highlight a "little bitty boy with a heart of steel," who prepares to march with his chief and stand firm with his tribe. Note the references to violence in this important variation of an Indian song, popularized by the Dixie Cups:

> My grandma and your grandma were
> sittin' by the fire
> My grandma told
> your grandma "I'm gonna set your flag on fire,"
>
> Talkin' 'bout hey now (hey now) hey now (hey now)
> Jocko mo feeno ah na ney,
> Jocko mo feeno ah na ney.

Looka my king all dressed in red
ko Iko 'n day
Bet you five dollars he kill you all dead
Jocko mo feeno ah na ney.

The song begins with a fireside scene of two grandmothers—not warriors—but quickly the tone shifts to battle: "I'm gonna set your flag on fire." This version of a traditional song emphasizes the deadly beauty of the king. In fact, the chief is supposed to represent resistance, bravery, control. The tradition of dressing up as Native Americans does not detract from the African Americans' own heritage; that heritage is reinforced through the call-and-response format of the traditional songs and percussive rhythms of West Africa. Above all, the chief "got fiyo—Ma day cootie fiyo"—"My chief has the fire." The particular figures and repeated tropes of the Indian songs showcase the chief as an exuberant and proud figure.

Another exuberant but ultimately tragic literary figure that seems to embody the city of New Orleans itself is the decaying southern belle, Blanche DuBois, frantically clinging to gentility and beauty as brutality and age move in. One cannot discuss the prominence of Louisiana literature without acknowledging the great playwright Thomas Williams, who found both his name, Tennessee, and his home in New Orleans. Originally from Mississippi and Missouri, Williams claimed that in his first visit to New Orleans he discovered a place where he could be himself. His love for the city shows even in his stage directions for the opening of *A Streetcar Named Desire:*

> The section is poor but, unlike corresponding sections in other American cities, it has a certain raffish charm. . . . It is first dark of an evening early in May. The sky that shows around the dim white building is a peculiarly tender blue, almost a turquoise, which invests the scene with a kind of lyricism and gracefully attenuates the atmosphere of decay. (scene 1)

What Williams found was a city whose landmarks and characters needed little embellishment. Thus he could have Blanche refer to actual locations that assume mythical dimension: "They told me to take a streetcar named Desire, and then transfer to one called Cemeteries and ride six blocks and get off at—Elysian Fields!" Originally naming the play "The Poker Fight," Williams kept hearing the clackety streetcar traveling through the Quarter until he acknowledged its call and renamed his masterpiece *A Streetcar Named Desire.*

A number of Williams's plays owe their birth to New Orleans and its carnival philosophy, their setting and their subject matter reflecting seeming contradictions of virtue and vice, gentility and brutishness, kindness and indifference. In the French Quarter one might expect violent passions and eccentric behavior, but Williams sets *Suddenly Last Summer,* perhaps his starkest play, in the Garden District, in the home of the respected Violet Venable. Williams shows that beneath the veneer of civility, the beasts stalk. Violet is pushing to have her niece Holley lobotomized to relieve her extreme distress and obsession with her cousin's death. The backdrop is a fantastical garden beautiful and deadly, housed within Venable's mansion. Slowly the tale unfolds of a mother/son pair whose excursions to exotic locales allowed them to fulfill their appetites for beauty, food, indolence, and affairs of the flesh—luring companions with their intellect, charm, and money. The mother became too old to attract, however, and the niece became an unwitting accomplice in procuring handsome males for the pleasure of her cousin. The son falls victim to a mob of starving boys who tear him to pieces as the cousin watches in horror. Fortunately for her, the doctor believes her story, and the mother must live with the knowledge that her and her son's appetites have led to death. Their love of beauty, so voracious it couldn't contain itself in art or landscape, or in spiritual aesthetics, extended to the flesh itself and, in carnival fashion, pressed toward the grotesque. The love of flesh reveals itself finally in a literal rending, even chewing of the flesh.

Like Violet, Blanche DuBois is a creature controlled by appetites who sees her beauty fading before an inevitable decay. However, Blanche is driven even more by a fear of death, as she declares, "What is the opposite of death—desire." On the flip side, however, she acknowledges that she has ridden this streetcar too often—that it has brought her to a place where she is not wanted and where she does not want to be. Williams said of Blanche that she was a creature that felt too much, was driven by a kind of fury. In Blanche's young life, desire and death became forever entwined in her young husband's suicide. When she learns of her husband's long association with another man, she expresses her disgust, which leads to his death. Mixing together guilt and hurt and a need to be desired, Blanche continues to call upon her charms, transforming from southern belle to middle-aged seductress to a fragile woman desperate for kindness from strangers. New Orleans's carnival demands too much of the flesh, however. She cannot escape its pull, as her brutish brother-in-law sees through her mask of virginal gentility. The ensuing assault breaks her illusions and sends her over the edge to insanity.

This attention to the flesh is a strong vein in New Orleans literature, emerging vividly in Anne Rice, who re-envisions the old-world vampire coming to the port city of New Orleans. Her first and perhaps best vampire novel, *Interview with the Vampire,* is set largely in New Orleans as Louis de Pointe du Lac retells his story to a reporter. Nineteenth-century New Orleans seems a prime location for extremes. Stately plantations exist just miles away from sordid city quarters, prosperous planters lord it over humans treated as property, and various types of humanity converge in the crowded streets. As Louis finds out, this includes the wandering undead. Louis succumbs, hating the creature he is turned into. He must live on blood but is loath to kill, existing for some months on rats. A man who loves beauty, Louis must live with ugliness. Rice gives a picture of a sophisticated, genteel society that is equally barbaric, unrefined, and cruel. Louis speaks of the land known for its sugar plantations: "There is something perfect and ironic about this land which I loved producing refined sugar. . . . This refined sugar is a poison. It was like the essence of life in New Orleans, so sweet that it can be fatal, so richly enticing that all other values are forgotten." Rice's vampire becomes the ultimate creature of carnival oppositions, living betwixt and between two worlds—the living and the dead.

THE UNIVERSAL APPEAL OF LOUISIANA LITERATURE

It is apropos to think of many New Orleans works featuring carnival, especially those imbued with comedy or appealing to the popular market, but Louisiana writers viewed as serious or philosophical also deal with carnival. Walker Percy's existentialist novel *The Moviegoer* focuses on a Gentilly businessman undergoing a search who, like Ignatius, spends much of his time watching movies and avoiding the crises of his own life. Binx wishes, however, that he could be like his uncle Julian, an easy Creole, leader of an established Mardi Gras krewe. Percy pays attention to the less exotic New Orleans, but again shows characters who inhabit the betwixt and between, who know that status, relationships, and personal philosophies may change at a moment's notice. Percy continues his intellectual, deadly serious comedies with Dr. Tom Moore, a physician convicted for selling drugs at a truck stop, who endures through *Love in the Ruins* and the aptly named *Thanatos Syndrome*. After spending two years in prison, Dr. Moore returns to Feliciana to find former patients appearing calmer, less neurotic, pleasant, and vacant. Thus he uncovers a plot to pacify the whole population by dispersing heavy sodium into the water. Luckily he is able to restore frustration and desire to the unknowing population.

Another novelist celebrated nationally is Ernest Gaines, whose works deal with universal questions of dignity, acceptance, and equality. They are firmly set in the Louisiana that Gaines grew up in. His works inhabit the rural landscape near False River and Pointe Coupée, giving the reader a look at the plantation system from the eyes of the African Americans who worked and lived on them. If one wants to learn about authentic Cajun and African American customs in Louisiana, Gaines is definitely an author to read.

In *The Autobiography of Miss Jane Pittman*, Gaines showcases the Louisiana landscape through one hundred years in the life of one exceptional woman born into slavery who endures into the twentieth century. Gaines also renders the plantation community in *A Gathering of Old Men*, where a group of old farmers rally to protect a black man falsely accused of murder. Community is strong in Gaines's novels, where pictures of daily life, work, food, church, and school are brought to life. In *A Lesson before Dying*, Gaines explores the racial setting of 1940s Louisiana, where it was virtually impossible for a black man to have a trial with a jury of his peers. Jefferson is in the wrong place at the wrong time, in the company of two men who start an argument and a shooting at a local grocery store. He is quickly convicted by the all-white jury, although the evidence is all circumstantial. There is no chance for another trial; and to add to the injury, his lawyer argues in his defense by ridiculing his face, demeanor, and race by claiming he did not have enough sense to plan a murder: executing him would be the same as killing a hog. Jefferson's godmother cannot suffer this indignity and prevails upon the white authorities to allow the reluctant black schoolteacher to hold sessions with Jefferson before his death to make him understand his humanity. Grant, the teacher, finds himself between two worlds. Highly educated and refined in temperament, he lives in a rude house, unpainted and unadorned, and teaches in a simple church whose wooden pews must serve as school desks and whose supplies are meager items handed down from white schools. Yet when this man known as professor seeks admittance to the house of Henri Pichot, head of the family for whom his aunt had worked for over fifty years, he must enter the back door and wait in the kitchen until summoned. He explains his position succinctly: "I tried to decide just how I should respond to them. Whether I should act like the teacher that I was, or like the nigger that I was supposed to be."

As Grant, out of love for his aunt and his girlfriend Vivian, continues meeting with a bitter Jefferson, there finally is a sense of redemption. Among the coarse law officials is one white deputy, Paul, who treats Jefferson and his visitors fairly; and through a dialectical struggle with the community's minister, Rev. Ambrose, Grant is forced to evaluate himself as a model for the community. What he comes to realize is that he is not the savior or even the hero, but Jefferson, the condemned man, can be that figure.

The story illustrates how those viewed as lowly in society can effect great change, especially if they show great love. The women who love Jefferson seem at first powerless, but they are the ones who manipulate the white officials into allowing Jefferson visitors. An emphasis on the body, the flesh, is also shown in this novel. Perhaps the strongest manifestation of love is in the food the women prepare. *A Lesson before Dying* is filled with gumbos, pork chops, coffee, chocolate cake, yams, greens, biscuits. Over and over again women express their love and their power in the meals they serve. One of the last remaining acts that Miss Emma can perform for Jefferson is to prepare meals for him to be taken to the prison. At first he is unable to accept her food, instead eating corn off the floor like the hog he has been labeled, but as he comes to believe in himself, he is able to accept the offerings of sustenance. The turning point for Jefferson occurs during a session with Grant, Rev. Ambrose, and Miss Emma, where she has prepared a special gumbo. When Jefferson refuses to sit, Grant does not give up. He tells him that simply eating his godmother's food will be a comfort to her and that he is still a living, breathing man, worthy of the great care Miss Emma takes in preparing the meal. While the Reverend and Miss Emma sit at table, Grant walks Jefferson around the room: "It would mean so much to her if you would eat some of the gumbo." Grant continues to talk to Jefferson about how his actions do matter and that he can be bigger than anyone who has ever lived on the plantation. The last information that Grant receives about Jefferson is that he walked to the chair a man. A model of manly dignity, Jefferson becomes a potential savior not only for the black community but for the white community as well, the innocent criminal who heals all the members as they learn about themselves and others.

FACT AS STRANGE AS FICTION

The best of Louisiana literature remains rooted in the peculiarities of locale—of landscape, population, and politics; and oftentimes real life looms stranger than fiction. It was a real-life Huey Long, after all, that declared "Every Man a King," who combined in himself the buffoon and the savant, the crusader and the corruptor, the humanitarian and demagogue. Two important artists, Robert Penn Warren and Randy Newman, could not escape Long's shadow in their stays in Louisiana and breathed literary life into the persona of the Kingfish. As a professor at Louisiana State University, Warren could see the marks of Huey firsthand and could interpret the greatness and tragedy of a man who believed that his own good intentions could trump personal appetites. In 1946, in *All the King's Men*, Warren creates Willie Stark, a figure that constantly evolves, overreaching and overextending proper bounds. Elected as the people's champion, he builds a political machine as ruthless as the ones he tears apart. Cronyism and kickbacks become the norm even as important reforms in education, transportation, and medicine are enacted. But, like the historical governor Huey Long, the fictional governor Willie Stark meets an inevitable, but surprising assassin. Willie's friend and employee, reporter Jack Burden, is left to figure out Willie's significance:

> I must believe that Willie Stark was a great man. What happened to his greatness is not the question. Perhaps he spilled it on the ground the way you spill a liquid when a bottle breaks. Perhaps he piled up his greatness and burned it in one great blaze in the dark like a bonfire and then there wasn't anything but dark and the embers winking. Perhaps he could not tell his greatness from ungreatness and so mixed them together that what was adulterated was lost. But he had it. I must believe that.

Robert Penn Warren's prize-winning novel succeeded in fashioning a literary answer to the complex enigma of Louisiana's most beloved and most hated governor.

In 1974, Randy Newman's *Good Old Boys* album showed that Long's persona continued to hang over the state—forty years after his assassination. With biting satire, Newman warns us to beware of the "naked man," to recognize racism and ignorance (in his highly sarcastic "Rednecks"), and to keep up Long's idea of "Every Man a King." In a song that he recorded for the album, Newman goes further than simply singing the governor's composition, he reinvigorates Long's persona with a title Long chose for himself, "Kingfish." Note the Kingfish's role in helping the little man:

> Who built the highway to Baton Rouge
> Who put up the hospital and built you schools
> Who looks after shit-kickers like you?
> The Kingfish do.

Newman goes on to chronicle Huey's battle against Standard Oil, asserting that "ain't no Standard Oil men" but "little folks like you and me" who will run the state. Both Warren and Newman realized the universal, archetypal figure in the very real man of Huey Long, and acknowledged how Louisiana itself would give birth to such a figure, even if, as Newman eloquently wrote, "They're trying to wash us away."

As seen through the literature of these two sojourners, where else but in Louisiana could a figure like Huey Long or Willie Stark emerge? Louisiana itself, especially up until the mid-twentieth century, was a mixture of rich natural resources and poor rural inhabitants, farmers of British or Irish ancestry, or of African, Italian, Spanish, Hungarian, or French descent, often living within a few miles of one another with a wary eye on one another's practices and customs. Louisiana grew accustomed to the shift of carnival and to the ability to laugh through tears, to this day ranking number 49 out of 50 states in education and healthcare but number 1 in enjoying life (a recent poll revealed Louisianians as some of the happiest folk in the nation).

THE LANDSCAPE IN VERSE

Louisiana's fascination with the carnival philosophy continues through the visions of poets who render the state's landscape in exquisite verse. Yusef Komunyakaa, born in Bogalusa, a paper mill town whose name means "the magic city," mixes scenes of natural beauty with poverty and violence. In "Song for My Father," the father is a strong figure bearing his son on a red bicycle's handlebars through a countryside fragrant with both honeysuckle and "stinking exhaust." The last image is the father steering "through . . . flowering dogwood like a thread of blood." Another poem, "My Father's Love Letters," shows a proud carpenter who can read elaborate blueprints but can write no more than his name. The poem blends admiration and disgust for this man, who had beaten his wife and now asks his son to help woo her back in writing:

> . . . This man,
> Who stole roses & hyacinth
> For his yard, would stand there
> With eyes closed & fists balled,
> Laboring over a simple word, almost
> Redeemed by what he tried to say.

Without sentimentalizing, Komunyakaa eloquently presents individuals living in a tangible poverty that infiltrates mind and spirit as well. Speaking of his own search for his place in Louisiana, Komunyakaa tells of retaking his grandfather's lost name, "affirming [his] heritage and its ambiguity."

In the same way, Darrell Bourque, state poet laureate from 2007 to 2011, strives to maintain heritage in his poem about the rural Cajun *courir de Mardi Gras*, the "run" of Mardi Gras, where participants chase down chickens and gather ingredients in a ritual killing and preparation of a special gumbo. In both French and English versions, Bourque explains how participants partake of another time, "forgetting" their masks and becoming "le feu et l'air": "fire and air." Celebrating carnival together, they do not remember their "separateness." Yet at the end of the ritual, they must acknowledge that they are not only fire and air, but earth as well. Carnival reminds that spiritual transcendence is not permanent; we must return to the body.

The blending of the spiritual and physical figures prominently in Bourque's poem "My Mother's Right Foot," which among other startling juxtapositions recounts a prayer addressed to the queen of heaven that moves from asking her to pray for the supplicant to "something about . . . bulls in the back pasture." Next the speaker is in the dehorning yard, blood spurting as shears crunch the base of horn and knives remove testicles. He responds by remembering aboriginal and classical dances in Crete, in Rome, in Mesopotamia. The poet ends his specific memory of working on a Louisiana farm with these statements: "I am calling blessed the arcs of blood. / I am saying this story is not about to end." Blood, sacrifice, family celebrations, and strife will continue.

Two other Louisiana poets, Jack Bedell and Pinkie Gordan Lane, also root their poems in landscapes and the peculiarities of locale. "In the Marsh" and "Baton Rouge" give complementary views of landscape: the natural and the manmade. Bedell personifies the bayou with its "black mud sucking [his] hip boots." Death reveals itself as the marsh "hovered" and "swirled" around a deer's body. Yet the final image is of the "marsh's breathing" encompassing death itself. In Lane's poem, "Baton Rouge," the city becomes a "great cat sprawled in the sun." Its oil refineries belch smoke, and rain "drips from her belly's felt need," while "the summer's sun vaporizes the tears of her ever present poor." Lane suggests a man-made landscape that has become a living organism, a cat "flip[ping] back on her boneless tail and purr[ing] herself to ambiance." According to Lane, some essential quality holds it back from manifesting ambition; instead "the city spins . . . simulating metropolis."

Former state poet laureate Brenda Osbey draws inspiration from the state's most complex metropolis, New Orleans. In *All Saints,* Osbey pays homage to New Orleans's inhabitants, living and dead. Detailing particular customs and rituals of mourning—carrying silver coins and bits of paper and fingernails, sprinkling cinnamon, making altars to remember the dead—Osbey venerates particular New Orleans saints and slave heroes, including St. Expedite (who supposedly arrived by post in a package marked for speedy delivery) and San Malo (who led a slave revolt in New Orleans at Chef Menteur in 1784). This exquisite book of poetry remembers the sacrifices of grandmothers who suffered indignities of factory work and of slaves who helped pave the very streets, forge the lacy ironwork, and develop the unique culture of the city. Osbey does not hesitate to include the ambivalent figure of Luis Congo, an African who was responsible for capturing slaves, sending many to their deaths. In explanation, Luis Congo's severed head boasts that he dared to make himself a king in a "nether land": "i captured and i killed and i did not look back," he says; but "i did not take from you your human qualities." Instead he sent them whole to the ancestors; they did not have to live as slaves in a strange land. Now the mighty man has been killed, beheaded by slaves, and begs for them to give him cool water. Even traitors have their place in history, Osbey suggests. Osbey celebrates the ancestors, imploring the reader to "wear the memory of the dead plainly." Indeed, in the first section, Osbey decrees that you should "live among your dead, whom you have every right to love." But, above all, in "The Seven Sisters of New Orleans," Osbey gives warning that those "outsiders" who try to rationally study Louisiana culture may instead find themselves fed, chatted, and comforted into making the place their home.

LOCAL COLOR

This strategy of writing from local color goes back to an early Louisiana writer, Kate Chopin, known mostly for her startling novel of female exploration, *The Awakening.* Chopin details the habits of wealthy Creoles and rural 'Cadians, clearly differentiating between these two groups of French descent. In *The Awakening* and in numerous short stories, Chopin highlights—somewhat stereotypically—the white Creoles as educated, graceful planters, physicians, or entrepreneurs while the Cajun men are rural, short, brown, and clumsy. Grand Isle, known today mostly for its excellent fishing, is portrayed as Louisiana's Riviera with hotels, bed-and-breakfasts, and bath houses. The local Acadians serve the wealthy Creoles who come from New Orleans to vacation. In two stories, "At the 'Cadian Ball" and "The Storm," Chopin further delineates the two French cultures. The heroine is Calixta, a young Acadian of spirit and beauty who is interested in the young Creole planter Alcée Laballière. Alcée is interested as well, but his serious interest lies in his Creole cousin Clarisse, who rebuffed a frenzied declaration of passion brought about partially by a ruinous storm that devastated the 900-acre rice crop. Upset, Alcée goes outside of his class to the 'Cadian Ball and finds Calixta, who has been trying to avoid Bobinot, her persistent, bumbling Cajun suitor. The two, obviously happy to be in each other's company, sit outside on a bench flirting. Before matters can proceed too far, however, Clarisse appears on the scene to whisk away Alcée. Without a second glance, Alcée leaves with his appropriate lover, while Calixta must trudge home followed by Bobinot. Knowing her love for Alcée is futile, Calixta tells Bobinot that she does not mind marrying him if he's still interested.

If the tale ended here, the reader would assume Chopin upholds Louisiana's cultural divisions and sees passion as a folly to be avoided through acquiescence to responsible relationships. However, there is a second story, "The Storm," unpublished in Chopin's lifetime. Calixta and Bobinot have been married for several years, as have Alcée and Clarisse. Another storm appears. This time Calixta is alone at home as Alcée rides by and must come in to seek shelter from the rain. Calixta and Alcée must close all windows and doors, even thrusting fabric under the door to keep out the insistent storm. The human storm of passion cannot be escaped, however, as the two fall into each other's arms and upon the awaiting bed. Chopin ends the tale with the two lovers' smiling good-byes, Bobinot and son returning to happy wife and mother, and Clarisse writing contentedly from Biloxi. Succinctly, Chopin states: "So the storm passed and everyone was happy."

The ending is not so happy for the heroine in *The Awakening*. Edna Pontellier is an outsider to Louisiana Creole culture who has moved to

New Orleans after her marriage. She is shocked by the free and familiar attitudes of the Creoles, their vitality, joking, and lack of prudery. However, she fails to read the culture accurately and believes a young Creole's constant flirting and devotion to her are serious. The society she has entered assumes a woman's continued chastity in the face of flirting and declarations of love by unattached males. Edna finds herself in that stage of betwixt and between. She has left behind her Protestant Kentucky upbringing but has not fully assimilated into the Catholic Creole society. She seems to awaken to desires of becoming an artist, of breaking the norms of society, of venturing "where no woman has ever gone before"; but in fact she begins to fall into a stupor of confusion. She reads Emerson but falls asleep doing so. She ventures to a secluded island with Robert, but feels oppressed with tiredness while attending a church service, retreating to a Cajun cottage to sleep away the afternoon. Chopin ends with a lyrical description of drowning, a suicide at once beautiful and awful as Edna ventures farther and farther into the Gulf.

In Chopin, those outsiders who fail to correctly interpret Louisiana cultures face grave dangers; but other Louisiana writers show that even insiders may become befuddled by their own state. James Wilcox, who was raised in Hammond, in Tangipahoa Parish, populates his novels with earnest, confused, everyday Louisianians whose lives are a blend of despair, irritation, and humor. For example, in *Modern Baptists*, Mr. Pickens, a plain, middle-aged assistant manager of the Sonny Boy Bargain Store, must deal with his more attractive, actor half-brother, who has just been released from prison. Of course, the brother, always referred to by his initials FX, immediately grabs the attention of the co-worker that Mr. Pickens has become so infatuated with that he has somehow managed to steal her watch. Mr. Pickens finds his inherited notions of propriety and responsibility slipping away. He has a reliable source of sexual satisfaction in Miss Mina, described as "attractive, clean, personable," and able to do "your income tax for you, if you wanted." Mr. Pickens remains firmly a Baptist, but declares he is a "modern" one. According to Pickens, drinking and dancing would be allowed in moderation. If you were unmarried at thirty, you could sleep with someone—"as long as you loved that person." If you were single at forty, adultery would be allowed—as long as no one would be hurt. With characters like Mr. Pickens, Wilcox carefully depicts this section of Louisiana, the Florida Parishes, which was not part of the Louisiana Purchase and for a brief time in 1810 was independent. Wilcox explains the Tory tendencies of early settlers and their differences from the French, just a few miles south, who considered a favorite food of the Anglo settlers, corn, to be pig food.

Three Florida Parish writers make special use of the landscape of southeast Louisiana. Issues of race, discrimination, and survival prevail in this "fallen paradise," as writer Dayne Sherman labels the area, a play on the state's motto of Sportsman's Paradise. Carlyle Tillery and Tim Gautreaux illuminate the lives of those who lived during the heyday of two timber industries, the pine industry and the cypress industry. Tillery writes of farmers who try to make a living in the cutover land after the harvesting of the longleaf pine. Published in 1951, *Red Bone Woman* follows the life of Mr. Randall, widowed farmer of some education whose loneliness forces him to contemplate a liaison with a young woman identified as a Red Bone. The Red Bones are a group separate from blacks and whites, believed by most to be of mixed white and black ancestry. However, the group itself will admit of no African American heritage and also denies Native American origins. Instead, they generally refer to themselves as Spanish whites, although there is no evidence of that heritage. Mr. Randall exhibits squeamishness about taking in Tempie. She sees it as wasteful to use water every day for a bath, but she works hard in the field and shows an interest in the farm that Mr. Randall's children did not. Still obsessed with his new wife's heritage, Mr. Randall fears that their first child will have "curled lips," indicating African American roots. To his dismay, Tempie's baby does have curled lips, but Mr. Randall tries to hide his revulsion. The narrative skips to the child's death from pneumonia a few months later, and then several years to Mr. Randall learning to love his children freely, finding them quite intelligent and eager to learn. He loses his reclusive stance to insist that his children be accepted into the local school. As the novel ends, the Red Bones have not fully moved from their betwixt-and-between status, yet there is an affirmation that love and understanding can effect change.

Setting his novel *Welcome to the Fallen Paradise* in the 1980s, Dayne

Fig. 6.1. Literary pursuit in the cutover. *Courtesy of Center for Southeast Louisiana Studies, Southeastern Louisiana University; Palmetto Collection*

Sherman continues the mix of tenderness and violence in Baxter Parish (resembling Tangipahoa Parish the most with bits of two other Florida Parishes, Livingston and St. Helena). Once again Louisiana's landscape crafts a culture built on familial loyalty, clannishness, subsistence work, and a propensity toward violence. A young man who had escaped the violence of his home parish by enlisting in the military returns after the death of his mother. Determined to honor his mother's memory and make an honorable living for himself, he buys land and a house in the northern part of the parish. Unknown to him, a family member of the former owner is refusing to relinquish his claim. The young man is threatened, stalked, and terrorized by a monster of violence, Cotton Moxley. This novel contains all the starkness of *Red Bone Woman* with the added gruesomeness of dog killing and Jesse's uncle being electrocuted through a successful sabotage. However, the land itself maintains a sense of promise. The narrator finds some justice in spending his violence on the unreasonable Moxley and some redemption in restoring his relationship with his high school sweetheart. Above all, in the midst of frustration and dismay, he comes to terms with a family measured by violence, loyalty, and love.

Violence, loyalty, and love are again key elements in perhaps the two most representative volumes of Louisiana life, Tim Gautreaux's fine short story collections *Same Place, Same Things* and *Welding with Children*. With both a keen eye and a finely tuned ear, Gautreaux brings to life the state we all love, even through our disappointments. In the title story from *Same Place, Same Things,* set in the Depression, the author writes of the strawberry farms that once dotted Tangipahoa Parish, showing what happens to a fertile land during drought. A traveling pump repairman encounters a lonely new widow who wishes to escape with him, but after sharing her gifts of dry sandwiches and strawberry wine, the repairman comes back to his mechanical sense and figures out from the wiring that the woman had in fact electrocuted her husband as he worked on the outside pump. Still, he feels compassion for her as he tells her it wouldn't help if he brought her with him. When she accuses him of having a hard heart, he simply states: "No ma'am. . . . I loved a good woman once, and I could love another. You can't come with me

Fig. 6.2. Music in the Piney Woods. *Center for Southeast Louisiana Studies, Southeastern Louisiana University; Palmetto Collection*

because you killed your old man." He learns that some people are perpetually desperate and dangerous.

In the title story of *Welding with Children*, a retired welder learns that if his grandchildren will have any chance at a decent life, he will have to take great care of them. He missed his chance with his own children, and now he will have to provide the appropriate environment, which means cleaning up his own yard first of all. After being taunted with the truth by a mean old farmer who refers to his vehicle as the "bastardmobile," Bruton describes the necessary purging: "A wrecker and a gondola came down my road, and before noon, Amos loaded up four derelict cars, six engines, four washing machines, ten broken lawn mowers, and two and one-quarter tons of scrap iron." Like many other Gautreaux characters, Bruton has a life-changing epiphany, hurtful but necessary.

Gautreaux also shines his light on Cajun culture. "Floyd's Girl" features the abduction of a young Cajun girl away from her father by her mother's Texas boyfriend. The neighbors fear for Lizette—"the gumbos [she] would be missing, the okra soul, the crawfish body"—and her daddy cannot bear for her to be taken to Texas. According to Floyd:

> There was nothing wrong with West Texas, but there was something wrong with a child living there who doesn't belong, who will be haunted for the rest of her days with memories of the ample laps of aunts, daily thunderheads rolling above flat parishes of rice and cane, the musical rattle of French, her prayers, the head-turning squawk of her uncle's accordion, the scrape and complaint of her father's fiddle as he serenades the backyard on weekends. The community rallies together, flying an old plane to overtake the Texan, dismantling his truck with blow torches; and when the small Cajun man is not able to beat the tall Texan, T-Jean's grandmere manages to insert the tip of her walker squarely into the foreigner's right eye. As the man heads to the hospital, Lizette heads back to her rightful home.

Another ensemble effort of Cajun community prevails in "Easy Pickings," where Marvin, an escaped convict, plans to rob an elderly woman. When he knocks out her dentures, she calmly picks them up and reinserts them; when he asserts that he could kill her, she replies, "But you can't eat me" as she "wag[s] a knobby finger in Big Blade's befuddled face." Mrs. Landreneaux plies Marvin, or Big Blade as he prefers to be called, with gumbo, dessert, and French-dripped coffee laden with brandy. As he tries to make his getaway with her as hostage, she fakes a heart attack, another elderly woman shoots the tires of his vehicle, and the deputy he had handcuffed in the kitchen appears in the yard to arrest him, carrying under his arm the oven door he was cuffed to. Far from being terrified by the experience, Mrs. Landreneaux invites Marvin to come back and play cards after his prison sentence.

Gautreaux's appreciation for Cajun culture shows in many of his stories, which all illuminate everyday, common people dealing with the shortcomings of life while finding bits of grace or at least arriving at a greater understanding of the world or themselves. Like Gaines, Gautreaux tries to depict the culture of Louisiana accurately, and in "Deputy Sid's Gift," he offers an eloquent statement about the need to purge the state of racial bigotry. The narrator is a well-meaning good ole boy, a former oil rig worker taking care of nursing home residents, who still feels that he isn't as kind as he appears. When his old junk truck is stolen, he enlists the help of Deputy Sid, the capable, immaculately dressed deputy of "Easy Pickings," to recover it. They find that a practically homeless, perpetually drunk black man has stolen it and is now living in it. When Sid asks Bobby if he truly wants it back, Bobby does not waver, outraged that someone would outsmart him. However, as time passes, Bobby changes from viewing Sid as a "black devil" to seeing him as an ally in trying to help Fernest Bezue. Unfortunately, they cannot help the self-destructive Fernest, but Sid offers this comfort when he tells Bobby of Bezue's death: "Don't feel like that. . . . We couldn't do anything for him, but we did it anyway." Bobby has learned true compassion and friendship from two men that he wouldn't normally see himself associating with. At the end of the story, Bobby and Sid sit together in the kitchen, drink coffee, and "cuss" the government.

WRAPPED IN CARNIVAL

Over and over in Louisiana literature, conflicting classes, contrasting ideologies, eccentric characters, a landscape of promise and heartache, and an overarching sense of failure and success being forever twinned whirl together. Novelists Gaines and Gautreaux, poets Bourque and Osbey, the chiefs of the Mardi Gras Indians, dramatic works such as *A Streetcar Named Desire* and *Steel Magnolias,* and new films and television series set in Louisiana, such as *True Blood* and *Treme,* continue to explore the true nature of carnival, that view of the world that acknowledges and celebrates the shift, that endures impermanence, and that strives to overreach or erase boundaries and divisions while at the same time letting them proliferate. Louisiana literature remains the keenest interpreter of a state perpetually flawed and bursting with promise; incomprehensible yet familiar: a paradigm both for living and for overcoming the American dream.

Fiction

The Best of LSU Fiction (2010), edited by Nolde Alexius and Judy Kahn

John Ed Bradley, *Restoration* (2003), *It Never Rains in Tiger Stadium* (2008)

James Lee Burke, *Cadillac Jukebox* (1996), *Creole Belle* (2012)

Robert Olen Butler, *A Good Scent from a Strange Mountain* (1992)

George Washington Cable, *The Grandissimes* (1880)

Kate Chopin, *The Awakening* (1899)

Moira Crone, *Dream State: Louisiana Stories* (1995), *The Not Yet* (2012)

John Dufresne, *Louisiana Power and Light* (1994)

Alcée Fortier, *Compair Lapin* (1894)

Ernest Gaines, *The Autobiography of Miss Jane Pittman* (1971), *A Gathering of Old Men* (1983), *A Lesson before Dying* (1993)

Tim Gautreaux, *Same Place, Same Things* (1996), *Welding with Children* (1999), *The Clearing* (2003), *The Missing* (2009)

Shirley Ann Grau, *The Hard Blue Sky* (1958)

Frances Parkinson Keyes, *Dinner at Antoine's* (1948)

Valerie Martin, *A Recent Martyr* (1987), *The Great Divorce* (1994)

Walker Percy, *The Moviegoer* (1961), *Love in the Ruins* (1971)

Anne Rice, *Interview with the Vampire* (1976), *Feast of All Saints* (1979)

Dayne Sherman, *Welcome to the Fallen Paradise* (2004)

Carlyle Tillery, *Red Bone Woman* (1951)

John Kennedy Toole, *A Confederacy of Dunces* (1980)

James Wilcox, *Modern Baptists* (1983), *Polite Sex* (1991)

Poetry

Darrell Bourque, *In Ordinary Light* (2010)

Yusef Komunyakaa, *Talking Dirty to the Gods* (2000), *Pleasure Dome* (2001)

Brenda Marie Osbey, *All Saints* (1997)

Uncommonplace: An Anthology of Contemporary Louisiana Poets (1998), edited by Ann Brewster Dobie

Drama and Film

Robert Harling, *Steel Magnolias* (1988)

Tennessee Williams, *A Streetcar Named Desire* (1947), *Suddenly Last Summer* (1958)

Band of Angels, directed by Raoul Walsh, 1957

Hard Times, directed by Walter Hill, 1975
Everybody's All-American, directed by Taylor Hackford, 1988
Belizaire the Cajun, directed by Glen Pitre, 1996
Eve's Bayou, directed by Kasi Lemmons, 1997
Divine Secrets of the Ya-Ya Sisterhood, directed by Callie Khouri, 2002
Beasts of the Southern Wild, directed by Benh Zeitlin, 2012

THE LOCAL DIET

MAGGIE HEYN RICHARDSON

Natives exalt it. Expatriates pine for it. Newcomers find it instantly beguiling. It's easy to argue that food is Louisiana's most compelling cultural feature. No other cuisine in America is as well defined or intact as that of Cajun and Creole fare, the former born of the ingenuity of poor farmers from Nova Scotia who settled in the state's bayous and prairie; the latter born of the cultural explosion that occurred in New Orleans beginning in the eighteenth century. In both cases, immigrants used traditions from home to transform the bounty of local ingredients, resulting in new foodways that have had notable staying power. But it isn't just the originality of the Louisiana menu that makes the culinary culture here so different. It is the way that food sets a certain tempo that guides our existence. Food in the Pelican State is the clockwork that makes life run.

Anyone who has moved to Louisiana experiences the enveloping nature of the culinary culture. Locals are forever discussing the perfect gumbo they cooked over the weekend, the redfish they fried at the fishing camp, the relationship they now have with this farmers' market vendor or that sausage maker, the proper formula for boiling crabs. Louisianians don't horde their food customs or secret them away from outsiders. They share them willingly and enthusiastically, inviting newcomers to tailgate parties at LSU's Tiger Stadium, where rabid home cooks smoke whole hogs in Cajun microwaves and prepare jambalaya in cast-iron pots, or to crawfish boils where the state's signature crustacean, scarlet and spicy, spills out onto newspaper-covered tables. After a dose of cold beer

Fig. 7.1. Crawfish boil. *Dustin Howes*

and a lesson in how to defrock a few pounds of mudbugs, a transplant's grip on wherever he or she came from loosens, and Louisiana, despite its historic warts and social struggles, starts to feel awfully charming.

Food is the great equalizer here, the glue that connects disparate groups, the constant in a place that has experienced more than its share of natural and manmade disasters, poverty, and general uncertainty. It is a conversation starter and the centerpiece of ongoing debates. Toss out, "Who makes the best po'boy (poor boy, po-boy)?" or "Who's got the best boudin?" and dug-in responses sally forth, rooted in the answerer's taste buds and loyalty to local purveyors.

Every region of the country claims distinct foodways, but the sheer volume of indigenous dishes and the enduring popularity of ingredients that spring from the local farms, waters, and fields are unique to Louisiana. The culinary ethos is remarkably preserved thanks to an overwhelming number of native-born residents—Louisiana has the highest of any state. This has locked in place the way food is prepared, served, and consumed, and the way rituals are repeated and handed down, from favorite snowball stands to tailgate spots. When natives do move away, they miss the local diet considerably, and they salve their longing by finding other Bayou State expats with whom they share Abita Beer and mail-order cracklin'.

Eating "local and seasonal" is the most popular American food trend in decades, but a deep commitment to regional provenance has always existed in Louisiana, where the relationship between residents and what they consume is rhythmic, passionate, and entrenched. It's hard to live here and not see the calendar through a culinary lens. January means that oysters from the rim of the Gulf of Mexico are at their peak—the same time mustard greens and fresh citrus fruits emerge from farms and backyards. King cakes appear in bakeries and grocery stores in rectangular boxes after January 6, the Feast of the Epiphany, and are consumed throughout Carnival season. They recede by Ash Wednesday, a sturdy Lenten tradition in a state where more than one-quarter of the population is Catholic.

By then, legions of crawfish are being trapped on farms and in the Atchafalaya Basin, and hauled in mesh sacks to the nearest seafood market. Concurrently, Louisiana's impressive strawberry crop peaks, and when it fades in late May, roadside stands and farmers' markets become awash in summer fruits—local blackberries, blueberries, figs, watermelon, and peaches.

For the state's hard-scrabble shrimpers, brown shrimp season begins in March and continues through the summer, when larger white shrimp take over. Blue crabs skittering in south Louisiana's network of estuaries peak in July, prompting locals to go in search of "full" crabs or "fat females" from their favorite seafood shops or dockside fishermen.

At that point in the culinary calendar, temporary snowball stands have sprouted across the state like crabgrass, selling mounds of syrup-drenched shaved ice, often in tall Styrofoam cups. Legacy stands, like Hansen's Sno-Bliz and Williams Plum Street Snowball in New Orleans, lie dormant in the fall and winter and open every spring to impatient loyalists hungry for classic flavors, such as orchid or nectar cream. In August, when the blanket of heat is at its worst, defiant crops such as okra, eggplant, and hot peppers still flourish, giving cooks something to work with before the fall crops emerge. While they're being harvested, another round of plants goes in the soil, including second-crop tomatoes, because the growing season in this subtropical state is nearly twelve months out of the year.

By Labor Day, the arrival of football season delivers four straight months of outdoor cooking ingenuity. Embellished grills, high-performance outdoor fryers, and expansive cast-iron pots yield mammoth servings of ribs, chicken and sausage jambalaya, fried fish, and smoked boudin on parking lots outside football fields across the state.

Then it's time for the holiday lineup. As in other parts of the American South, cornbread dressing supplants white-bread stuffing during family meals, the result of the historic cultivation of corn. But Louisiana's holiday tables include dishes not often found elsewhere, like seafood-stuffed mirliton, duck and andouille gumbo, turtle soup, corn and crab bisque, rice dressing, scalloped oysters, bread pudding, pralines, coffee with chicory, and orange-infused, boozy café brûlot.

The calendar is ruled by food, but beyond that, natives and anyone who has lived here long enough to soak in the culinary culture share a kind of shorthand about how it should be prepared and enjoyed. Cajun and Creole recipes start with chopped and sautéed onions, celery, and bell pepper, a combination referred to as the "Holy Trinity," as well as roux, the backbone of gumbos, soups, stews, courtbouillon, and étouffées, made by sautéing equal parts of flour and oil with a watchful eye.

Louisianians also fall back on food-related absolutes, which can seem noticeably absent elsewhere in the world. Coffee is always brewed strong and sometimes includes chicory. Lunchtime should provide easy access to fried seafood po'boys and blue-plate specials with candied sweet potatoes or smothered okra. Mondays are the traditional day for red beans and rice, a throwback from the weekly washday in New Orleans when women needed a fuss-free meal. On Fridays, fried catfish is still a regular special in restaurants, derivative of the traditional Catholic fast. During Lent, this practice reaches fever pitch when creative seafood specials dominate Friday menus and locals stop for sacks of boiled crawfish and their accompanying potatoes and corn at the end of the work week.

Fig. 7.2. Flowering peach in Ruston. *Simone Mhire*

The state has a palpable collective food culture, but its diverse regions and their varying natural environments have also produced their own food identities. North Louisiana and central Louisiana share commonalities with the culinary cultures of Texas, Arkansas, and Mississippi, but they are also known for Ruston peaches and Cenla pecans and watermelon. Sandwiched between the two areas in northwest Louisiana are Natchitoches and its famed meat pies, and the town of Zwolle with its longstanding tradition of tamale making. Both result from Spain's hold on territory west of Natchitoches in the eighteenth century when Spanish soldiers served a local fort, Los Adaes. When the fort closed, many solders remained in the area, bringing empanadas (meat pies) and tamales with them. Their descendants still live in these communities today.

Meanwhile, a drive along Interstate 10 through Acadiana leads to dozens of tucked-away Cajun community meat markets and their links of fresh pork boudin. Farms north of Baton Rouge deliver plump blueberries, while the state's lower parishes have the right climate to yield oranges, grapefruits, and kumquats.

From jambalaya to crawfish étouffée to gumbo, Louisiana's famed dishes stem from auspicious geography and a complex immigrant mix. Native Americans, African and Caribbean slaves and their descendants, Haitian, Spanish, German, Italian, Croatian, and Hungarian immigrants, and the French Canadians exiled from Nova Scotia known as Cajuns, all contributed to the culture by using what was available to feed their families. These groups were later joined by immigrants from Vietnam, the Middle East, and Latin America, who continued to meld local ingredients with their particular traditions.

Throughout Louisiana's history, immigrants found a humid, subtropical climate and diverse natural regions, including marshes, hills, delta farmland, and valleys—winning conditions for trapping, hunting, fishing, and cultivating. The state's generous growing season supports 30,000 farms today, which produce top crops like corn, sugarcane, pecans, and sweet potatoes. Louisiana is also the third-largest producer of rice in the United States, a thrifty staple introduced in the state in the eighteenth century that figures large in gumbo, étouffée, jambalaya, and other signature dishes.

Louisiana's food culture is tightly bound to water, a result of its vast coastline and wetlands. The state is the number-one producer of crawfish, alligator, oysters, and shrimp in the United States, and it supplies one-quarter of all the seafood in the country. Just north of the coast, the prairie parishes between Lafayette and the Louisiana-Texas border feature conditions perfect for supporting two important staples in the same pond system: rice and crawfish. Stretching further north, delta farmlands have a long history of growing soybeans, corn, and sweet potatoes.

These natural assets feed the state economy and fuel its residents' characteristic joie de vivre. Local ingredients undergird family dinners, weddings, funerals, parties, fundraisers, and holiday celebrations. They are also vital to more than four hundred regional festivals, taking center stage at the Ponchatoula Strawberry Festival, the Breaux Bridge Crawfish Festival, the Louisiana Pecan Festival in Colfax, the Tamale Fiesta in Zwolle, the Jim Bowie Barbecue Duel in Vidalia, and the Jambalaya Festival in Gonzales. Food is something to share and to celebrate in Louisiana, and few cultures do it more publicly.

———— ✦ ————

If food is a window into Louisiana's reverie, it also makes the state's rash of modern tragedies more poignant. Hurricanes Katrina and Rita in 2005 decimated the seafood industry, hitting hard the family shrimpers who already live on tight margins. Five years later, many of these fishers had successfully rebuilt their operations, only to have them disrupted again when the Deepwater Horizon oil rig exploded in the Gulf in 2010. As oil threatened to seep into the wetlands, the state of Louisiana called for a freshwater diversion, which flushed the marshlands but dramatically changed the salinity by introducing too much freshwater into brackish waters. About 80 percent of the oyster beds were wiped out. There is also the ongoing urgent battle of coastal wetlands erosion. A parcel of wetlands the size of a football field is taken over by water every 38 minutes in an area that is home to two million people, a base of operations for the offshore oil industry, and habitat to countless species.

When Hurricane Katrina slammed into southeastern Louisiana on August 29, 2005, and caused a breech in New Orleans's precarious levee system, the city's tea-saucer topography was no match for floodwaters. Houses, businesses, restaurants, and nearby farms were leveled as the death toll reached 1,836. Thousands relocated and many never returned. What Hurricane Katrina didn't accomplish was finished a month later when Hurricane Rita caused billions in damage in southwestern Louisiana and sent an unwelcome storm surge back to the state's battered east side.

The events produced countless stories of government ineptitude, loss, and pain. Outside of cable news stories, under-the-radar tales revealed the storms' impact on closely held family traditions.

One was about personal recipe collections. For decades, readers of the now-downsized *New Orleans Times-Picayune* had clipped recipes from its venerable Food section, stuffing them into kitchen drawers, notebooks, and other cubbies. Stained and yellowed, many were enlisted annually by home cooks during family celebrations. They were, of course, part of the storm's panorama of loss. Storm victims would eventually put their lives back together, many outside of New Orleans. But when the time came later to prepare traditional family dishes—an attempt at reclaiming order—residents felt the storm's blow again. Their recipes were gone. It was indeed possible to find other formulas for gumbo, étouffée, or bread pudding, but a personal collection that predated the Internet had no doubt included irreplaceable favorites. Moreover, for decades the *Times-Picayune* had published treasured recipes from New Orleans's local chefs, whose restaurants were like houses of worship. Storm victims' recipes had been more than sets of instructions; they were tethers to memory. And they were lost.

Or were they? Two months after the storm, the *Times-Picayune* undertook a simple but stirring bit of activist journalism. At the suggestion of a reader, food editor Judy Walker began a column in late October 2005 that linked wistful locals whose collections had been ruined with their lost recipes. Their letters to the Food section consistently reported two things: personal storm sagas and the need to cook dishes that reminded Katrina victims of a better time. For many living outside of New Orleans, finding the recipes was especially important.

Walker and her team found some of the requested recipes in the *Times-Picayune*'s salvaged archives, and others in the personal collections of readers whose homes had been spared. They were shared each week in the Food section.

Later, Walker and food columnist and author Marcelle Bienvenu turned the column into a cookbook, *Cooking Up a Storm*, which documented the project and provided a collection of the city's cornerstone recipes. Home-kitchen favorites were joined by famed cocktails like the Ramos Gin Fizz, Galatoire's eggnog, and the Fairmont Hotel's Sazerac, and dishes like beignets, eggs Sardou, and the former Schwegmann's Grocery Store's spaghetti and meatballs, which was run in its newspaper ads.

The rebuilding effort that took place after Hurricane Katrina was fueled by a powerful desire to preserve the area's character. But this fierce need to hang on to tradition isn't reserved for storms, as shown in the quiet resurgence of a near-endangered Louisiana dish, Creole cream cheese.

Many with roots in New Orleans and south Louisiana recall Creole cream cheese, a fresh cheese made from raw milk clabbered with rennet, strained, and enriched with a final addition of fresh cream. The tradition was alive and well in the first half of the twentieth century, when home cooks crafted it from raw milk in the same manner that fresh, unripened cheeses were made in old-world Europe. It was also widely available in grocery stores and through local dairies.

The modern usage of the word "Creole" connotes spiciness, but Creole cream cheese is anything but. Its mild flavor and easy consistency made it a family staple especially popular among children and the elderly. Typically served for breakfast, Creole cream cheese is slightly tangy and can be steered sweet or savory. Common applications were to top it with fresh fruit and sugar, or spread it on dense toast with salt and black pepper.

Creole cream cheese's wobbly trajectory over the last century illuminates the difficulty indigenous dishes everywhere often face. It also demonstrates their hold on the people of Louisiana.

By 1986, all of the original local dairies that once made Creole cream cheese in Louisiana had closed or were bought by national conglomerates. Furthermore, home cooks had lost the ability to purvey raw milk. Creole cream cheese was on the verge of extinction until Dorignac's Grocery Store in Metairie began producing a version. While it was a welcome return, its authenticity was often debated by persnickety longtime fans.

Then in the late nineties, the Mississippi-based family dairy Mauthe's began selling hand-crafted Creole cream cheese at the Crescent City Farmers Market in New Orleans. Their wildly popular product, helped along by New Orleans cooking instructor, radio host, and author Poppy Tooker, triggered interest in Creole cream cheese among a new generation of local food fans and the culinary preservation group Slow Foods USA. For a time, Creole cream cheese was also made by Chef John Folse and Co. and by Smith Creamery.

Katrina interrupted Mauthe's operation, and owners Kenny and Jamie Mauthe struggled for several years to bring it back. By 2012, they had finally returned to farmers' markets in both Mississippi and Louisiana, where fans of the dish welcomed them with stories of childhoods filled with Creole cream cheese and declarations that Mauthe's version tasted like what they remembered.

It's not hard to find similar die-hard culinary customs in Louisiana, such as how to achieve the proper balance of ingredients in gumbo, the right ratio of spice to water for boiled crawfish, or the manner by which rice—the keystone of so many of the state's dishes—should be prepared.

For Lionel Key, a Baton Rougean of Creole descent, that culinary custom is making authentic filé, the fine, green powder sprinkled on gumbo to enhance its flavor and thicken its consistency. It is believed to have first been produced by the Choctaw Indians who lived along Louisiana's bayous and who traveled by canoe to New Orleans to sell their product at the French Market.

Key learned his craft in 1982, but the tradition has been in his family since 1904. That year, his blind great-uncle, Joseph Willie Ricard, then nine, was given a hand-carved 120-pound, 3-foot-high cypress mortar and pestle by his uncle, Gerard Ricard. Making filé would become the young man's trade and would be one of the means he used later to support a wife and four children in the town of Rougon.

Key grew up watching Ricard, known as "Uncle Bill," use both ends of the wood pestle to pound dried sassafras leaves first into papery flakes, then into fine powder. The blind Ricard had achieved accuracy through

Fig. 7.3. Boudin. *Dustin Howes*

a keen ear and years of pounding. At thirty-two, Key finally asked his great-uncle for instruction.

When Ricard died in 1985, Key, then a UPS driver, took up making filé. He has been featured in national publications and on television shows, and his filé has been used in top Louisiana restaurants and is sold at farmers' markets and festivals. He is one of a small number of surviving artisan filé-makers today.

Of all foods in Louisiana's culinary repertoire, boudin is arguably the most emblematic, reflecting the ingenuity that springs from rural, agrarian thrift. Boudin, after all, makes fast work of the tougher parts of the pig and of organ meats, which are boiled together until soft and tender, then ground, mixed with spices and the ultimate recipe stretcher, fluffy white rice, and stuffed into a sausage casing.

Stretching east to west across south Louisiana are dozens of traditional family-owned Cajun meat markets that produce boudin as well as other signature stuffed, trussed, and smoked meats. Boudin is a mainstay. Likely the oldest such shop that makes it is Bourgeois' Meat Market in the small town of Schriever, an outpost situated in the state's southern reaches between Thibodaux and the oil town of Houma. The spot first opened in 1891 and today is run by Donald Bourgeois, grandson of founder Valerie Jean-Batiste Bourgeois.

In Valerie's day, the bayou country's small towns were plentiful but disconnected. He figured they needed a mobile meat market. Slaughtering a single cow or pig at a time, Valerie traveled until he sold each cut. Refrigeration eventually allowed him to open a store on Schriever's Main Street, where he made sausage, boudin, and the poor man's terrine made from pork shoulder and split hock called hog's head cheese.

Valerie's son Lester took over in 1949 and continued turning out the meat market's fare. Lester's son, Donald, began working there as a young man and runs the shop today.

Donald was minding the market in the late eighties when he inadvertently introduced a new product for which the meat market remains known. He had made a small amount of beef jerky for himself in the smokehouse out back when a silver-tongued oil field salesman and regular customer named Chick Breaux dropped by the store. Donald offered a sample to Breaux, who liked it so much he asked Donald to sell him a special batch. Breaux believed it would be an effective tool for buttering up secretaries on sales calls.

Donald acquiesced, and soon the word got out to other customers. Today, the shop sells one thousand pounds of jerky a week with lines that can snake out the front door. It is made in an ancient smokehouse that predates the convenience of convection and requires Donald to add hardwood every two hours and manually shift small fireboxes to evenly distribute heat. Donald has resisted modernizing the smokehouse for the sake of flavor. He has also shunned the addition of nitrates and other preservatives.

The meat market's 120-year quest for consistency is further demonstrated by its steadfast production of red boudin, a version in which blood from a slaughtered pig is cooked and added to the pork and rice, intensifying its flavor. When the state of Louisiana tightened regulations concerning production of red boudin, Lester Bourgeois fought for a contingency. Today, the market is just one of two that continues to make red boudin.

Recently, Donald's son, Beau, interrupted a Ph.D. program in mathematics at Tulane University to return home and join the family business. Early each weekday, he's at work in the back creating the signature items on Bourgeois' hand-scrawled menu.

For the boudin, Beau and the shop's longtime employees cook down about 2,500 pounds of pork shoulder and 60 pounds of liver in a stainless-steel pot overnight until it's tender, after which they painstakingly separate the meat from the bone. They grind it, mix it with rice, chopped green onion, parsley, and spices, and then load it into a pressurized sausage filler. From this cylindrical, waist-high machine, the boudin is squirted carefully by hand into natural sausage casings and tied off in one-pound links..

Mopping his brow, Beau says he likes the rhythm of the work in the back. He enjoys the physical demands of an old-school smokehouse and of moving around pots so large they're placed on wheels and pulled with an iron hook. Every day that he makes boudin, smoked sausage, and head cheese, Beau becomes a keeper of one of Louisiana's rare culinary traditions.

By the time the store opens at seven, the line at the front counter has already begun to form.

Apple, R. W., Jr. "It Takes More than a Crayfish to Make a Cajun Wiggle." In *Far Flung and Well Fed: The Food Writing of R. W. Apple, Jr.*, 74–81. New York: St. Martin's, 2009.

Bienvenu, Marcelle, and Judy Walker, eds. *Cooking Up a Storm: Recipes Lost and Found from The Times-Picayune of New Orleans.* San Francisco: Chronicle Books, 2008.

The Christian Woman's Exchange—Creole Cookery. 1885. Reprint. Gretna, La.: Pelican Publishing, 2005.

Hearn, Lafcadio. *La Cuisine Creole.* 1885. Reprint. Bedford, Mass.: Applewood Books.

Jacobsen, Rowan. *The Geography of Oysters: The Connoisseur's Guide to Oyster Eating in North America.* New York: Bloomsbury, 2007.

Roahen, Sara. *Gumbo Tales: Finding My Place at the New Orleans Table.* New York: Norton, 2008.

Severson, Kim. *Spoon Fed: How Eight Cooks Saved My Life.* New York: Riverhead Books, 2010.

Trillin, Calvin. "Eating Festively." In *The Tummy Trilogy*, by Trillin, 92–103. New York: Farrar, Straus and Giroux, 1994.

———. "Missing Links." *The New Yorker*, January 28, 2002, 46–51.

Tooker, Poppy. *Crescent City Farmers Market Cookbook.* New Orleans: Marketumbrella.org, 2009.

Tucker, Susan, ed. *New Orleans Cuisine: Fourteen Signature Dishes and Their Histories.* Jackson: University Press of Mississippi, 2009.

LOUISIANA POLITICS
POPULISM, REFORM, AND DISASTER

WAYNE PARENT

From the Hollywood-dramatized antics of Governor Huey Long in the 1920s to the high-stakes blame game after 2005's Hurricane Katrina and the 2010 oil spill, Louisiana politics seems to explode into the national spotlight fairly frequently. Over the years Louisiana has gained a reputation for its politics, and it is not one that other states envy. V. O. Key in his classic 1949 book *Southern Politics in State and Nation* opened his chapter on the state by asserting "Louisiana is sui generis, just like Huey." And sui generis, or "one of a kind," it remains.

The reputation for uniquely vibrant politics, with a never-ending list of larger-than-life personalities and high drama, is a reputation that most Louisianians likely grudgingly accept or even embrace. Louisiana has been called a carnival, a festival, a gumbo, and more—a characterization with some merit and that can be understood as it connects to some unique features of the state.

LONGISM

One way to understand the roots of Louisiana's political carnival in the twentieth century is to understand the appeal of the three people that dominated the state from the 1920s until the end of the century. Huey Long, his brother Earl Long, and Edwin Edwards were all governors who

Fig. 8.1. Historian T. Harry Williams talking with U.S. Senator Russell Long, who is holding a picture of his father, Huey P. Long. *Russell B. Long Papers, Mss. 3700, Louisiana and Lower Mississippi Valley Collections, LSU Libraries, Baton Rouge, La.*

are household names in Louisiana. Huey's son Russell Long was U.S. senator for almost forty years and chair of the Senate Finance Committee for fifteen. Outsiders look and wonder why they were so powerful. A closer look at Louisiana itself will reveal those answers.

Huey Long's reign over Louisiana, first as governor, then from Washington D.C. as U.S. senator, is irresistible fodder for journalists, authors, and artists alike. Long has been the subject of high-profile, award-winning works of nonfiction and fiction, both in print and on film. The appeal is easy to understand. Huey Long fashioned himself as a fierce champion of the underrepresented common person and blazed his way to power with bravado and unrelenting pursuit. Huey Long stories are legend in the state, and they mostly involve Long crudely or rudely and certainly loudly confronting the establishment.

Long succeeded in Louisiana in ways that might not have been possible elsewhere. On first glance he appears to be like many "common folk" politicians in the South leading up to the Great Depression and beyond.

When Huey became governor in 1928, a vast majority of Louisianians, like the citizens in much of the Deep South, were very poor, undereducated, and with quite limited access to public services like roads, hospitals, and schools. Also like most of the South, Louisiana was home to a significant minority of African Americans, who were without even more, including fundamental political and civil rights. At the time of Huey Long's rise to power, increasing numbers of poor, undereducated white citizens who lacked adequate public services were acquiring the right to vote and becoming the ascendant crucial force in Louisiana politics and whose support provided an unmistakable path to political power.

Aspiring southern politicians in similar situations generally found success by appealing to these newly enfranchised masses through rhetoric of racial division and conflict. It was easy, even if destructive, to gain votes of poor whites by making villains of poor blacks. These populist politicians had little money to use to meet concrete economic needs of poor whites, so they won with racial emotional, psychological appeals instead. The opposition to slavery in Long's family background made that option fairly untenable. Fortunately for Long, the situation in Louisiana differed from that of other states in the Deep South in two key respects that allowed him to run as a populist emphasizing the needs of the poor without resorting to racial rhetoric. First, oil had recently been discovered in Louisiana, and the taxes associated with it began to fill government coffers. Money was available to deliver real goods without the need for recourse to emotional racial appeals. Second, racial rhetoric in New Orleans and French Catholic Louisiana would have met with limited success anyway. New Orleans was a commercial center with a significant population of African Americans that had never been slaves, and the more rural French south Louisiana didn't have the history of racial conflict that existed in most of the remainder of the Deep South. Therefore, Long was a full-speed, powerhouse economic populist in a state that could provide goods and services to a newly voting citizenry that desperately wanted and needed them. Until his assassination in 1932, he was wildly popular among the masses.

Huey Long's economic populism, drawing on the vast resources provided by oil and gas severance taxes, created a high-stakes politics where the government controlled the money and where every election determined who was able to spend the spoils. Louisiana citizens who could vote (for much of the century, distinctly not most African Americans) understood the dynamic and participated in greater numbers than most of the rest of the South. The combination of a population that desperately needed services and an oil gusher of money to provide them set the stage for the flamboyant, circuslike politics that became the state's trademark. Louisiana's constitution allowed governors to serve only one term, creating an environment of nonstop electioneering and a consistently highly competitive, volatile, and participatory political atmosphere unlike anywhere else in the region.

EARL LONG AND THE CIVIL RIGHTS ERA

Earl Long was very different from his older brother in that he never became a national figure and never received the same kind of awestruck notoriety as Huey. Nevertheless, he served as governor longer than Huey, arguably had more of an immediate impact on the state, and his toughest challenges and eventual demise taught us a lot about how Louisiana would confront the most fundamental change in southern politics in the century, the civil rights movement. Earl, like Huey, was a master of poor people's politics but, like Huey, was not comfortable with using racism to appeal to voters. During Earl's rise to power and early career, this predilection was not a major obstacle. But, as A. J. Liebling in his highly acclaimed and wonderfully written 1961 biography, *The Earl of Louisiana*, explains with insight and detail, it was the race issue that would spell Earl's political demise and ultimately the end of Long-style economic populism, or "Longism," as it is called in Louisiana.

What we learned from Earl's governorship in a most spectacular fashion was that while Louisiana may have been somewhat less susceptible to the flames of racism that were being fanned by politicians of the time, it was certainly not immune to them. Even though parts of south Louisiana and New Orleans allowed greater numbers of African Americans to vote before the Voting Rights Act of 1964 than in fellow Deep Southern states, attempts to facilitate racial progress nonetheless met with ferocious resistance. As Liebling explains so well, it was Earl Long's interest in racial progress that provoked his notorious rant in the state capitol that sent him to a mental hospital in Texas, and then ultimately back to a hospital in Louisiana, where he used his political finesse to make a triumphant return as governor. The incident, which was the subject of newspaper and magazine articles and theater newsreels throughout the country, caused a nationwide sensation because of its carnival-like story-line. More significantly, however, it showed that the Longs of Louisiana were only able to quiet the seething racial tension that lay beneath the political surface during their years as governor, not make significant advances. And, indeed, Louisiana had its share of racial conflict that could not be ignored and would rise again and again throughout the century.

After the Civil Rights and Voting Rights Acts of the mid-1960s, together with the sometimes harsh white reaction that followed, Louisiana politics found a new equilibrium. It was defined by the election in late 1971 of Louisiana's first French Acadian governor, Edwin Edwards, who was enormously popular and, after the constitutional change in the previous decade, was overwhelmingly re-elected to the second of what would be four terms to absolutely dominate Louisiana politics for the next thirty years. His stunning triumphs and tragedies fit seamlessly into classic Louisiana political high drama and in the end even added a few exclamation points.

THE EDWARDS ERA FROM GOOD TIMES TO BAD

Edwin Edwards's first victory after winning an extremely close Democratic primary over future U.S. senator J. Bennett Johnston was a celebration of Louisiana's ethnic diversity. Since the Voting Rights Act of 1965, the state's voting population had finally come to resemble its population as a whole. Edwards campaigned directly to and overwhelmingly carried the state's newly enfranchised African American population, roughly a third of the state and a quarter of the electorate. He was also a representative of the southern European population in the South, known elsewhere mainly for its rural Acadian French and urban New Orleans French and Spanish populations. In his first term, he appointed unprecedented numbers of African Americans and women to high-profile positions and was a symbol of Louisiana's newly inclusive populism. Like the Long brothers before him, Edwards rewarded his friends and punished

Fig. 8.2. Edwin Edwards with Castro Carazo in 1972, while Edwards was serving his first term as governor. Carazo composed the official fight song of Louisiana State University, still in use today. *LSU Photograph Collection, RG #A5000, Louisiana State University Archives, LSU Libraries, Baton Rouge, La.*

his enemies, and thanks to the continued influx of oil and gas revenues, he had almost unlimited power to do it. Indeed, by the 1970s, almost 40 percent of the state's budget revenues were oil and gas related. It was a politician's dream: spend the money on the people who supported you and, in that most Louisiana of spirits, "Laissez les bons temps rouler!"— let the good times roll.

In this atmosphere, and with a flourish in 1975, despite the howls of journalists, good-government groups, and even political scientists, three months before he ran for re-election, Edwards easily convinced the legislature to pass new election rules that happened to benefit him enormously. He created the Louisiana open election system, which scrapped the sacred party primary system for a free-for-all where all candidates regardless of party run in one election and the top two, again regardless of party, meet in a final showdown. If a candidate receives a majority in the first round—and this is what incumbents who wanted to avoid a general election against a member of the other party relished—the election is over. Edwards won his re-election that way in 1975, and that, combined with a new constitution he passed soon after taking charge, elevated him to the legendary governor status occupied by Huey and Earl Long.

Edwards's and Louisiana's fortunes changed dramatically and rapidly two years after the completion of his second term. On the surface, Louisiana politics appeared to be forging into a more contemporary political system. In 1979, Congressman David Treen became the first Republican in modern times to be elected governor, and with his election the party had not only snagged the state's premier office but increased its "bench," as several well-known officials became Republican. In his first years in office, Treen did what Republicans are elected to do—he cut taxes—and built a reputation of honesty and integrity, if not efficiency. Then the price of oil plummeted, and Louisiana's economy went down with it. Everything changed. The flow of money that had allowed money to be spent by Democrats and taxes to be cut by Republicans suddenly slowed to a trickle.

Treen could not recover politically, and Edwards, promising to bring the good times back, roared to a third term in what was then the most expensive nonpresidential race on record. Not only did the economy continue to take a hit, but Edwards's actions during that time caused him and the state tremendous grief. He was accused of selling prized hospital permits during the time he was out of office. His third term was dominated by trials. The first ended without a verdict, and he was acquitted in the second. While the court system of Louisiana found him not guilty, the people of the state, according to public opinion polls, resoundingly did not.

By 1980, Louisiana was beginning a long economic downturn, and Edwards was beginning a decade of defending himself in court, ultimately unsuccessfully. In one of the most bizarre twists in a state known for them, he would have one last hurrah before that final trial and conviction. Edwards ran for re-election in 1987 but pulled out of the runoff and was succeeded by upstate congressman Buddy Roemer, who ran on a reform message. An increasingly angry and frustrated electorate, still feeling the impact of low oil prices, overpowered Roemer's term. When

Roemer ran for re-election in 1991, that anger found its voice among the white population in former Ku Klux Klan grand wizard and then state representative David Duke, and the African American population turned to Edwards. Roemer was squeezed out of a runoff spot, leaving Louisiana with a choice between Duke and Edwards. "Vote for the Crook, It's Important" was the bumper sticker that encapsulated the mood of the electorate as Edwards cruised to a most unlikely fourth term, in which he was unable to turn the state around. Soon afterward, he was indicted on charges regarding casino licensing, and this time he was sent to prison. Louisiana's freewheeling political culture and its modern face would never be the same.

REFORM AND DISASTER

When V. O. Key referred to Louisiana as one-of-a-kind, he was not characterizing its charismatic politicians and their colorful language. He was referring to a politics of corruption and dirty deals. In 1949, referring to the Louisiana of the first part of the twentieth century, Key was unrestrained in his characterization:

> Few would contest the proposition that among its professional politicians of the past two decades La. has had more men who have been in jail, or who should have been, than any other American state. Extortion, bribery, peculation, thievery, are not rare in the annals of politics, but in the scale, variety, and thoroughness, of its operations the Long gang established, after the death of the Kingfish, a record unparalleled in our times. Millions of dollars found their way more or less directly to his political heirs and followers. From the state treasury, from state employees, from gambling concessionaries, from seekers of every conceivable privilege, cash flowed to some members of the inner circle.

Louisiana has a long history of being characterized as a den of political bribery, fraud, vice, and sleaze. Most Louisianians, of course, hope that is a part of the nature of Louisiana politics that is quickly losing ground.

The decrease in oil-related revenue and the high-profile trials and eventual conviction of four-term governor Edwards appeared to steer Louisiana politics into an unprecedented era of reform. Up until this

Fig. 8.3. Oak tree felled by storm on state capitol grounds. *Dustin Howes*

time reformers would be elected every few years. However, after the mid-1990s, the reform message was a necessary and winning one. In 1995 and again in 1999, Republican Mike Foster was elected as a reformer. And in 2003, the runoff between reformers Kathleen Blanco and Bobby Jindal was heralded as a new page in Louisiana politics, producing either the first woman governor in Louisiana or the first Indian-American governor in the United States. Blanco won and was reasonably popular and successful until disaster struck in the form of the devastation following Hurricanes Katrina and Rita. President George W. Bush and Governor Blanco both suffered politically because of their responses. Blanco chose not to run for re-election and was succeeded by her former opponent Bobby Jindal, who won the gubernatorial election easily. Two years into his first term, Governor Jindal faced a disaster of his own in the BP oil spill in the Gulf of Mexico and, perhaps learning from his predecessor's mistakes, received much higher public marks for his performance. In the course of a few decades, Louisiana had transformed from a state known for populism, bravado, and "letting the good times roll" to one hobbled by disaster and responding with continuous calls for reform.

THE KATRINA EFFECT

In the weeks and months after the world watched the devastation of Louisiana's largest city, New Orleans, and shortly afterward a much less publicized, but severe and damaging Hurricane Rita affecting the remainder of the Louisiana coast, predictions about the political impact of these catastrophes abounded. Most discussions centered on the partisan effects of the loss of thousands of mostly African American, mostly Democratic voting citizens of New Orleans. Indeed, within days of the disaster in 2005, commentators were questioning the fates of Democratic governor Kathleen Blanco, Democratic and African American New Orleans mayor Ray Nagin, and even Democratic U.S. senator Mary Landrieu, whose re-election was three years in the future. Their individual fates speak well to the complex impact of the aftermath of Katrina. Governor Blanco received blame for her handling of the situation, didn't run for re-election, and was succeeded by Republican Bobby Jindal. On the other hand, Senator Landrieu benefited from the perception that she had been a consistent and persistent voice for Louisiana after Katrina, and was re-elected.

The political impact on New Orleans itself presented a more complicated story. Mayor Nagin was not given high marks for his handling of the situation. However, the widespread concern in the African American community that New Orleans would no longer have a black voice prompted him to be re-elected less than a year after the devastating event, while New Orleans was still at the very beginning stages of rebuilding. Four years later, as citizens returned to the city from which they had fled, there emerged a sense of hope alongside the sense of frustration at the slow pace of rebuilding. By this time, racial considerations in the African American community were subdued as Mitch Landrieu, the white Democratic lieutenant governor who lost to Nagin four years prior, emerged triumphant in the mayor's race with a substantial majority of black support.

Statewide, the hurricanes and the BP disaster that followed five years later didn't alter the course of Louisiana politics. Rather, they reinforced trends that were in place before these disasters. Continued and reinvigorated emphasis on reform politics was the primary result.

DEMOCRATIC RESILIENCE FOLLOWED BY
REPUBLICAN SURGE

Concurrent and completely intertwined with the transformation of Louisiana's political culture was a transformation of party dynamics in the state. As in much of the South and for the same reasons, Louisiana's party system was a dominant one-party Democratic system until the mid-1960s. One striking difference, however, was that with the emergence of Longism in the 1920s, the one-party system was effectively split into two easily identified, enduring factions. The "Longites" were poorer and working-class voters who supported the Longs and their programs of spending on hospitals, roads, schools, and a plethora of public works initiatives. The "Anti-Longs" were middle- and upper-income voters who supported Long-opposition positions for lower spending, lower taxes, and government reform. This bifactional system worked effectively from

Huey Long's ascendance to power in 1928 until the voting rights movement in the early 1960s.

Partially because of the familiarity with voting along economic lines, the emergence of the Republican party in the South after the Voting Rights Act had obvious economic as well as racial and social dimensions. To be sure, newly enfranchised African Americans voted loyally with the Democratic party, the party of Presidents John F. Kennedy and Lyndon B. Johnson, who had forged their successes. As in much of the rest of the South, many whites that resented these successes broke their solid allegiance to the Democratic party and began to vote more and more for Republicans. However, Democrats in Louisiana fared somewhat better during the emergence of the two-party South than their counterparts in surrounding states. Indeed, Louisiana was the last southern state to elect a Republican to the U.S. Senate, in 2004. Democrat Bill Clinton easily carried Louisiana in 1992 and 1996 when Republicans George H. W. Bush and Bob Dole were winning in much of the South—notably in Mississippi and Alabama—by very large margins.

In the 1970s, 1980s, and 1990s it was fairly obvious why Louisiana was more competitive for Democratic presidential and U.S. Senate candidates than the otherwise comparable states of Mississippi and Alabama. First, the new and proportionally large African American vote in the three states was more urban in Louisiana. African Americans were voting for Democrats and were turning out at greater rates in the more organized urban areas of Louisiana. Second, the southern European Catholic regions of south Louisiana were trending Republican, but not as fast as the northern European Protestant, overwhelmingly Baptist areas in north Louisiana, Mississippi, and Alabama. These two factors gave Democrats a more level playing field in national elections in Louisiana during the last few decades of the twentieth century and made it a target state for both parties at that time.

As the century closed, however, the Democrats' fortunes began to wane. The 1996 open-seat U.S. Senate election was won by the Democrats but foreshadowed a significant shift in political fortunes toward the Republicans. In that election, State Treasurer Mary Landrieu met former state representative Louis "Woody" Jenkins in a race that she was favored to win mainly because Jenkins was perceived as an out-of-the-mainstream conservative Republican. As the election neared, a former Catholic archbishop denounced Landrieu because of the Democrat's position on abortion and strongly urged Catholics to vote for the Republican. He was effective, and Landrieu's wire-thin margin held up only after weeks of examination in the Senate. The message from that election was clear and evident in the voting patterns. Catholics in south Louisiana were voting increasingly Republican. That change in party dynamic led Republican presidential candidates George W. Bush and John McCain to big victories in 2000, 2004, and 2008 and helped David Vitter become the first Louisiana Republican to be resoundingly elected to the U.S. Senate in 2004. In national elections, Louisiana had moved from being a swing state to a solid Republican state.

The Republican success in nationally oriented elections was trickling down to the governance of the state as well. Republicans began winning the governorship and statewide offices, and dramatically increasing their numbers in the legislature as well. After the 2007 statewide elections and 2008 national elections, in almost any statewide contest the Republican party label was clearly beneficial. The striking exception to this pattern was and is Democratic senator Landrieu herself. She managed to win re-election in both 2002 and 2008 despite national partisan trends moving against the Democrats in Louisiana. Her re-elections underline a second factor in national partisan trends in Louisiana almost as significant as the shift toward Republicans.

AN ELECTION SYSTEM THAT DISCOURAGES
PARTY LOYALTY

While Democrats win the governorship in very Republican Kansas and Republicans win Senate seats in Democratic Massachusetts, Louisiana's record of voting against general state partisan trends is reinforced by a surprisingly resilient election system that shuns party institutions completely. As discussed above, in 1975 Governor Edwin Edwards successfully created a system where all candidates regardless of party participate in a single election requiring a runoff between the top two vote getters (regardless of party) if no candidate reaches a majority. This election method was implemented at exactly the same time that the Republican

Party was beginning to be competitive in the state. Since there were no party primaries, party registration was, except for occasional elections of party officials and for occasional presidential primaries, meaningless. One effect was clear: with Republicans viable and as Democrats began voting consistently for Republicans, there was no need to bother to change party registration, and therefore party registration in Louisiana was a uniquely poor measure of partisanship. Without meaningful registration or participation in party primaries, the parties themselves lost a useful tool for party loyalty. One of the most deceptive phrases to an outsider in contemporary Louisiana politics is, "I'm a registered Democrat, but I'm voting for the Republican in this election." It is very likely that the person voicing it had been voting Republican for decades, but there was absolutely no need to change party registration. The pride in partisan autonomy allowed Democrats like Senator Mary Landrieu to stress local, individual issues, thereby disassociating her candidacy from partisanship.

In 2008, this pattern was striking. Louisiana was one of the few states to vote even stronger for the Republican presidential candidate in 2008 than in 2004, reflecting the powerful Republican swing of the last decade. Democratic senator Landrieu was the Republicans' top target. Her relatively easy win was most telling in the areas of suburban New Orleans, normally strongly Republican. However, even though Louisiana was in the midst of a brief period in which party primaries were used, her campaign de-emphasized her party ties and stressed her relentless support for initiatives for the New Orleans area after Hurricane Katrina. Her victory was largely due to unprecedented support in these strongly Republican New Orleans suburbs.

From 2006 through 2010, Louisiana experimented with returning to party primaries for federal elections, but the legislature voted to end the experiment after November 2010. Therefore, the rules that reinforce nonpartisanship have resumed (although this brief period of election normalcy will likely confound and confuse outsiders attempting Louisiana voting analysis for years to come). With the primaries so short lived, weak partisan attitudes and weak party institutions will likely continue to be a hallmark of Louisiana politics.

A STRONG, PERHAPS DECLINING, CULTURE OF
POLITICAL PARTICIPATION

While Louisiana's election rules discourage partisanship, they obviously don't discourage participation. Indeed, if there is one consistent and enduring aspect of Louisiana's political culture that has changed little since the 1920s and the days of Huey Long, it is a highly engaged electorate with many opportunities to participate. The evidence is clear in every aspect of Louisiana government and governance. Louisiana's participatory society is likely a result of two characteristics unique to the state. First is the strong economic populist politics forged after the flow of resources into the government with the discovery of oil in 1912. Second is the mix of three highly conscious ethnic groups of roughly equal proportions: rural and urban African Americans, southern European Catholics in New Orleans and south Louisiana, and northern European "Bible Belt" Baptists in north Louisiana. This pairing of well-defined ethnic diversity with a tradition of populist governance has led to a combustible mixture of volatile politics (see Parent, *Inside the Carnival,* for an extensive discussion of this phenomenon).

The evidence of a participatory, unstable politics is found throughout the political system. Louisiana has had eleven constitutions, more than any other state, including the second longest in the history of the United States. Louisiana's laws require the direct election of almost every office possible from a long list of statewide officials to judges at every level. Louisiana's legal system, like that of no other state, is based on the French rather than British system, which allows the legislature rather than the judicial branch to decide on the specific applications of the law. Until the oil bust in the 1980s, Louisiana was at or near the very top in per capita campaign spending as well. Voting participation, while about average nationally, is typically the highest in the South, home to most of the lowest voting segments of American society, the lower socioeconomic classes. The use of referenda in the state is widespread in the form of amendments to the constitution, with a long list of constitutional amendments on almost every statewide election ballot where they are allowed.

Because the oil and gas severance funds flowing into the government were a cause of these participatory populist practices in Louisiana, the fairly abrupt drop in that revenue in the 1970s had some impact on these practices. Campaign spending has retreated to fairly normal levels as the money for contributions has decreased. The state has reduced the number of elected statewide officials, notably removing the country's only elected commissioner of elections in 2004, and that is a trend that is likely to continue. However, perhaps because of the prominence of disasters such as hurricanes and oil spills, many of the participatory habits formed during a century of politics remain. Government officials from all over the country noticed that the Louisiana electorate was attentive and demanding during the aftermath of Hurricane Katrina and of the BP oil spill. The resilience of that sense of political efficacy, fostered during decades of a fairly populist democracy, will be fascinating to watch.

THE GOVERNOR, LEGISLATURE, AND COURTS

One of the most intriguing aspects of the office of governor in Louisiana is that most citizens and elected officials, especially legislators, voice the opinion on television, on radio, and in newspaper interviews that Louisiana has the most powerful governor in the nation. However, studies in political science that compare powers of governors across states show something very different. Indeed, Thad Beyle's study ranks Louisiana's governor at about the national average.

The perception is significant, however, and the result of some understandable reasoning. Huey Long, Earl Long, and Edwin Edwards were all known for ruling with an iron hand and passing most legislation that they wanted. Indeed, until the early 1990s there is no record of a governor's veto being overridden, and very few have been overridden since that time. While Louisiana's governor officially has about average power, the informal or cultural power of the office remains. In the absence of a strong and politically powerful legislature, that is a situation likely to continue.

While Louisiana's legislature has had some notable and spectacular confrontations with the governor over the years, these confrontations are very much the exception, and the legislature in Louisiana, while structurally fairly strong, is a politically weak force compared to the governor. The most telling evidence is in the selection of the leadership. Each chamber, as in most states, has a membership elected from single-member districts that don't overlap, with the House the larger body at 105 members and the Senate at 39 members. Each elects a leader, the Speaker of the House and president of the Senate, who sets the agenda and selects most of the committee membership and all of the chair and vice chair positions of all standing committees. With rare exception, the legislature has informally deferred to the wishes of the governor, and that choice has been the choice of the governor. Since the 1990s, Louisiana has had several Republican governors but only recently a Republican majority in either chamber. However, the leadership has often been a Republican or, failing that, a Democrat sympathetic to the governor. Rarely are there signs of political will in the legislature to act in disagreement with the governor, even when they are of opposite parties or represent different factions in the same party.

Despite its reluctance to resist the governor, Louisiana's legislature has evolved over the years. Significant changes occurred in the 1970s to professionalize and streamline the workings of the legislature, giving it the capacity to become a powerful force in politics. In addition, a limit of two consecutive terms was instituted in the 1990s, allowing for greater turnover in the chamber. And finally, Republicans, and to a lesser extent women, have grown significantly in power in Louisiana's legislature. In 2007 the parties almost reached parity in both chambers, with the Democrats holding a slight majority in each.

A most telling characteristic of Louisiana's political system is the courts system. All judges in the primary courts system—the Supreme Court, the Courts of Appeals, and the District Court—are directly elected. Even though there are periodic calls for reform to systems of appointment and election and even though reforms have affected the other institutions, the courts have remained directly elected. This is a clear impact of Louisiana's populist heritage. In addition, the basic legal framework is not precedent and common law, the English-based system used in the federal courts, but rather a legislatively enacted code based on the French legal system. In a state that ranks among the highest numbers of criminal cases per capita, attorneys per capita, and people incarcerated per capita, the court system is an active and particularly relevant part of Louisiana's democracy. Therefore, the judiciary system is a primary example of how, despite Louisiana's evolution and various reforms that have occurred, the state remains a fundamentally unique political animal.

IS LOUISIANA POLITICS STILL UNIQUE TODAY?

Louisiana certainly has a history of colorful, flamboyant politics. However, time has smoothed the edges a bit. The cold, unrelenting eye of public access through television and the Internet has made the shenanigans of politicians less appealing and more consequential. The gush of oil-related money that encouraged political deal making has slowed to a small stream. The power relationships and contours of the broad ethnic mix have changed, and with them political party politics has changed as well. Louisiana will likely remain intriguing, though. Centuries of norms of behavior, often reinforced in law and institutions, will likely keep Louisiana politics a source of fascination well into the twenty-second century.

BIBLIOGRAPHY AND FURTHER READING

Beyle, Thad, et al. *Politics in the American States: A Comparative Analysis.* Boston: Scott, Foresman, 1983.

Bridges, Tyler. *Bad Bet on the Bayou: The Rise and Fall of Gambling in Louisiana and the Fate of Governor Edwin Edwards.* New York: Farrar, Straus, Giroux, 1992.

Horne, Jed. *Breach of Faith: Hurricane Katrina and the Near Death of a Great American City.* New York: Random House, 2008.

Hrebenar, Ronald J., and Clive S. Thomas, eds. *Interest Group Politics in the Southern States.* Tuscaloosa: University of Alabama Press, 1992.

Key, V. O. *Southern Politics in State and Nation.* New York: Vintage Books, 1949.

Leibling, A. J. *The Earl of Louisiana.* Baton Rouge: LSU Press, 1970.

Maginnis, John. *Cross to Bear.* Baton Rouge: Darkhorse Press, 1992.

———. *The Last Hayride.* Baton Rouge: Darkhorse Press, 1984.

Parent, Wayne. *Inside the Carnival: Unmasking Louisiana Politics.* Baton Rouge: LSU Press, 2004.

Rose, Douglas, ed. *The Emergence of David Duke and the Politics of Race.* Chapel Hill: University of North Carolina Press, 1992.

Williams, T. Harry. *Huey Long.* New York: Bantam Books, 1970.

Wright, Richard. *Kingfish: The Reign of Huey P. Long.* New York: Random House, 2006.

SEEING AND HEARING LOUISIANA
MUSIC AND FILM

— + —

"HOW DID WE END UP AT THIS PARTY?"
—A FERAL LOUISIANA PLAYLIST

ALEX V. COOK

Louisiana is a crucible of American music. The roots of blues, jazz, country, and rock 'n' roll can all be seen as byproducts of the massive cultural collisions that made Louisiana. And while understanding these stylistic lineages is crucial to understanding American music, it's in the aberrations where Louisiana sings itself. The wild hollers of outsize egos, the willingness to let styles and traditions cross-pollinate into new forms of music, the comfort with things being a little crazy is the real sonic story of Louisiana. It is in this spirit that I steer away from the heroes of New Orleans jazz and the revered Cajun pioneers and instead attempt a fractured portrait of the true, wild Louisiana in twenty tunes.

KEITH FRANK AND THE SOILEAU FAMILY BAND,
"READY OR NOT," FROM *READY OR NOT*

Keith Frank's sentiments in "Ready" are pretty universal—especially since the Delfonics had hits with the refrain that makes up most of the song's lyrics:

Ready or Not
Here I come
Gonna find you and
Make you want me

But it reveals perhaps an unintentional truth about zydeco, the music of which Keith Frank is a master. Zydeco is an elusive music, R&B-inflected, accordion-driven Cajun dancehall music performed in backwoods nightclubs far off the tourist trail. I've seen Keith Frank play at the Hot Spot in Church Point, the Pat Davis Lounge on the far side of Cecelia. I've seen him where I was one of the only people in the club; I've also seen him in bars packed to overflowing, the band illuminated by nothing more than the lights on their crackling amps.

Even when you can find the club Keith Frank is playing, it's difficult to get a read on the song. "Ready or Not" is typical for a Keith Frank "song."

Fig. 9.1. Teddy's Juke Joint, Zachary, Louisiana. *Dustin Howes*

I say "song" because they tend to turn into medleys. "Ready or Not" gives way to an "All the Jazz" chant over Wes Montgomery–style guitar licks. Frank is not afraid to include soul, hip-hop, classic rock—I swear I once heard his accordion do the dive-bomb wail of "Kashmir"—anything in the name of zydeco. Zydeco exists perhaps as more of an assertion than a fixed style of music, evolving with the times. In the mid-1970s, Keith Frank joined in his father Preston's Family Zydeco Band at age four and eventually took over when his father retired.

JOE FALCON, *CAJUN MUSIC PIONEER*

Louis Michot of Lost Bayou Ramblers turned me onto this record while discussing what Cajun music really is. Falcon, with his wife Cleoma Breaux, made what is generally considered the first Cajun record, *Allons à Lafayette,* in 1928 for Columbia. *Cajun Music Pioneer* was recorded in 1963 at the tiny Triangle club in Scott, Louisiana, just west of Lafayette. Despite almost four decades of Cajun music committed to recordings previous to this one, it feels like Joe Falcon and his band are the first pack of wild animals to barge out from the woods. They still clatter like a kicked-over bar table, tearing at their instruments like wild animals.

The reason the recording happened is that Cajun music was on the verge of becoming a museum piece, a folk style practiced in earnest by elder players in their twilight. Michot found resonance in these wild, rocking recordings as a kid who wanted to be in Guns n' Roses instead of the Balfa Brothers. Here was the music of his parents amped up for the honky-tonks, seemingly a feral reminder that all things, even the sweet two-steps and waltzes of Cajun dance halls, once had fangs and claws.

ROBERT PETE WILLIAMS, "PRISONER'S TALKING BLUES," FROM *ANGOLA PRISON BLUES*

Dr. Harry Oster described Angola this way in his 1969 book *Living Country Blues:* "Enclosing some three thousand caged and womanless Negroes, this huge prison is a fertile breeding ground for the blues." It was in the breeding ground that he first encountered Robert Pete Williams.

Williams was born to a sharecropper in Zachary, Louisiana, in 1914 and grew up playing the style of blues found at picnics and fish fries. In 1956, Williams shot a man in a night club and landed in the state penitentiary at Angola, and seemingly the blues style he embodied was trapped in with him.

Williams's lyrics speak with alarming clarity about hard luck and harder women over a percolating rhythmic playing, a style of blues that faded with the electric blues that players like Louisiana's Buddy Guy played in Chicago. It wasn't until the folk revival of the 1960s that his music found its first wide audience, at the 1964 Newport Folk Festival. There, Williams became a torchbearer of the real blues, unspoiled by the marketplace and popular appeal.

Williams's "Prisoner's Talking Blues" consists of a spectral recitation of regret, a plea for mercy over a skeletal guitar line. The song radiates the meditative sadness of the prisoner, the wrongly accused (Williams maintained the shooting was in self-defense), the forlorn. It's a blues that cuts to the bone of despair. The fact that Williams survived, that the music he plays survived, is a testament to the human spirit of which the blues is built.

DOUG KERSHAW, "DEVIL'S ELBOW," FROM *DEVIL'S ELBOW*

Doug Kershaw's song "Louisiana Man" was the first song broadcast back to the earth from space, by the Apollo 12 mission in 1969. Not to belabor a pun, but Doug Kershaw is that far out. Kershaw's is a mix of Cajun and country dipped in moonshine and stirred by his lightning-fast fiddle hand. He's an embodiment of Louisiana's innate musicality. In the song "Devil's Elbow," he is asked why he's such a great fiddle player, graced with the "Devil's elbow." He answers with a more ridiculous question: "Go ask the eagle why it flies and why God graces its skies with rainbows!" Asked and answered.

His first hits made Doug Kershaw Louisiana's ambassador to the psychedelic era, parlaying an appearance on the first episode of Johnny Cash's variety TV show in 1969 and a week at the Fillmore East opening for Eric Clapton in the early 1970s. Kershaw's place in music is at the nexus of country, Cajun, and classic rock, a neon three-sided pyramid that emerges from the swamp during a full moon, perhaps answering that 1969 broadcast from space, the soul of the Louisiana Man sent skyward with a flourish from the Devil's elbow.

BEAU JOCQUE AND THE ZYDECO HI-ROLLERS, "THE HUCKLEBUCK," FROM *PICK UP ON THIS*

Once, at La Poussière dancehall in Breaux Bridge, I saw a band announce they were gonna do "The Hucklebuck," and a good ol' boy in attendance slapped his knee and shouted, "Yee-haw!" perhaps implying an additional, "Finally!" "Hucklebuck" speaks to the wild, aggressive side of Cajun music, obscured by an endless parade of romantic ballads. In fact, if there is any flesh connection to the tune with the same name that Chubby Checker, Frank Sinatra, and Otis Redding all recorded, Lake Charles zydeco monster Beau Jocque cooks it right off the bone. "Hucklebuck" is the only discernible human utterance that occurs in the song.

The rest is a glossolalia of grunts and snarls occurring at the breaks. The Sinatra version may walk you through the steps, but Jocque leaves you to follow your instinct. That good ol' boy threw his gal around the dance floor like he was being judged for distance, and the only other people willing to venture out on the boards were those prepared to catch her. Beau Jocque's primal zydeco inspires such action in a man.

Beau Jocque (Creole for "big guy"; his birth name is the equally grand moniker Andrus Esprit) took up the accordion after being laid up by a work accident, and shortly after, he became the guttural muscle behind zydeco in the late '80s and really the model for much of the contemporary zydeco bands. Jocque freely mixed the traditions of Clifton Chenier (who himself played fast and loose with musical styles) with Motown swing and rock swagger. Jocque's tunes seem almost perfunctory brackets in which the intense rhythms defining them can be summoned from the deep well of feral humanity. Jocque allegedly partied himself into a heart attack that ended his reign as the new King of Zydeco in 1999, but his music lives on in the wild stomp of south Louisiana dance halls.

"I'm a King Bee" might just be the coolest-sounding song in popular music. The skeletal rhythm pounded out by J. D. Miller's house band is like footsteps in the dark. The guitar sparks like a bulb hanging on a frayed wire from the ceiling. Slim Harpo's harmonica might as well be played by a ghost. The only thing that feels immediately present in the song is Slim's nasal voice, boasting of the potency of his stinger, threading to buzz 'round your hive.

The legends involving how Miller captured this sound in his little studio in Crowley verge on the apocryphal. Some say it was the chicken crates he used to dampen the sound, some say it was a problem in the soundboard. What matters is not how the beguiling reverb that marks this tune was created, but where the echoes of it landed. This song arguably launched the British blues fascination that strangely reignited American interest in its own root sound. The Rolling Stones put a version on their first album, perhaps as a sinister counterpoint to the Beatles' fascination with the more socially acceptable Little Richard. An early incarnation of Pink Floyd recorded the tune, perhaps attracted to its spectral qualities. The Doors have done it, as have the Grateful Dead. No doubt countless other bands have wrapped their mic cords around it, but it remains Slim's tune.

James Moore—the Slim Harpo name granted later by the media-savvy producer J. D. Miller—was born in Lobdell, Louisiana, in 1924. Moore played with his brother-in-law Lightnin' Slim (Moore played as Harmonica Slim; you had to be slim back then) until his own music career took off in 1957 with "I'm a King Bee." While the tune may have launched a thousand psychedelic ships seeking the raw and true heart of the blues, Moore only did music on the side, running a trucking business in the 1960s while having a no. 1 *Billboard* R&B single with "Scratch My Back" and other hits. Harpo passed away in 1970, missing an opportunity to participate in the blues revival of the hippie era. I'm tempted to speculate how deep that echo might have been with Canned Heat's horsepower behind him, but then I can't think of anything sounding much cooler than the original tune.

"You Are My Sunshine" is such a huge song that it is bigger than the outsize character that recorded it. The most famous song ever written about a horse was penned by Jimmie Davis, sharecropper's son, country singer, movie star (you might remember him from classics like *Cyclone Prairie Rangers* and *Square Dance Katy*), and governor of Louisiana for two nonconsecutive terms, beginning in 1944 and 1960. He fought the powerful populist Long family as a staunch segregationist—his 1927 master's thesis was titled "Comparative Intelligence of Whites, Blacks and Mulattoes"—but all of that rich detail hides in the shadow of a song everyone knows about a horse.

Davis's recorded output is as multifaceted as his biography, filled with lonesome downers and lively jump blues tunes, cowboy rambles, solemn gospel numbers, and even a couple of risqué hillbilly songs (seek out "Tomcat and Pussy Blues" if you can find it) from his early days. A lesser-known number titled "I Got News for You," a 78 recorded for Capitol in 1949, perhaps captures the outsize spirit of Jimmie Davis. It begins by addressing the lonely, commiserating with the dark nights of soul searching for what slipped through one's fingers, as a steel guitar guides the melodrama. Then suddenly he announces, "What you need is a trip! A trip on the Davis ship! Go to bed children and quit your crying. Come take a ride on the Sunshine Line!" A train whistle sounds, and Brother Jimmie delivers a sermon aboard a train bound for unfettered positivity. It's a weird tune but a great one, but then what else do you expect from a man who, among his many achievements, taught the world a song about loving a horse.

SISTER GERTRUDE MORGAN, "LET'S MAKE A RECORD," FROM *LET'S MAKE A RECORD*

In 1938, Columbus, Georgia, housewife Gertrude Morgan heard a voice telling her to become an evangelist, and she left her family for the streets of New Orleans to start an orphanage. In the mid-fifties, God spoke to Morgan again, telling her she was the Bride of Christ and that she was to channel her ecstatic ministry through art. She thus became widely known as a folk artist and a French Quarter fixture, replete in white habit, talking about the Book of Revelation and Jesus riding with her on an airplane.

Morgan began making paintings of her visions on pieces of scrap wood and scrawling poems on any available sheet of paper. In 1970, she recorded a spellbinding album of prayer chants accompanied by the rattle of her tambourine.

The opening title tune of *Let's Make a Record* consists of little more than repetition of "Let's make a record for my Lord." She enlists you, Ezekiel, and all who listen in the task. A minute in, she stops short, her persistent tambourine still rolling on its own momentum. "Hold it! Hold it!" she cries. "Give up Lucifer! He's no good! A demon! A lying one!" before sliding back into her trance.

It's tempting to tie this wide-eyed ritual music to New Orleans's storied (and often misrepresented) voodoo side, but I believe Sister Morgan is tapped into the currents of good and evil rubbing together in south Louisiana. Her tambourine is a telegraph message from the eternal, sparking in the heat.

MR. QUINTRON, "SWAMP BUGGY BADASS"

The real testament to the power of New Orleans R&B is not simply its reach, or the place its practitioners hold in the pantheon of popular music, but how it draws people back into it, how it is expansive enough for anyone willing to get funky to carve their niche in it. Take Mr. Quintron, aka Robert Rolston, an Air Force kid with origin myths rooted in Mobile and Germany who cut his teeth in Chicago, now the king of the New Orleans underground.

He plays an organ fronted with the grill from Ernie "Mother-in-Law" K-Doe's Cadillac, complete with working headlights. The minimalist yet manic beat comes from an invention (patented) of Mr. Quintron's called the Drum Buddy, an optical rhythm machine that uses a spinning perforated coffee can to dictate the rhythm, kind of like a player piano reel for a post-civilization funk fertility ritual. He holds court at the Spellcaster Lodge, a club in his Ninth Ward neighborhood, or at the Saturn Bar, a ramshackle, painting-festooned establishment on St. Claude Avenue.

The show usually begins with his partner Miss Pussycat's puppet show, a death and intrigue–filled tableau of surrealist proportions, quickly devolving into a room full of sweaty, writhing bodies shouting along with "Swamp Buggy Badass" and countless other tributes to his adopted Louisiana home. Recently, Q's art has been sanctioned with month-long residency/performance at the New Orleans Museum of Art, which resulted in the album *Sucre du Savage*.

The version of "Swamp Buggy Badass" appearing on the *Swamp Tech* album doesn't sound like much, mirroring in some ways the stripped-down bounce rap scene with which Quinton is connected, but like bounce, and much of New Orleans music in general, the song takes over a room when it's played live. It takes on the throb of New Orleans's musical pulse, runs it through the bohemian filter that makes the city such a great place, and, in that moment, is the only music in the world.

WARREN STORM, "PRISONER'S SONG"

When you see Warren Storm on stage singing his 1958 "Prisoner's Song," you realize you may have never seen a real performer before. Storm still plays the bars and festivals around his hometown of Abbeville, but he plays them like he's Johnny Mathis or Elvis or Wayne Newton or some super-performer combination of the three. Storm got his start as a drummer in J. D. Miller's house band, backing up a number of the early blues and country singles that came out of that studio, but it's his swamp pop hits from the 1950s and 1960s that made him a star.

Swamp pop is a music more defined by its embrace than by place or even time. It is basically Cajun, blues, and zydeco musicians from Acadiana playing New Orleans R&B in response to the rise of rock 'n' roll. Traditional Cajun music was largely wiped off the map by the juggernaut of country music radio in the 1960s, and rock 'n' roll pretty much finished the job. Through swamp pop, performers like Storm found a way to stay relevant, and curiously, it is through this timeless and anachronistic style that they remain so.

Turn on Cajun and swamp pop-centric radio stations KBON or KPVI on a ride through Acadiana and you'll hear a Warren Storm song at least once an hour. Show up with the throngs, young and old, packing the

Lamar-Dixon Expo Center in Gonzales during the Swamp Pop Festival, and Warren is still the brightest star in the sky. To a large segment of defiant Louisianians, Storm's star has never faded. His powerful voice throws off the dust coating these tired oldies hits and makes them sound fresh and alive.

DALE HAWKINS, "SUZIE Q"

It is a curious thing to be remembered as an architect of the swamp rock boogie, but really, listen to "Suzie Q" and try to describe it any other way. That riff, provided by James Burton, makes it one of the most endearingly cool songs in popular music. Like many country musicians in Shreveport in the '50s, Dale Hawkins jumped on the rock 'n' roll bandwagon when Elvis took over from Hank Williams as king. Hawkins could rock, but it's the roll that really defines his songs.

Hawkins's tunes held close to the swing of the blues; his first single was a cover of Willie Dixon's "My Babe." Listen to the element of danger that embodies "Suzie Q." The drums are like tree branches slapping the side of a shack in a wind storm. The guitar sounds like it was strung with barbed wire echoing through a chicken coop. The solo is more of a screech.

I got to see Dale Hawkins perform just months before he passed away in 2010. At seventy-three he'd lost none of his menacing spark, "Suzie Q" sounding as wild as if it had just wandered out of the woods.

THE METERS, "CHICKEN STRUT," FROM STRUTTIN'

The true sound of the New Orleans that many of us know is the wild yet expansive funk of the Meters, often gravitating from one theme or riff to the next like the crooked line one follows from the house to the restaurant to the bar to another bar to "how did we end up at this party?" on into the next morning's hangover.

Experts will proclaim Struttin', the 1970 third album from the band, as a lesser work, lacking the well-oiled mechanics of the Meters, but it captures the loose haze of a night out in New Orleans with imperfect precision. New Orleans is a city mapped out on a warped grid, land implausi-

Fig. 9.2. New Orleans street music. *Dustin Howes*

bly under the water, where compass directions are eschewed for uptown, downtown, toward the river, or toward the lake. It's a place where community and chaos have an understanding, where you are early if you aren't an hour late, jangling in a little disoriented and sweaty like "Chicken Strut" wondering where the party's at. For the most part, it's right there.

DR. JOHN THE NIGHT TRIPPER, "GRIS-GRIS GUMBO YA YA," FROM *GRIS-GRIS*

There is perhaps no more narcotic a song than "Gris-Gris Gumbo Ya Ya." The thinly veiled swamp shaman act Dr. John performs on this song mirrors the drug problem that would plague him for decades. It's psychedelic blues drift by like the deepest of bong hits, like an opiate fog. It's less a song proper than it is a tune inscribed by a ghost.

Mac Rebennack was already a well-established musical figure in New Orleans by 1965 when he made off for Los Angeles, escaping a drug charge, to record his debut album in the heart of the psychedelic sixties. Rebennack originally wanted New Orleans singer Ronnie Barron to front the band Dr. John, but someone counseled Barron against it, so Rebennack slid into the role that would define not only him but New Orleans music in the minds of many.

"Right Place Wrong Time," his hit from the 1973 smash *In the Right Place,* became the first interface with New Orleans R&B since Fats Domino, and "Such a Night," from that same album, featured in The Band's famous Last Waltz concert, cemented Dr. John as a gruff, lovable funky uncle. But it's the early records, the loose, sinewy ones where the blues drift on waves of humidity, smelling like the streets of New Orleans after a warm summer downpour, staggering like an afternoon drunk, that tap into a deeper, wilder, and truer New Orleans. Not everyone in the city is a voodoo-spouting junkie hipster, but chances are they at least know somebody who knows somebody who is, and has a little bit of that scent on them.

TONY JOE WHITE, "ROOSEVELT AND IRA LEE," FROM *CONTINUED*

Tony Joe White, the psychedelic, deep-voiced son of Oak Grove, Louisiana, is best known for his hit "Polk Salad Annie," but he's sung about crooked sheriffs, homemade ice cream, race relations, even trolls ("Even Trolls Love Rock and Roll"). Tony Joe White fits the wide swath of his backwoods Louisiana upbringing into his swamp boogie.

My favorite tune of his, though, involves the story of Roosevelt and Ira Lee. It's a rambling moonlit tale of two boys going bullfrogging when "Right away, they knew the night was gonna be a bummer" and Ira Lee steps on a water moccasin.

It's not really that much of a tale. The two hightail it out of the swamp to steal chickens instead. What's great about the song is that it is cut straight from the psychic humid of Louisiana childhood. If you grew up with access to the Louisiana swamps, you'll find yourself in Roosevelt and Ira Lee, days percolating like Tony Joe White's funky rhythm section, danger murmuring like his baritone, adventure searing like his guitar. You listen to Tony Joe White and check yourself for snakebites.

LIL' BOB AND THE LOLLIPOPS, "I GOT LOADED"

Every band in Louisiana does "I Got Loaded." All of them. Cajun bands, zydeco bands, swamp pop, blues bands. I'm willing to bet you could get a Louisiana church choir to bust into it just by standing up in the pew to testify:

> Last night
> I got loaded
> On a bottle of gin, a bottle of gin

My favorite version is that by swamp pop titans Lil' Bob and the Lollipops. They rend it straight enough as the horn-laden dance tune it remains today. Partly, it is Lil' Bob's backstory that makes it for me, how a young Camille Bob from Arnaudville, Louisiana, traded a horse for his first set of drums. How he was run out of town for making time with a white woman at an Acadiana roadhouse (which one depends on who is telling the story).

Partly, it's the ebullience Lil' Bob brings to the song. He and the song are effortlessly happy, swinging from the rafters joyous over life's simplest pleasures, and retelling the tale over another bottle.

WEBB PIERCE, "BACK STREET AFFAIR," FROM *SO MANY YEARS*

Webb Pierce's mournful twang over the breezy sway of pedal steel and banks of fiddles sounds like the most natural thing in the world yet is the work of a most calculating individual. By age fifteen, the West Monroe teenager had the first of many radio shows. After a stint in the army, he had a second show with his young bride in Shreveport, "Webb Pierce with Betty Jane, the Singing Sweetheart," while working at the Sears and Roebuck around the corner from the station. It seems like quite a feat for such a young man, but it was only the beginning for Webb Pierce.

He and Betty Jane divorced after both were awarded contracts by 4 Star Records in California, and he signed on with a fledgling radio program back in Shreveport called *Louisiana Hayride*. He paid young girls to scream from the front row, creating a buzz; that buzz got him a new deal with Decca Records, where he scored massive hits with "Wondering" and "That Heart Belongs to Me."

The final piece to the puzzle was Pierce filling the slot at the Grand Ole Opry after Hank Williams was fired. That, and his hit "Slowly," introduced the pedal steel guitar into the country music vernacular.

"Back Street Affair" is a serpentine variant of the sad-sack pity songs Hank Williams made famous. "They say you wrecked my home/I'm a husband that's gone wrong" he laments to his mistress. He's not lonesome to the point of crying; he's instead bemoaning his reputation in the community.

Pierce lived an extravagance country music had never seen. He commissioned famed tailor Nudie Cohn, creator of the Nudie Suit, to line a pair of convertibles with silver dollars and built a massive guitar-shaped pool at his Nashville home, which became a popular tourist attraction. He stayed with Decca into the late '70s, long after he was a hot radio commodity (though he did score a 1982 hit, a duet with Willie Nelson revising "In the Jailhouse Now"). After a lifetime of excess, he succumbed to pancreatic cancer in 1991, revered among fans of classic country music, and largely forgotten by everyone else.

RUFUS JAGNEAUX, "OPELOUSAS SOSTAN"

There were other south Louisiana hippie bands, but Rufus Jagneaux is the only one people can remember and they don't necessarily remember it fondly. In his book *Swamp Pop: Cajun and Creole Rhythm and Blues,* Shane Bernard discusses the controversy surrounding "Opelousas Sostan": "The popularity of 'Sostan' with the south Louisiana public infuriated some cultural activists and musical purists, who regarded the song as an offensive parody of Cajun music and culture." That was the first thing that attracted me to the song. Acadiana culture has a tendency for hyperbolic reverence (for good reason; if they didn't care so much, the whole culture would have died out decades ago), and "Sostan" takes a lighthearted view of it, building a hazy, hippie rambler out of this one scene.

Opelousas Sostan
Used to come this way
On his way to sing his song,
"I can hear the jukebox play."
"Mais, I can hear the jukebox play.
Allons 'vec moi! Bon temps rouler."

Teenaged Benny Graeff had written the tune while spending the winter in a Tennessee commune and through his uncle, who happened to be a member of the Boogie Kings, set up a session at Floyd Soileau's studio in Ville Platte and recorded one of the most endearing songs in the pantheon of Acadian music.

The other reason I love the song is because it wasn't a radio hit per se —a number of DJs were gun-shy about it—but it was a jukebox smash, where people voted with nickels and dimes in every diner and honky-tonk across the state. To this day, you put Rufus Jagneaux on in any Acadian hole in the wall and the whole bar will come alive singing, "I can hear the jukebox play."

BOBBY CHARLES, "STREET PEOPLE," FROM *BOBBY CHARLES*

There are plenty of people that will hold up Gram Parsons as the true master of Cosmic Americana, but I would offer up the sorely undersung self-titled solo album by Bobby Charles. If you remember sweet old Bobby at all, it's for the massive hits he wrote for Fats Domino and Bill Haley. Leonard Chess signed him after hearing his audition of a tune he wrote, "See You Later, Alligator" over the phone, supposedly not knowing Charles was a white Cajun boy from Abbeville, Louisiana. His successes of the '60s include penning "Walking to New Orleans" for Fats Domino and "(I Don't Know Why I Love You) But I Do" for Clarence "Frogman" Henry. After a while, he drifted away from the business.

Charles had some important friends, namely The Band's Rick Danko, who rounded up his Band-mates as well as David Sanborn and Dr. John to record *Bobby Charles* in 1972. Critics loved it for its effortless, sleepy charm, but even an appearance in The Band's Last Waltz couldn't put Bobby Charles on the map.

Perhaps it's the inherent marginality in the songs that's kept them from a wider popularity. Charles sings of "Hangin' out with the street people / they got it down" with the ease of a drifter padding in from a morning train-yard drink. It's maybe the friendliest song about transience, understanding that the path he's chosen is not the norm. "Some people would rather work / you need people like that," he concedes as he disappears, chuckling into the last embers of the sunset, hitting up whoever's around for change.

BOB CORRITORE AND CAROL FRAN, "I NEEDS TO BE BE'D WITH," FROM *HARMONICA BLUES*

Carol Fran is many things: a seemingly unsinkable legend of Louisiana's blues heritage, a testament that sexy doesn't dissipate with age, but, most importantly, a master of the fine art of cuttin' up. Carol Fran has been, is, and will forever be the smack-talking, entendre-doublin' upstager of any scene she appears on.

Take this tune from Bob Corritore's *Harmonica Blues* album. Bob's harmonica comes on like a freight train descending from heaven, but when Carol Fran opens her mouth, he might as well have sat out on the session.

> I've been a lover all of my life
> Ain't never thought about bein' nobody's wife
> I got a sweet sugar daddy
> who comes around when I want him to
> talkin' about right now.

It's like a shotgun blast of female sexuality.

Fran was born Carol Martin in 1933 in Lafayette, Louisiana. A gig singing jump blues with Don Conway took her to New Orleans, where she recorded her classic 1957 debut, "Emmitt Lee," for Excello. Fran performed with Guitar Slim, Lee Dorsey, and any Louisiana blues outfit that could keep up with her. Fran almost made the big time in the early '60s; it's largely agreed that if Elvis hadn't done "Cryin' in the Chapel," it would be known today as a Carol Fran song.

Fran married guitarist Clarence Hollimon and spent the '80s with him in Texas, but relocated to Lafayette after his death. In her seventies,

Carol Fran still can command a stage with the same unflinching sexual banter and barrelhouse voice.

DALE AND GRACE, "I'M LEAVING IT ALL UP TO YOU"

Dale Houston was already a star when Sam Montel heard him play in a Baton Rouge bar in 1960 and suggested he team up with a girl from Prairieville by the name of Grace Broussard. Grace had a local following, singing with her brother Van Broussard, but when Montel heard her and Dale perform the Don and Dewey tune "I'm Leaving It All Up to You," he knew there was something special.

Dale and Grace's rendition is the pinnacle of country sweetheart ballads, their love waltzing in on a dream cloud of strings onto radio stations and jukeboxes across America. They had the number-one song in the country when they stood on a Dallas street corner along with Bobby Vee and the rest of Dick Clark's travelling Caravan of Stars to wave at President John Kennedy's procession moments before that shot rang out.

The duo had a second, lesser hit with "Stop and Think It Over," but the times had changed in 1964. The British Invasion was in full swing and fans lost touch with their style of country sweetness, and the duo disbanded. Still, though, if you tune in to any classic country station on the AM radio of the soul and wait until things get still, Dale and Grace will start singing to each other, and there is nothing else in the world but that harmony.

— ✦ —

AUTHENTICITY AS A CONUNDRUM IN EIGHT LOUISIANA FILMS

ZACK GODSHALL

AUTHENTIC NEW ORLEANS

Elia Kazan, one of the greatest directors of actors ever to make films, made perhaps the most famous New Orleans film of all time and undoubtedly one of the great literary adaptations ever put to screen—Tennessee Williams's *A Streetcar Named Desire* (1951). One year earlier, Kazan made another New Orleans film—*Panic in the Streets* (1950)—which, despite its simple characters and strained plot, remains one of cinema's most authentic depictions of the Crescent City. Taking tips from the Italian neo-realist movement, Kazan intermingles local voices and faces with those of trained actors as he puts his cast and crew on the New Orleans streets and sidewalks and in its dark warehouses and dreary alleyways. Ultimately, the film dramatizes the multicultural hodgepodge of New Orleans with hardly a trace of cliché or stereotype. They even get the accents right.

Another classic, which seems to feature more Italian accents than local ones, is the oddly beautiful 1980s existential, Beckettesque, independent hipster-flick *Down by Law* (1986). While the cast features two iconic musician-songwriter-actor-artists (Tom Waits and John Lurie, both of whom contribute to one of the coolest soundtracks ever) and an Italian actor-director-comedian (Roberto Benigni), and while the story depicts small-time hoods, prostitutes, a radio DJ, a European tourist, the Orleans Parish Prison, and the Louisiana swamp, the stylized direction of Jim Jarmusch and the stunning black and white cinematography of Robby Müller render all of these overwrought tropes deadpan, oddly comedic, and absolutely mesmerizing.

AUTHENTIC CAJUN

Woe to he who claims to have captured the authentic Cajun experience on film, for there is likely not another group of people so steadfastly concerned with the slapdash ways they have been objectified and represented in film than Cajuns. And so it is with a sense of trepidation that I, a non-Cajun Louisianian, suggest two exemplary films about Cajun life.

It is not possible to write of Cajun films without including some discussion of the Louisiana-born filmmaker Glen Pitre, the unofficial godfather of Cajun film. Before attending college at Harvard, Pitre was making low-budget French-language films in Lafourche Parish, "Westerns on the Bayou," so-called. However, he is best known for his breakout film *Belizaire the Cajun* (1986). In the spirit of diversity, I recommend a lesser-celebrated work of Pitre's, *The Scoundrel's Wife* (2002). Filmed near Pitre's home in Lafourche Parish and replete with shrimp boats, Cajun dancehalls, and a drunk Catholic priest played wonderfully by Tim Curry, *The Scoundrel's Wife* puts a twist on the classic Odyssean story, albeit told from a widowed Penelope's point of view, and sets it on the Louisiana bayou. I first saw this film at a multiplex in Lafayette when I was in college, and I still recall the sense of pride and bewilderment felt among those in attendance, for how unusual it was for everyone to see their unique corner of the world projected before them as if the screen itself were a mirror.

Les Blank and Chris Strachwitz's documentary *J'ai été au bal* (1989) uses a number of Louisiana musicians and a few local historians to tell the story of Cajun music and zydeco, two musical folk traditions distinct in all the world. As with all of Blank's films, he lets the folk do the talking, and the singing and the playing and the dancing and shouting and eating. Needless to say, *J'ai été au bal* celebrates what it documents. As such, the film is as much a carnival as it is a document, parading proudly the genius of the inventors and ambassadors of Cajun music and zydeco.

AUTHENTIC SWAMP

What happens when Hollywood comes to the swamp? A band of privileged outsiders invade and coopt what they will for their own purposes? Ill treatment of the locals at the locals' expense so the studios can profit? A stealing of the seemingly prehistoric landscapes for marketing and distribution purposes? Walter Hill's swamp movie, the cult classic *Southern Comfort* (1981), seems to do these very things while remaining a completely original and, dare I say, sensitive illustration of the Louisiana swamp and its people. Part western, part horror, part war allegory (the film's plot bears a strong resemblance to the narrative of America's involvement in Vietnam), *Southern Comfort* is an anti-exploitation exploitation film.

While *Southern Comfort* remains something of a conundrum, always teetering on outright camp, it's impossible to deny the film's atmospheric achievement—from its eerie score to its rendering of the swamp as an evocative region of primal beauty, a place equally savage and comforting. And if *Southern Comfort* verges on camp, then Louisiana's other great swamp movie, Robert Flaherty's classic *Louisiana Story* (1948), comes dangerously close to being kitsch. Funded by Standard Oil, this carefully scripted "documentary" about a Cajun family who makes a deal to allow an oil company to drill in their swamp predicts a seemingly hospitable codependence between the people of south Louisiana and the oil and gas industries.

However, despite being backed by one of the biggest of all oil companies, *Louisiana Story* manages not to be a simple propaganda film. Flaherty, a storyteller and a poet first, doesn't simply tell you facts about the swamp and its people. Rather, he asks you to dip your fingers in the water, to feel the trees and taste the wetness in the air, to smell the flora and to imagine what creatures lurk in the darkness just beyond the surface. Flaherty refuses an overt politicization of his material, but he does allow at least a few implications to loom large—that an innocence has been lost and that we have witnessed the end of nature as it once existed as a place of mystery, danger, and wonder. And so when the oil company appears by literally blasting its way into the earth, the viewer, especially the Louisianian, cringes. Come what fortunes may, a treasure not made by man is now forever gone.

AUTHENTIC COMMUNITY

Depicting the effects of a civilization given over to ruin forms the basis for the short film *Glory at Sea* (2008), made by the filmmaking collective Court 13. Now better known for their first feature film, the award-winning indie hit *Beasts of the Southern Wild* (2012), Court 13 is a group of 20-somethings who moved to New Orleans shortly after Hurricane Katrina hit in August 2005 intent on fashioning from the smithy of Louisiana's soul a mythic and transcendent piece of cinema. While only twenty-five minutes long, *Glory at Sea* stands as one of the most profound cinematic achievements to emerge from the self-sufficient–DIY–digital filmmaking movement, or any filmmaking movement for that matter. While the film portrays an unspecified post-hurricane wasteland popu-

Fig. 9.3. Scene from the short film *Glory at Sea. Courtesy Court 13*

lated by a desperate and disjointed community of characters seemingly pulled straight from Greek and biblical myth, the film represents the spirit of New Orleans and coastal Louisiana with such specificity and authenticity that the fantastical setting and plot feel more real than those of any comparable documentary or "realistic" film. Though its setting is tragic, the film ends in triumph, for the devastated community is not content merely to endure its tragic fate. Their collective spirit drives them to prevail and overcome.

Before Court 13 moved to New Orleans, Baton Rouge had its own filmmaking collective of sorts, headed by Steven Soderbergh. Well known for breaking boundaries in the film world, Soderbergh continues to work with a core group of collaborators, a number of whom he met while in high school in Baton Rouge. And of all his films, none speak more to the spirit of collaboration and community than his bizarre Baton Rouge mind-bender *Schizopolis* (1996). A complete cinematic conundrum, the film seems like it could have been made anywhere by almost anyone, but the knowing viewer soon recognizes something completely uncanny, completely homegrown, and perhaps something uniquely Louisianian. Most of the cast and crew are from Baton Rouge, and one can feel the spirit of camaraderie that pervades nearly every frame. These filmmakers weren't worrying about marketing and distribution nor casting a bunch of Hollywood wannabes—not even thinking about how the film would further their careers. They were just enjoying the process. And as such, the film is something of a celebration of a number of qualities ever-present in Louisiana culture. Community. Independence. The carnivalesque. The bizarre. The mundane. The nonsensical. Conflict and discontinuity. And as the *Schizopolis* DVD menu suggests, it is "inspired by rumors, bald-faced lies, and half-remembered dreams." It's frustratingly impenetrable and intrinsically flawed, but if you let it, it can be a rollicking good time, which is perhaps exactly as it should be.

FURTHER READING

Aswell, Tom. *Louisiana Rocks! The True Genesis of Rock and Roll*. Gretna, La.: Pelican Pub. Co., 2010.

Bernard, Shane K. *Swamp Pop: Cajun and Creole Rhythm and Blues*. Jackson: University Press of Mississippi, 1996.

Brasseaux, Ryan A. *Cajun Breakdown: The Emergence of an American-Made Music*. New York: Oxford University Press, 2009.

Broven, John. *South to Louisiana: The Music of the Cajun Bayous*. Gretna, La.: Pelican Pub. Co., 1983.

Cook, Alex V. *Louisiana Saturday Night: Looking for a Good Time in South Louisiana's Juke Joints, Honky-Tonks, and Dance Halls*. Baton Rouge: LSU Press, 2012.

Koster, Rick. *Louisiana Music: A Journey from R&B to Zydeco, Jazz to Country, Blues to Gospel, Cajun Music to Swamp Pop to Carnival Music and Beyond*. Cambridge, Mass.: Da Capo Press, 2002.

Laird, Tracey E. W. *Louisiana Hayride: Radio and Roots Music along the Red River*. New York: Oxford University Press, 2005.

Oster, Harry. Living Country Blues. Detroit: Folklore Associates, 1969.

Savoy, Ann Allen, ed. and comp. *Cajun Music: A Reflection of a People*. Eunice, La.: Bluebird Press, 1984.

Tisserand, Michael. *The Kingdom of Zydeco*. New York: Arcade Pub., 1998.

Documentary

Bayou Maharajah: The Tragic Genius of James Booker. Directed by Lily Keber. 2013.

Invisible Girlfriend. Directed by David Redmon. 2009.

The Pirogue Maker. Directed by Arnold Eagle. 1949.

Tchoupitoulas. Directed by Bill and Turner Ross. 2012.

T-Galop: A Louisiana Horse Story. Directed by Conni Castille. 2012.

Fiction

Angel Heart. Directed by Alan Parker. 1987.

Bad Lieutenant: Port of Call—New Orleans. Directed by Werner Herzog. 2009.

Hush . . . Hush, Sweet Charlotte. Directed by Robert Aldrich. 1964.

Passion Fish. Directed by John Sayles. 1992.

Schultze Gets the Blues. Directed by Michael Schorr. 2003.

THE ARCHITECTURE
OF LOUISIANA

J. MICHAEL DESMOND

Europeans and Africans, Protestants, Catholics, and Jews, have been in
Louisiana now for some three hundred years, Native Americans long
before that. They have all left their marks. There have been many moments of discovery, originality, and invention in the architecture of the
state along the way. Since ancient times, a work of architecture has been
evaluated according to three aspects: how well built and stable its construction, how well it provides for the activities it was built to house,
and how beautifully or meaningfully it accomplishes these things. It is
this last aspect that typically differentiates a work of architecture from
a simple building, a cathedral from a filling station. A town hall or a
church helps us to understand the world we live in and how we live in it
together by representing to us our civic, religious, or other shared values
and ideals. Above all else, such building is a social act, one aspect of the
shaping of culture, of people, and of place. In the history of any people,
the early years are formative periods during which ways of life and patterns of belief are established. An architecture that represents social values can only arise as those are developed. This has certainly been the
case in Louisiana. The building practices of the first century of European
and African settlement here were largely elemental—struggles with materials, technologies, and environments. Only as Louisiana moved into
its second century did we see a more general mastery of these allow a
full range of expression to appear in a century dominated by a variety of

historical models. Our third century was one of phenomenal growth and expansion that saw many kinds of architectural invention as well. We stand today at the beginning of the fourth.

The story of architecture in Louisiana begins in the distant past, many thousands of years ago. Native American mound sites predominate; other uses were more ephemeral and did not leave traces enough for us to distinguish. The mounds here are among the oldest-known locations of human building in the Western Hemisphere. The great diversity of these sites can be organized into groups enclosing central spaces or plazas, and individual or free-standing mounds. Examples of both of these types, such as Watson Brake, Raffman, and the LSU mounds, are between 5,000 and 6,000 years old. The group of mounds at Poverty Point, while not the oldest in the state, is the largest. This site flourished around 1500 BC and was built by what may have been the first complex human culture in the United States. Poverty Point lies along Bayou Macon at the edge of the Mississippi River floodplain in the northeast corner of Louisiana. It consists of a series of concentric rings of low earthen mounds describing a central plaza with a larger T-shaped mound, sometimes referred to as the "bird mound," beyond the western edge opposite the plaza. This site marks one beginning of the great Mississippi Valley culture of indigenous peoples, reaching from Louisiana northward, eventually culminating in such ancient cities as Cahokia near present-day St. Louis.

There are hundreds of mound sites found throughout the state. In almost every case, we know very little about the use of the site and its associated structures and are left to conjecture according to what we can determine about configuration and context. The LSU mounds in Baton Rouge, for example, do not contain burials and were apparently never large enough to support structures. They are, however, located at the last spot on the continent where one can stand on high ground and see the great river without the threat of flood, before it winds its way southward to the sea. There is only one river system of this size in North America, and only one place with these characteristics. While Native American buildings of the colonial and earlier periods do not exist in Louisiana, there are a few early European descriptions and drawings that give us an idea of the basics, the most notable of which are the Alexandre de Batz *Temple des Sauvages Cabane du Chef* of 1732, and the Jean Baptiste

Michel Le Bouteux *Veuë du Camp de la Concession de Monseigneur Law, au Nouveau Biloxy, Coste de la Louisianne*, of 1720. These depict lightweight structures made of small-diameter wooden poles and sticks, some set into the ground, others suspended between, and covered with mats woven of a variety of local plant materials.

French Creole building began in south Louisiana as adaptations of traditional Norman French medieval wood-framed mortise-and-tenon construction with the wood directly in contact with the ground. The open spaces in these early wood frames in Louisiana were typically filled with a mixture of mud and moss, or some other binder adapted from Native American practices and known as *bousillage*. Soon these buildings were being built above the ground, raised on short brick piers when possible, to protect the structure from ground moisture and termites. By the mid-eighteenth century the influence of French Creoles from the West Indies, who had been building in a tropical climate for much longer, began to be felt. The pattern of the raised cottage quickly became the norm, with larger houses raising the entire structure above a brick utilitarian ground floor. Galleries were added to the earliest European-inspired examples to provide extra living space and to create shade, leading to the characteristic kick in the profile of the roofs of these early buildings. It is a tradition that remains alive today in many floodprone areas of the state.

The LaCour House in Pointe Coupée Parish, c. 1735, exemplified these practices. Although it has been moved, it may be the oldest surviving building in the Mississippi Valley. Otherwise, the most outstanding surviving examples date from the earliest years of the nineteenth century and show the development of two widespread regional types: the French Creole and the Acadian raised cottages. Clear examples of these two traditions can be found in the Spanish Customs House (1807) on Bayou St. John in New Orleans and the Pierre Olivier Du Closel House (c. 1815), known as Acadian House, at Longfellow-Evangeline State Park near St. Martinville.

A varied collection of early Louisiana buildings illustrating these and other construction types have been collected at LSU's Rural Life Museum in Baton Rouge. Beginning in the 1970s, structures representing the variety of Louisiana's rural buildings have been moved to this extended outdoor museum to create areas devoted to describing life in the plantation

Fig. 10.1. Ursuline Convent in New Orleans (1749–1753)
Historic American Buildings Survey, Richard Koch, photographer

and upland South cultures in the nineteenth century. At the other end of the state, the Germantown colony near Minden in Webster Parish has a valuable collection of nineteenth-century log cabins, illustrating the use of that rather different technology in the wooded hills of north Louisiana.

As was the case in most colonial settlements, there were a number of buildings constructed in the early years in New Orleans that owed their origins directly to European traditions and power structures and reflected these influences more than the evolving indigenous practices. In this line, the Ursuline Convent designed by François Broutin is among the oldest buildings in the state, completed in the early 1750s. This building replaced an earlier one that had been built with wood directly in contact with the ground. The replacement is a masonry structure with a Norman roof truss. This imposing structure helped to establish a strong and lasting presence of the Catholic church in New Orleans and throughout the state and remains one of Louisiana's most important historic buildings (fig. 10.1).

Individual residences of increasing substance came into being with the growth of plantation estates after the perfection of sugarcane refining in 1795. (See Barbara Bacot's essay "The Plantation" in the book *Louisiana Buildings*.) The large houses of these planters up and down the regional waterways reflect the early slave-based agricultural economy in Louisiana, first of cotton and indigo, then sugarcane. Parlange, near New Roads in Pointe Coupée Parish, is among the most impressive remaining examples of a large house built in this French Creole vernacular, and is still lived in by the original Parlange family. Family traditions date the building to the 1760s, while historians have pegged it around 1820. The house faced the Mississippi when it was built, but the great river has long since moved away, leaving the building to face a "false river" today. In this magnificent early Louisiana house, we see the fullest development of a large umbrella roof, shielding the walls of the dwelling on all sides and surrounding it with extensive exterior galleries open to the river breezes that are more likely to be effective at this height. The main floor is composed of two central drawing rooms, one slightly larger than the other, with bedrooms at either end; to the rear, small dressing rooms frame a backside porch. The irregular measure of the house and its gallery is typical of many of these buildings, where notions of architectural formality or pretense were overcome by simple pragmatic requirements. This is evident in the way in which the rhythm of doors along the main elevation is irregular and does not correspond to the pattern of the porch structure, leaving the later central stair to be centered on a blank wall (fig. 10.2). While Parlange is perhaps the most outstanding example of this early hybrid tradition extant today, others still standing include Destrahan (1787–1790) and Homeplace (c. 1800) Plantations in St. Charles Parish, Oakland Plantation (1818) at the Cane River Creole National Historical Park in Natchitoches Parish, Austerlitz Plantation (c. 1832) near Parlange in Pointe Coupée Parish, Whitney Plantation (1790, 1803) in St. John the Baptist Parish, and Magnolia Mound (1815) in Baton Rouge. In many ways, these noble and expressive structures are the most Louisiana of buildings.

The coming of the Americans and the Anglo influence after the Louisiana Purchase in 1803 brought different kinds of social complexity to the state's architecture. The large plantation houses became more formal

Fig. 10.2. Parlange Plantation in New Roads (1750–1830)
Historic American Buildings Survey, Richard Koch, photographer

in their designs, more premeditated, and more reflective of imported sensibilities. The first fully imported and self-conscious architectural style brought to New Orleans in these years was the so-called Federal style, an Americanized version of the English Georgian. This red-brick architecture with white stone trim and typically green painted shutters reflected the first flush of early nineteenth-century economic growth in the newly established territory. It was the primary building idiom in the newly established American sector just upriver from Canal Street. It also was used extensively in Baton Rouge in the years before the Civil War. Today much of this building stock has been lost, with the prim "Thirteen Sisters" of Julia Row (1832–33) in New Orleans and the Warden's House/Prison Store (1838–39) from the old Louisiana State Penitentiary in Baton Rouge being perhaps the most prominent remaining examples.

The influx of northern interests also brought an enthusiasm for the cool rationality of the Greek Revival and along with it in 1817 America's first professional architect, Benjamin Henry Latrobe. His Bank of Louisiana on Royal Street in New Orleans is one of the first examples in the state exemplifying the increase in sophistication that came in with the nineteenth century. Here we see innovation in structure and form combined with attention to correct classically inspired detailing. Latrobe was the first fully trained European architect to work in the United States, having a career along the Eastern Seaboard before moving to New Orleans. Unlike his decidedly Greek-inspired Bank of Pennsylvania in Philadelphia, this one brought the banking floor right down to the level of the street for the first time, thus not simply imposing historical precedents but adapting these to the informality of southern life and culture.

At the beautiful Evergreen Plantation and its group of associated buildings on what is known as the German Coast approximately fifty miles upriver from New Orleans, we can see the sense of order typical of the Greek Revival mode beginning to take effect. Evergreen, first constructed in 1790 by Christophe Haydel, was similar to his brother's house now known as Whitney next door, as noted by Karen Kingsley. In 1832 Haydel's grandson Pierre Clidamont Becnel extensively remodeled the house. Becnel had studied in Philadelphia and brought with him a more refined sensibility of the Greek Revival than was seen in other contemporary Louisiana homes and their detailing. The hint of a central pediment, with exquisite dual spiraling front stairs and Venetian front door and window ensemble below, suggests a central-plan hall even though the French Creole plan of the earlier house was kept. The main house exhibits a widow's walk and was flanked by an exemplary symmetrical arrangement of garçonnières, pigeonnières, kitchen, and plantation office. To the rear, in stark contrast to the refined and cultured image presented by these groupings of style buildings, still stands one double row of one-room slave cabins reaching back away from the river almost one thousand feet to the sugar mill and plantation cane fields beyond. Altogether, this series of buildings presents one of the most finely executed ensembles of its time in Louisiana, rivaled perhaps only by Uncle Sam Plantation across the river.

Some fifty miles farther upriver in Ascension Parish, the exquisite Greek Revival–style house known as Bocage displays a refined and inventive massing and proportion. A house was purportedly built on this site as early as 1801 by Emanuel Marius Pons Bringer of Hermitage Plantation as a wedding gift for his young daughter. The house took its current form as a result of renovations, probably by James Dakin of New Orleans in 1840 after a fire. This somewhat smaller house became one of the most exquisitely proportioned and detailed of the period and remains today a unique vision (fig. 10.3). On the interior, the presence of refined ornament suggests the influence of a pattern book such as Minard Lafever's *Beauties of Modern Architecture,* published in New York in 1830, as Mills Lane has noted. This building is prim, sparse, and elegant in ways well beyond most of its peers along the river. Compare it to Ashland nearby, built a year later, to see a house with a more modern full central hall, similar square piers, and full entablature, which misses the subtleties of Dakin's work at Bocage.

Fig. 10.3. Bocage Plantation near Darrow (1837).
Courtesy Marion Rundell, photographer

A building such as Bocage is a uniquely individual creation, standing apart from the trend toward standardization in domestic vernacular building that developed in Louisiana throughout the nineteenth century. While there continued to be a range of inventive residential design, producing many elaborate large houses throughout the state, it was the standardization of types exhibited throughout latter nineteenth-century New Orleans neighborhoods that is one of our most remarkable accomplishments, producing what is undoubtedly the most extensive and certainly the finest collection of wood-framed houses in the world.

The Greek Revival architectural style was adopted by the U.S. government for a series of imposing governmental buildings located in prominent port cities on the Atlantic and Gulf Coasts in the early and mid-nineteenth century, ranging from the U.S. Customs House in Boston (1837–47) to the Treasury Building in Washington, DC (1836–42). The U.S. Customs House (1856) at the foot of Canal Street in New Orleans, by Alexander Wood and later James Gallier, was the last of these built and the largest. Here the Greek inspiration was combined with Egyptian-influenced detailing to provide an imposing federal presence in the state. The earlier U.S. Mint (1835–38), at the opposite end of the Vieux Carré on Esplanade Avenue, was designed by William Strickland and is now being used by the Louisiana State Museum. The finest Greek Revival institutional building in Louisiana, however, may be the old New Orleans City Hall, now known as Gallier Hall, built between 1845 and 1851. Designed by James Gallier, it sits on Lafayette Square in the new American sector. Its clean lines and innovative use of different stone make this imposing and authoritative building one of the finest examples of its type in the country. The Greek Revival spread through the state over the next decades, affecting virtually all kinds of building. St. John's Episcopal Church (1844–45) in Thibodaux, one of the oldest Episcopal churches in the Mississippi River valley with its tall, plain windows and austere detailing, is an example of the clean rationality this architectural idiom could provide. The beautiful and recently renovated St. Martin Parish Courthouse (1854–59) in St. Martinville, across the Atchafalaya, is another Louisiana representation of this first national American architectural style.

As the nineteenth century wore on, the white, almost abstract per-

Fig. 10.4. Grace Episcopal Church in St. Francisville (1858–1860).
State Library of Louisiana

fection of the Greek Revival was displaced throughout the state by the more romantic and evocative inspiration of the Gothic Revival. As early as 1838, one of the finest religious interiors in the South was constructed for the Gothic St. Patrick's (1838–40) on Camp Street in New Orleans, designed and begun by James Dakin, then finished by James Gallier. This church, which sits across Lafayette Square from the Greek Gallier Hall, has a unique interior stained glass fan vault surrounded by an eclectic array of false Gothiclike vaulting suspended from the church's timber truss roof structure. Today St. Patrick's is the oldest existing church in New Orleans.

Some of the finest examples of this period in Louisiana remain today in small Gothic-style parish churches built in wood and brick throughout the state. The earliest extant ones, such as St. Paul's in St. Gabriel and St. Paul's across the river in Bayou Goula, are early nineteenth-century creations. By the 1870s buildings such as Grace Memorial Episcopal in Hammond, Christ Episcopal in St. Joseph, and St. Andrew's Episcopal in Clinton followed the example set by Richard Upjohn and other northern architects in adapting the newly invented wooden balloon framing to Gothic details and sympathies. Some of the finest small churches throughout the state are examples of this style built in red brick. Buildings such as Grace Episcopal (1858–1860) in St. Francisville and Christ Episcopal (1853–54) in Napoleonville, surrounded today by their century-old cemeteries and live oak groves, offer a palpable experience of living history, the integration of the natural and the manmade (fig. 10.4).

During this period, many government agencies followed the lead of James Dakin's Louisiana State Capitol (1847–52) in adopting some variant of the Gothic style into public service. Kingsley notes that Dakin used this mode because it allowed him to depart from the overworked Greek and Roman civic models with an innovative flair. The castellated walls and towers of this building dominated the Baton Rouge skyline for over seventy years. Left in ruins after the Civil War, the building was restored in 1880 by William Freret from New Orleans, who added the grand spiraling cast-iron central staircase and stunning multicolored stained glass dome (fig. 10.5). It was used as the capitol until the present one was completed in the 1930s, and serves today as a museum of the state's political history. This institutional Gothic style was also used in

Fig. 10.5. Interior of the restored Louisiana State Capitol building in Baton Rouge (1852 and 1888). *State Library of Louisiana*

Fig. 10.6. Louisiana Institution for the Deaf and Dumb and the Blind (1851–1858), since demolished. *Office of Public Relations Records, RG #A0020, Louisiana State University Archives, LSU Libraries, Baton Rouge, La.*

the now-lost Deaf and Dumb Asylum in Baton Rouge (fig. 10.6) and the original LSU building in Pineville.

This eclectic mix of Greek and Gothic inspirations blossomed in the years after the Civil War into a full range of architectural expressions from the classic to the romantic, with everything in between. In Catholic church design, this ranges from the neo-Gothic Church of the Ascension of Our Lord in Donaldsonville (1875–90) to the more Roman and early Christian–influenced St. John the Evangelist in Plaquemine (1926–27). There are thousands of churches from almost every denomination across the state during this broad time period in which experimentation combined with duplication. The sometimes florid and overwrought detail contrasts with a stark and economical purity to produce a beautiful depth of experience in support of our many religious rituals.

By the last quarter of the century, the Gothic models were being replaced by the more robust forms of a Romanesque revival. This revolution was largely engineered by the Louisiana native H. H. Richardson, one of the first Americans to attend the prestigious École des Beaux Arts in Paris. The Richardsonian Romanesque that came out of his Boston office in the 1870s swept across the Midwest and into the South during the last years of the nineteenth century. In Louisiana, it flourished in a number of expressive courthouses and jails across the state, including the Grant, Bienville, Ascension, and old Rapides Parish courthouses. The Pointe Coupée Parish Courthouse (1902) in New Roads is perhaps the most substantial of these remaining today; many have been lost. The great Louisiana architect Richardson, however, has only one building in the state—an unbuilt project for a library in Michigan that was reworked after his death as the Howard Memorial Library (1886–89) off Lee Circle in New Orleans and is now part of the Ogden Museum of Southern Art.

By the turn of the century, the historically accurate if limited inspiration of Greek and Roman models as expressions of authority and social order gave way to an equally expressive Beaux Arts classicism. These buildings were in part inspired by the splendors many Americans saw at the 1893 World's Columbian Exposition in Chicago, the so-called White City. In Louisiana, as in so many other places around the country, light-colored brick was combined with stone trim and detailing in a wide variety of building forms juxtaposing a pedimented façade with a central dome, or at least the impression of a dome given by a white painted cupola. This style flourished in courthouse design in particular, as can be seen in Calcasieu, Beauregard, Vernon, and Tensas Parishes today. The B'nai Zion Temple (1914), later used by the Knights of Columbus, and the Scottish Rite Temple (1916–17) built in Shreveport by Neild and Olschner are among the finest examples of this idiom. At the other end of the state, the Touro Synagogue (1907) of New Orleans, while built in this general pattern, has a somewhat more Byzantine expression.

Up to this point, architectural explorations in Louisiana fell into two broad periods, the colonial and the eclectic. In the first of these, Louisianians struggled to create new lifestyles and to adapt their inherited ideas about building to the materials and environment of this new place. This began with timbers laid on the ground and culminated in the large raised plantation houses of the 1790s–1810s, with occasional European-financed buildings of more substance representing institutional interests. The expanding success of the region's economy, its growing social complexity, and the coming of the Americans with their Anglo sensibilities ushered in a century of more eclectically articulate designs and increasingly sophisticated building technologies. Throughout the nineteenth century, buildings in the state ranged through classical and medieval models of all kinds, adapting these forms and feelings to every landscape and institutional type. By the 1920s this eclectic or adaptive mode would change as Louisiana moved into a third century, one of more invention and experimentation.

The twentieth century was characterized by broad changes in population, economic patterns, technologies, and transportation. The years following the First World War saw a boom of public building that peaked with the extensive programs of the New Deal. The Art Deco style that appeared during this period contrasts with the preceding strictly eclectic mix by fostering the inventive exploration of new massing profiles based on a nascent "functional" reading of the purposes and objectives of the buildings. This can be seen in the Caddo Parish Courthouse (1926–28) in Shreveport. Not far away, Samuel Weiner's design for the Shreveport Municipal Auditorium (1928–29) displayed a richly colored and textured mantle of architectural detail and ornament expressive of the exuberance of the arts draped over a simple functional massing of entry façade, auditorium box, and theater flyloft with offices tucked into the corners. This building has been known as the "Cradle of the Stars" because it was home to the *Louisiana Hayride* country music radio program, and its splendid auditorium saw some of the most definitive early performances of such stars as Johnny Cash and Elvis Presley. Huddie "Leadbelly" Ledbetter, James Brown, Aretha Franklin, Bobby "Blue" Bland, and B.B. King are just a few of the well-known African American artists that have performed here. In the Louisiana State Exhibit Building (1937–38), by Neild, Somdal, and Neild, we see an eccentric circular gallery completely surrounding an inner courtyard and fountain juxtaposed with a forcefully simplified grand entry portico where again function and symbolism are rudely, if inventively, combined.

While the Art Deco style appears in such notable central Louisiana buildings as the current Rapides and Natchitoches Parish Courthouses (both 1939–40), it was in the more southerly and urban parts of the state that it had its greatest impact. The interior of the Shushan, or Lakefront, Airport in New Orleans is one of the finest examples of this style in the country. Here it represents the attempt to step outside of the historicist or eclectic bent of traditional architecture in search of an expressive fluidity highlighting a sense of luxury and progress. The use of fine materials and sculptural and ornamental elements express the image of flight.

While the overall form of the building is more conventional than that of, say, Eero Saarinen's TWA Terminal at Kennedy Airport in New York thirty years later, one can see this as one beginning of the drive to find new ways of reflecting and finding inspiration in the marvels of modern life.

Without doubt, two of the most magnificent buildings in Louisiana, "Big Charity" Hospital (1937–39) in New Orleans and Huey Long's new Louisiana State Capitol (1931–32) in Baton Rouge, express the representation of aspects of modern life cloaked in Art Deco garb. Both were designed by the New Orleans firm of Weiss, Dreyfous & Seiferth. At Charity we see the inventive massing required to give over 2,600 hospital beds natural light on a dense downtown urban site. The beautiful entry ornamental panel speaks to the central importance of health in the productivity of modern industrial society. At the Capitol we see the administrative tower reaching for the sky, providing a beacon as it rises between the two flanking chambers of the state's representative government. The large ceremonial stairway, one of the grandest in the country, leads up to a central lobby with some of the most beautiful public art in the state. Jules Guerin's murals depicting the abundance of the earth are complemented by a masterful exterior sculptural program as the building rises 450 feet—the highest state capitol in the country (fig. 10.7). It is a skillful adaptation of Bertram Goodhue's design for the Nebraska State Capitol (1922–32).

Our sense of architecture in Louisiana owes much to the Public Works Administration projects. Many dozens if not hundreds of institutional buildings of all kinds were sponsored or affected by the variety of federal building projects of the 1930s New Deal era. This building boom gave us schools, universities, hospitals, courthouses, and many other buildings and infrastructure projects. The influence of the Art Deco style used on a range of public buildings, including courthouses in St. Landry, Jackson, St. Bernard, Iberville, and Caldwell Parishes, has helped to establish this architectural idiom as the most common and authoritative representation—indeed the very image—of state government in Louisiana. This has been strengthened in recent years by the Louisiana State Capitol Park concept, where we see contemporary architects return to the use of a compatible architectural language in a sculptural, less directly functional manner.

Fig. 10.7. New Louisiana State Capitol with sculpture by Lorado Taft
and C. M. Godd (1932). *State Library of Louisiana*

The period between the world wars saw the first high-rise (6–9 stories) commercial building in Louisiana. While New Orleans had the most of these—as many as the rest of the state combined—Baton Rouge also saw a number of impressive structures, such as the Reymond Building (ca. 1920–22). In general, these buildings follow an example such as Louis Sullivan's groundbreaking Wainwright Building in St. Louis.

The Louisiana cultural landscape has seen other kinds of large, domineering structures over the years, beginning perhaps with the great sugar refineries. These structures, from small-scale individual planter operations as exemplified by the Rosalie Sugar House (c. 1850) in Rapides Parish, to the large ones still in use today such as those making up the Cinclare Sugar Mill Historic District (1855–1945) in West Baton Rouge Parish, organize the visual and economic structure of their landscapes for miles around. The large, even gargantuan, timber mills—the Great Southern Lumber Company of Bogalusa, the Louisiana Cypress Lumber Company in Ponchatoula, the Minden Lumber Company, among many others that once existed across the state—sent timber to an expanding national economy in the first decades of the twentieth century.

Along with Louisiana's extensive forests, the great river has produced an architecture of its own. While the flotillas of nineteenth-century steamboats that once visited Louisiana by the hundreds have almost all gone, on any given day fully half the barges in the United States are in Louisiana. Although these are dispersed and cannot be seen from any single vantage point, the large Mississippi River bridges that tower over our flat lands do give us views of the great oceangoing vessels that ply the river daily.

Beginning in 1908, the coming of the Standard Oil refinery in Baton Rouge marked a change of scale, both economic and physical. The petrochemical plants and refineries that dot the south Louisiana landscape have not yet been romanticized the way our sugar mills and the abandoned steel mills in other parts of the country have. A significant structure associated with the industrial complex that has grown up over the last century was the remarkable Union Tank Car dome in north Baton Rouge. At 384 feet across, this geodesic structure, first envisioned by Dick Lehr and engineered by Buckminster Fuller, was for decades the longest span structure in the world. It has recently been lost.

Following the restrained invention of the Art Deco period, the explosive decades after the Second World War saw perhaps the richest period of expansion, innovation, and exploration in the state's architectural history. This time was characterized by the desire to look beyond the simple repetition of traditional models, and in the best work to understand and reinterpret their accomplishments in support of new social and economic forms. This inspiration touched the design and conception of houses, schools, churches, and public buildings of all kinds. Louisiana's system of public education in particular saw unprecedented investment through the 1950s and 1960s, and a small group of architects in the southeastern corner of the state responded with thought and form. In particular, the growing international firm of Curtis and Davis and the iconoclastic Charles Colbert in New Orleans stand out. The more significant of these buildings for elementary and secondary education utilized new materials in the exploration of inventive solutions that took advantage of the region's mild winter climate by integrating classroom wings, covered areas, and surrounding playgrounds and open areas. Colbert's Hoffman Elementary School of 1948, designed before air conditioning was in common use, initiated the pattern of finger schools, where rows of single classrooms open on two sides to light and air flow with protected playgrounds in between. This inventive building was an example of the abandonment of historical types in favor of pragmatic or functional objectives. Following a few years later, the Thomy Lafon, Avery Alexander (McDonogh 39), and St. Frances Xavier Cabrini schools by Curtis and Davis, and the Mahalia Jackson (McDonogh 36) and Phillis Wheatley schools by Charles Colbert, established the city of New Orleans as one of the most innovative centers of architecture for education in the country. The Wheatley school raised the body of the building some 12 feet above the ground to provide a sheltered play area by using grand steel trusses. This heroic building won a 1954 National AIA design award and was published around the world. Colbert raised the active spaces above the floodplain while providing shade and shelter, both modern adaptations of traditional Louisiana building principles made possible by the use of new materials and patterns of thought. Unfortunately, these groundbreaking school buildings are all now lost.

Of the many buildings that Curtis and Davis added to the New Orleans cityscape, perhaps none so embodies the aspirations of the period as well as the New Orleans Public Library, completed in 1958. Built on the site of the former Orleans Parish Courthouse and Jail (itself a remarkable late nineteenth-century specimen), this paradigmatic modern building exemplifies the attitude toward flexibility and openness as a programmatic and symbolic objective characteristic of the period. Its concrete frame allows various volumes and functions to sprawl and rise through the building while maintaining a sense of spatial continuity with the surrounding city. An aluminum sun screen protects the dominantly glass exterior envelope from the sun and rain. On a smaller scale, the Miller Memorial Library (1956) and the Southeastern Louisiana College Cafeteria (1954) in Hammond, both by John Desmond, continued these themes, allowing the spacious canopy of surrounding live oaks to be an ever-present factor in the sense of the interior, bringing to Louisiana the spacious and progressive modernism of such international architects as Mies van der Rohe and Eero Saarinen.

Church design in Louisiana was also affected by the design aspirations of the period, especially in the case of the Catholic church. The Vatican II initiative of the early 1960s encouraged the exploration of new and different spatial arrangements, as was seen in such buildings as the churches of St. Francis Cabrini in New Orleans by Curtis and Davis and St. Pius X in Baton Rouge by Desmond. These and other churches pulled the altar into the sanctuary while dramatizing the sense of a central focus in spaces meant to be more "participatory." One of the most successful of these buildings was Our Lady Queen of Heaven Church in Lake Charles, designed by Curtis and Davis in 1971, with Robert Biery as project architect (fig. 10.8). From the exterior, this building appears as a retreating collection of white painted-brick walls enclosing courtyards and entry while tracing a horizontal pattern through the rhythm of vertical pine tree trunks on the site. The sanctuary, covered by a hovering, singular, and abstract wood-covered box, is lowered into the ground. As one walks up to the building, the process of discovery is gradual, unpeeling a layer at a time as walls give way to courts which open through plate glass expanses to an uninterrupted sanctuary space. As the visitor moves inside, the great central room slowly descends into the earth, focusing

Fig. 10.8. Our Lady Queen of Heaven Church, Lake Charles, Louisiana (1971).
Courtesy Philip Gould, photographer

attention on the altar and congregation gathered beneath an overhead light well, with views of pine boughs along the flanking sides. It is a functional plan made elegant by classic modern minimalist detailing, attention to materials, and spatial continuity. The goal was to produce an informal and inclusive space that allowed a sense of the congregation and its members to dominate rather than overt historicist statements of the ritual.

The design of houses during this postwar boom saw the adaptation of modern materials and spatial explorations to the climate, and the influence of traditional forms, perhaps more than with any other building type. Again this effort was led by a rather small group of architects in the central and southeastern parts of the state. Houses by Curtis and Davis, Charles Colbert, and John Lawrence of New Orleans, John Desmond in the Florida Parishes, and Sam Short and A. Hays Town in Baton Rouge explore ways to extend a casual living space outward into the environment at a variety of scales.

In the rolling pinelands north of Lake Pontchartrain, Desmond developed a series of houses in the 1960s that took advantage of the larger lots possible outside of the urban environment. The Duncan House of 1962 in Covington is a prime example. Here a very private street side opens up at the rear to the wooded vistas of the lot. The shared spaces of family life are defined by discrete architectural elements and furnishings under a broad, gathering pitched roof, punctuated by a brick hearth. The use of natural materials, a color scheme based on the environment, and the raised or floating character of the structure and floors all combine to tie the building to an articulate experience of place. The house, when seen from the rear, can be seen as furthering design strategies explored by Frank Lloyd Wright, and by Walter Gropius in the design of his own first American building.

The ideal of combining the potential of modern materials and contemporary spatial and programmatic ambitions with a respect for traditional forms and specific local contexts may be most successfully realized in the LSU Union building of 1964, designed by John Desmond and located on the campus of the state's flagship university in Baton Rouge. The original core of the LSU campus was designed in 1922 by the St. Louis German-American architect Theodore Link. His tightly woven cruciform-shaped quadrangle was built on an earlier preliminary scheme of Frederick Law Olmsted Jr. of Brookline, Massachusetts, locating key programmatic buildings at focal points in the design. The entire ensemble follows an Italian Renaissance inspiration through the use of stucco, tile roofs, arcaded passages, and Tuscan columns in the creation of one of the finest building groups in the state (fig. 10.9). The goal of the LSU Union from the start was to turn the traditional concept of a boxy student union/cafeteria inside out, opening it to the vibrant life of the campus (fig. 10.10). The building was located between the majority of student dormitories and the historic academic classroom core in a grove of dedicated live oaks. The architect responded by raising the roof on exuberant cast-in-place concrete columns, opening the communal spaces of the building to the beautifully textural space of the live oak canopies while invoking the broad plane of the university's Parade Ground beyond. The surrounding campus circulation walks were oriented through the building to put it literally at the center of campus life. The beauty of its design lies in the way in which this functional ambition is expressed in an optimistic openness. While the building contrasts dramatically with the more tightly regulated massing of the classroom buildings beyond, the use of compatible materials and textures, and formal references to arches and pebbly stucco, tie it to its place. In general, the

Fig. 10.9. LSU Campanile and surrounding buildings in Baton Rouge (1922).
Courtesy East Baton Rouge Parish Library

university has not been able to add such richly textured buildings to its original campus. Today, however, a new gymnasium by Tipton Associates of Baton Rouge is one of a series of buildings by this firm for the University Laboratory School demonstrating that the potential still exists.

Louisiana does not have many such coherent building ensembles; planning has not generally been one of the state's best accomplishments. There are, however, a few such groups that stand out. At the heart of old New Orleans, in Jackson Square, one finds perhaps the most outstanding new-world example of an old-world ideal urban composition, lying at the center of the town, facing the river, providing a locus for the church and flanking government buildings, and then framed by the regular rhythm of the beautiful Pontalba Apartments (fig. 10.11). This is the ideal model of reasoned, civic space first described in the Italian Renaissance. It

Fig. 10.10. LSU Union in Baton Rouge (1964). *Courtesy Jim Zietz, photographer*

expressed symmetry, hierarchy, governmental and societal order sanctioned by religious authority. The central Place d'Armes, now converted to a green public park, ties these architectural expressions together with a reference to the sky and a statue of Andrew Jackson on horseback. It is the finest European square in the United States. Among other successful ensembles are the original core campuses of Dillard University in New Orleans (1935–36), Southeastern University in Hammond (1932–39), and the University of Louisiana at Lafayette. All of these began with purposeful arrangements of supporting buildings also expressive of ideals of unity and order. The Academy of the Sacred Heart near Grand Coteau (1821, 1939) and the Jackson Barracks in St. Bernard Parish (1834–35) also fit this institutional model.

Today, the best contemporary architecture of Louisiana finds opportunity in the challenges facing us, incorporating the significant aspects of each situation into the search for pragmatic and symbolic form expressive of our common aspirations. While New Orleans has lost most of its innovative midcentury modern schools in the last few years, the firm

Fig. 10.11. Jackson Square with St. Louis Cathedral, the Cabildo, Presbytère, and Pontalba Apartments in New Orleans. *Mss. 1534, Louisiana and Lower Mississippi Valley Collections, LSU Libraries, Baton Rouge, La.*

of Eskew + Dumez + Ripple is among those continuing that legacy of innovation in design. Their recently completed L. B. Landry High School in Algiers organizes a large, complex program around exciting new spaces, bringing a sense of identity to a community and optimism to public education. This dynamic new campus was quickly and efficiently designed and built after the previous school was damaged in Katrina and utilizes the best of contemporary design practices, including a rooftop photovoltaic array to supplement energy usage and an integral stormwater management system. It also succeeds in organizing a large and complex program, including a 650-seat auditorium, a black box theater, a 1,000-seat competition gymnasium and basketball court, and a smaller gymnasium, along with classroom "houses" and a full complement of rehearsal spaces for the 900-member student body—all brought together into easy functional zones gathered around a dramatic and efficient interior lobby and stairway sequence giving the community of students a window onto the skyline of their city. This high school had been, and now will continue to be, an important monument in the city's African American community.

Fig. 10.12. Shaw Center for the Arts in Baton Rouge (2005), opposite the
Old State Capitol. *Courtesy Jim Zietz, photographer*

At the other end of the cultural spectrum, the Shaw Center for the
Arts in Baton Rouge, by Schwartz/Silver Architects of Boston and completed in 2005, brings together an array of local arts institutions in a
public/private collaborative agreement literally woven into the urban
fabric of downtown Baton Rouge. The LSU Museum of Art, the Manship Theater, the LSU School of Art Gallery, the Arts Council of Greater
Baton Rouge's Community School for the Arts, and LSU's Laboratory for
Creative Arts and Technologies combine with a number of restaurants,
a street-level coffee shop, and a rooftop observation deck offering spectacular views of the city and the Mississippi River. Sitting adjacent to
James Dakin's Old Louisiana State Capitol and across the street from the
city's historic water tower standpipe and newly created park, this ambitious new building utilizes a state-of-the-art cast-glass layered exterior
skin system wrapped around a series of intertwined boxlike masses that
is opened up by a soaring-through block lobby while reaching over adjacent existing buildings and rising to the height established by the Capitol

(fig. 10.12). The color and overall form of this building both defer to the historical significance of the Dakin building while bringing to life a new vision of an exciting urban Louisiana. The public rooftop terrace offers some of the most outstanding views available throughout the entire Mississippi River valley. This complex celebrates the role of the arts in our communities by means of a building that invents new spatial and iconic forms while drawing on the best of our past. This is something one sees much more of in Europe than in the United States, but as this country matures, many such opportunities to blend the new with the old lie before us.

The goal of tying the new to the old, of deriving inspiration for the future from the character and elements of our shared cultural environment, can also be seen in the Louisiana Sports Hall of Fame and Northwest Louisiana History Museum, recently completed in Natchitoches (fig. 10.13). Designed by Trahan Architects of Baton Rouge, the understated exterior of this fascinating new building is wrapped in a slatted copper system that varies only slightly across the skin to create vision and shade opportunities. This gently modulated skin draws back at the building's main public entry on Front Street at the northern end of downtown Natchitoches, facing the beautiful Cane River, the location of several historic Louisiana Creole plantations and their significant related buildings. Here one is drawn in by a sensuously curving interior landscape of cast-stone panels curving in three dimensions in patterns inspired by the meandering channels of the region's bayous and rivers. A central lobby and circulation core reach upward to skylights through two floors of unencumbered surrounding exhibition space that gives the museum function great flexibility while at the same time making a dramatic statement about the nature of the public realm. This is a forward-thinking building that brings the most advanced technology and design to the creation of an ambitious new vision of the possibilities of architecture in Louisiana.

The new St. Landry Parish Visitor Center, by Ashe Broussard Weinzettle Architects of Alexandria, along I-49 near Ville Platte, also makes use of the old while looking to the future. Recycling here has a literal as well as iconic dimension. This humble but sophisticated structure reuses a variety of locally found traditional materials such as salvaged longleaf

Fig. 10.13. Louisiana Sports Hall of Fame and Northwest Louisiana
History Museum, Natchitoches, Louisiana, 2013. *Courtesy Trahan Architects,
Tim Hursley, photographer*

pine and brick, recycled asphalt and locally sourced sandstone, combining these with a photovoltaic film system, a rotary wind turbine, and an integrated stormwater collection and irrigation system. The building contains visitor information materials in an open central lobby and a publicly available lecture hall with adjacent covered exterior areas. The dominant horizontality of the site and adjacent highway inspired thoughtful massing and detailing strategies that integrate the building and its beautiful gardens.

All of these recent buildings respond to their physical contexts in creative ways as they explore relationships between the new and the old in providing settings for activities they house. This is what characterizes so much of the best architecture in the state. The forms of a Bocage, a St. Andrews, a Charity Hospital, or an LSU Union were all daring in their day; they were explorations of our relationships to each other and to the world around us, explorations of what these might mean. The architecture of Louisiana has seen three centuries of such experiment and invention in the context of both tradition and a changing world. The experience and values of our forebears recorded in the architecture they built enrich our lives in so many ways, giving us one of the richest traditions of building in the United States. Today, as we face the challenges and possibilities of the future, the preservation of the best of this heritage must be an active part of moving forward with vigor and invention.

FURTHER READING

Edwards, Jay D. *Louisiana's Remarkable French Vernacular Architecture, 1700–1900*. Baton Rouge: Department of Geography and Anthropology, Louisiana State University, 1988.

Kingsley, Karen. *Buildings of Louisiana*. New York: Oxford University Press, 2003.

Lane, Mills. *Architecture of the Old South: Louisiana*. Savannah: Beehive Press, 1997.

Leighninger, Robert D., Jr. *Building Louisiana: The Legacy of the Public Works Administration*. Jackson: University Press of Mississippi, 2007.

Poesch, Jessie, and Barbara SoRelle Bacot, eds. *Louisiana Buildings, 1720–1940: The Historic American Buildings Survey*. Baton Rouge: LSU Press, 1997.

LOUISIANA AS CENTER FOR THE ARTS

RICHARD ANTHONY LEWIS

For more than two centuries, owing to geographic location and robust growth, Louisiana has offered a vital marketplace for development of the arts. Commercial opportunity was an especial characteristic during the antebellum period in New Orleans, where the population grew from about 10,000 in 1809, to more than 24,000 by 1815, nearly 50,000 by the mid-1840s, to over 160,000 on the eve of the Civil War. The plantations along the River Road, towns, and other concentrations of wealth attracted an astounding number and variety of artists, architects, craftsmen, decorative artists, and photographers. While populations and fortunes became less stable after 1861, the lure of profit and notoriety continued to attract artists. Still, the arts of Louisiana have been marked by a peculiar blend of conservatism and innovation. Patrons tended to prefer styles that were considered ten or twenty years out of fashion elsewhere. Yet they also selected among a panoply of novel styles offered by artists trained in academies and apprenticeships all over the world. Not until the eve of the Civil War did native artists emerge in great numbers, and the state continues to attract numberless émigrés. This distinction—the dynamism sparked by a continuous influx of "foreign" artists competing with natives, together with the value placed on tradition and the familiar—has made Louisiana an exceptional center for the arts for over two hundred years.

José Francisco Xavier de Salazar y Mendoza, the earliest identified Louisiana artist of substance, painted portraits to the exclusion of other subjects. Trained in Mexico City, Salazar followed the late-Baroque manner

Fig. 11.1. *Marianne Celeste Dragon (or Dracos)*, attributed to José Francisco
Xavier de Salazar y Mendoza, c. 1795. Oil on canvas, 37¼ × 30¼ in.
Louisiana State Museum, Gift of John T. Block, 05750

popular in the thriving new-world capitals under the sway of Spanish influence. Salazar's patrons constituted a who's who list of Louisiana's colonial influentials, including Père Antoine, James Wilkinson, Bishop Luis Ignatius Peñalver y Cardenas, members of the Montegut and McCarty families, and Don Andrés Almonaster y Rojas. To contemporary eyes, Salazar's style appears naïve and awkward, charming as it is. Yet his portraits are embedded with a complex symbolic program—inclusion of specific flowers alluding to motherhood, gestures implying one's place in the social hierarchy, or physiognomic details underscoring the sitter's moral character.

The sitters for Salazar and his many followers represented an astonishing medley of ethnic identities. Owing partially to the contests over identity and power in Creole Louisiana, portraiture probably accounted for about 85 percent of artists' output in Louisiana during the antebellum period. The remainder was mostly religious art, much of which has not been preserved, as well as scenic and theatrical art, trade signs, the occasional engraving or lithograph, political banners, and other ephemera. Many artists, including the obscure French artist known only as "F. Godefroy," emulated Salazar in a retrograde colonial manner well into the 1820s, even though they were well versed in more current European styles. A number of competent miniaturists, mostly trained in Europe, worked in Louisiana during the late colonial and early national periods. Ambrose Duval, Jean-François Vallée, and the husband-wife team of Antonio and Nina Meucci produced a number of small portrait keepsakes and mourning pictures, adhering to the international style characterized by a dot-and-stipple technique. Most, if not all, artists working in Louisiana during the colonial period had received training in Europe or Latin America.

THE EARLY NATIONAL PERIOD

A preference for the colonial style persisted through the opening years of the nineteenth century. Edmund Brewster, an artist of middling talent from London via Philadelphia, arrived in 1819 and created a stir with his portrait of the beloved former Grand Inquisitor, Père Antoine. Expectations and tastes shifted almost overnight. The earliest identified art criticism, appearing in the *Louisiana Gazette* in mid-April 1819, suggests

Fig. 11.2. *Portrait of a Woman*, Matthew Harris Jouett, c. 1824.
Oil on canvas, 30 × 25. *Louisiana State Museum, T0002.1966*

that Brewster's cool and precise style was something of a revelation: "We had persons among us styling themselves 'Portrait Painters,' but except in a few instances, their paintings required a lable [*sic*] on them to enable even a friend to suspect for what they were designed." The critic's implicit target is the generalization of features advanced in colonial art; suddenly, such conventions seemed outdated. Louis-Antoine Collas arrived in 1821, bringing the latest French neoclassical style marked by cool precision, riddance of superfluous detail, and intense focus on the countenance. Top-notch Yankee artists such as John Wesley Jarvis and John Vanderlyn, together with Kentuckian Matthew Harris Jouett, were also in Louisiana by this point, bringing an essentially English style of portraiture then popular in urban art centers such as New York, Boston, and Philadelphia. Jouett in particular followed Gilbert Stuart's example—bravura brushwork and strong, warm characterizations of appearance.

Collas, Vanderlyn, Jarvis, and dozens of other painters—ranging from the academic to the naïve—tended to visit New Orleans between December and March, coincident with the winter social season. Depending on one's talents and industry, earnings could be high—Jarvis claimed to have made $6,000 in a single season (and spent half of it). In 1821, John James Audubon journeyed by flatboat to New Orleans from Kentucky with an outsized ambition to become a leading portrait painter. Audubon's early portraits fit squarely within the tradition of plain painting, or limning, practiced in the city by artists such as the obscure Mr. Feuille. Audubon was disappointed by the harsh reception he received from Jarvis and Vanderlyn, as well as a lack of commission, and thus turned his attention to another project—an illustrated work of ornithology designed to surpass the recent work of Alexander Wilson. He accomplished this daunting feat in spectacular fashion with the publication of *Birds of America* (1826–1838), a double-elephant folio featuring 435 species.

The early 1820s also witnessed the beginnings of a local printmaking industry, together with a market for decorative arts including furniture, porcelain, ironworking, and textiles. Brewster's engraving *La Père Antoine de Sedella* (c. 1820) is counted among the earliest local prints; other important early printmakers include Jules Manouvrier, Jacques Belaume, and the firm Pessou and Simon. However, as Jessie Poesch wrote, "The earliest prints representing Louisiana were created by artists who had never set foot in the region." The same may be said of the decorative arts, though enamel decoration of porcelain emerged as a thriving industry in the late 1820s, best represented by German-born decorator Rudolph T. Lux, who worked in the early 1850s. A local tradition of cabinetmaking emerged in the late eighteenth century and expanded greatly after about 1830. Artisans, notably Prudent Mallard, the brothers William and James McCracken, François Seignouret, and free man of color Dutreuil

Barjon and his namesake son proffered local interpretations of high European and American styles. Most firms sold both imported and locally produced furniture, together with china, linens, and other household items. As with painters, most furniture makers and dealers were émigrés from France, Germany, or U.S. cities north of the Mason-Dixon line.

THE AGE OF PARTISANSHIP

Wealth and cultural practices drove the demand for the fine arts, especially portraiture, which answered a need for extravagant display among elite planters and merchants eager to establish their place within the social hierarchy. Architecture, theater, the opera, the decorative arts, buildings, fashion, music, and other forms of expression reflected a predilection for conspicuous display. For Louisiana patrons, especially members of the Creole elite, the French neoclassical style of Jean Joseph Vaudechamp and Jacques Amans telegraphed sophistication, underscoring connection to the most fashionable painting coming out of the École des Beaux Arts in Paris. Their paintings are cool and restrained, distinguished by strong drawing and modeling composed of multiple thin glazes. However, details such as lace collars or cravats were highlighted with thick impasto dashed with bravura and *facture* similar to Jouett's practice. The cool neoclassical style remained popular in Louisiana well into the 1850s, practiced by artists ranging from luminaries of the academy, such as Charles-Jean-Baptiste Colson and Louis Nicholas Adolphe Rinck, to those with marginal training such as C. R. Parker or Francis Martin Drexel.

Other mostly European artists introduced novel styles during the 1830s, most notably Franz Joseph Fleischbein. Strange hair styles, pinched waists, attenuated limbs, and planar treatment of forms suggest the impact of the emerging German Biedermeier manner. Vaudechamp and Rinck, among others, began incorporating features of the emerging international style in the late 1830s. A few years later, "Plantation Baroque" painters such as the German exile Johann Wilhelm Rümpler, Mainer Charles Octavius Cole, and Englishman William Henry Baker fused the cool precision associated with neoclassical painting with a warm, sentimental style. Their portraits of children in particular are

Fig. 11.3. *M. Carti*, Charles-Jean-Baptiste Colson, c. 1837.
Oil on canvas, 36 × 29 in. *Louisiana State Museum, 01002*

laden with symbolic overtones that underscore the emergence of Protestant middle-class values in Louisiana. The profusion of competing
styles—Spanish, French, German, Italian, English, and American—reflected the diversity of Louisiana's population. Patrons' sundry prefer-
ences parallel attempts to establish hegemony in the social and political
arenas during a period of fierce partisanship.

Fig. 11.4. *Family Picnic*, Olidé P. Schexnayder, c. 1900.
Glass plate negative, 8 × 10 in. *Louisiana State Museum, 1998.001.16.033*

While portraiture remained dominant, artists of this period also advertised the ability to tackle a range of subjects. For example, Fleischbein and Dominique Canova listed the ability to paint a dizzying assortment of landscape, genre, religious, and mythological subjects. If such works were commissioned in large numbers, little has survived. The meticulous topographical gouache drawings by Marie Adrien Persac, the small landscapes of Robert Brammer, and the handful of genre scenes focusing on Native Americans by Albert Boisseau are counted among the few extant easel-sized landscapes. The press and published reminiscences also suggest high demand for scenic paintings, mostly related to the theater or opera, pastimes of astonishing popularity across class lines during the nineteenth century. Excepting a handful of drawings and the panoramic canvases of John Antrobus and Hippolyte Victor Valentin Sebron, we have only a vague sense of pre–Civil War Louisiana scene painting.

In March 1840, Jules Lion held the first recorded exhibition of photographs in New Orleans, though fellow French artist J. B. Pointel du Portail had a month earlier announced that he would show his daguerreotypes.

It is not known if the latter exhibition took place—or if du Portail worked with Lion—but du Portail did mount an exhibition in Baton Rouge in 1844. Both Lion and du Portail appear to have abandoned the new medium in preference for lithographs and paintings, but within the space of fifteen years, the city was flooded with daguerreotypes, ambrotypes, tintypes, and *cartes de visite*. Most of the earliest photographers, including Lion, Frederick Law, Felix Moissenet, John Hawley Clarke, and William Watson Washburn, concentrated on portraits, following the conventions associated with miniatures.

Photography relieved artists' burden to create a likeness but also undercut the market for painting, especially the intimate miniature. Many painters of the era, such as Fleischbein, also worked as photographers. Most nineteenth-century Louisiana photographs were oriented to the commercial market and thus are valued largely for their documentary function. Samuel T. Blessing, John Norris Teunisson, and Theodore Lilienthal produced city views with a high degree of compositional acumen though a somewhat antiseptic eye. Others, such as Jay Dearborn Edwards, George François Mugnier, and Olidé P. Schexnayder, took photographs that possess a depth of feeling that extends beyond mere capturing of appearance. Their photographs were precedent to iconic twentieth-century practitioners such as Robert W. Tebbs, Fonville Winans, Ernest J. Bellocq, and Clarence John Laughlin.

THE POSTBELLUM PERIOD

The later nineteenth century witnessed an expansion of genres—still lifes, landscapes, grand commemorative paintings, cityscapes, and scenes of daily life. However, as with the postwar economy in general, margins were slim, and artists adapted. One result was the growing popularity of crayon portraits, hybrid photographic drawings that were much cheaper than oil paintings. Hardship and a growing sense of camaraderie led artists to create the first formal associations, such as the Cup and Saucer Club and Artists' Association of New Orleans near the century's end. William Henry Buck, Andres Molinary, Achille Perelli, Paul E. Poincy, George David Coulon, and Bror Anders Wikström, all artists of industry and ability, took the lead in organizing exhibitions and

Fig. 11.5. *Man Hanging from Oak Tree in Swamp*, Richard Clague Jr., c. 1864.
Oil on canvas, 12½ × 16¼ in. *Louisiana State Museum, 1998.088.1*

art classes. Though often overlooked today, painters François Bernard and Alexandre Alaux were recognized as leading masters during the last half of the century, and their meticulous, almost photographic canvases commanded top prices.

A notable postwar development was the rising popularity of easel-sized landscapes. Trained in Paris to follow Barbizon style, Richard Clague Jr. led a small cadre of landscapists including Buck, Molinary, Charles Giroux, William Aiken Walker, Joseph Rusling Meeker, and Marshall J. Smith. Members of Clague's circle often worked outdoors, or *en plein air*. Some, such as Buck, also made landscape photographs. At least on the surface, their painting appears to be straightforward, naturalistic depictions of bayous and other distinctive Louisiana scenes. It is curious that a pronounced taste for landscape painting did not emerge earlier,

as it had in the Northeast and Middle Atlantic regions. Even more striking is the paucity of maritime subjects. A handful of artists including
Elizabeth Lamoisse drew harbor views, but only Edward Everard Arnold
and James Guy Evans concentrated on ship portraits before the 1880s.
After this, Captain William Lindsey Challoner, August Norieri, and Theodore S. Hacker constitute a short list of Louisiana maritime artists—a
genre largely out of favor by 1920. Why this market did not evolve in one
of the most active ports in the United States is puzzling. Sculpture too
remained underdeveloped throughout the nineteenth century, notwithstanding a few key figures such as neoclassicist Philippe Garbeille and
self-taught wood carver Pierre Joseph Landry.

THE MODERN ERA

Founded in 1896, Newcomb College set a standard for female education, drawing national attention to development of the arts in the Deep
South. As stewards of the Newcomb curriculum, the brothers William
and Ellsworth Woodward introduced an Arts and Crafts aesthetic em-
boldened by regional flair. Newcomb is best known for art pottery but
concentrated as well on drawings, paintings, textiles, examples of book-
binding, metalwork, and other decorative arts. The Woodward brothers
also introduced Louisianians to Impressionism twenty years after it had
caught on in New England. Perhaps more importantly, they fired the
burgeoning passion for historic preservation that resulted ultimately in
the creation of the Vieux Carré Commission in 1936 to administer the
second dedicated historic district in the country.

Artists benefited from institutional foment during the first part of the
twentieth century. The Louisiana State Museum (1905), Delgado Museum (now known as the New Orleans Museum of Art, 1911), and The
Historic New Orleans Collection (1966) helped focus attention on both
the fine and decorative arts in Louisiana. A loosely associated group of
artists formed in New Orleans during the 1920s, today known by the
somewhat disparaging term "French Quarter School." Artists such as
Knute and Collette Pope Heldner, William Spratling, and printmaker
Morris Henry Hobbs catered to the burgeoning local tourist industry
and growing interest in American history. Along with writers such as

Fig. 11.6. *Tea set with stylized tea tree blooms*, Newcomb Pottery,
Henrietta D. Bailey, decorator, Joseph Fortune Meyer, potter, 1906.
Earthenware. *Louisiana State Museum, 1975.001.46 .49-53*

Sherwood Anderson, Tennessee Williams, and William Faulkner, French
Quarter artists celebrated the unique, roughshod, and booze-soaked aspects of the South's acknowledged capital of sin, documented a few years
earlier in Bellocq's photographs of Storyville's notorious ladies.

During the Great Depression, the arts in Louisiana were invigorated
by an infusion of new artists such as Alvyk Boyd Cruise, Xavier Gon-
zalez, Clarence Millet, Conrad Albrizio, Frances Benjamin Johnston,
and Hans Mangelsdorf. Under the capable leadership of preservation
architect Richard Koch, sculptor Angela Gregory, and painter Caroline
Wogan Durieux, artists and architects of all stripes descended on the
state, funded by the Federal Art Project (FAP), Historic American Buildings Survey (HABS), and other alphabet-soup agencies administered by
the Works Progress Administration (WPA). These artists created thousands of prints, murals, architectural sculptures, photographs, drawings,
and graphic designs, often adhering to the aesthetics of social realism or
a conservative interpretation of Modernism. The balance between male
and female artists during this period is striking. The Depression and

early postwar period also offer a rare example of sociopolitical critique. Durieux and John McCrady stood in strident opposition to what was in their estimation a self-reflexive, apolitical art of the previous generation, offering instead their own left-leaning vision. Not until the late twentieth century would pointed social commentary again become a central feature of Louisiana art.

With the termination of the WPA, the shift away from art making as a primary function of Newcomb College, and dissolution of so many arts organizations in the 1940s, Louisiana lost a great deal of its prominence as an international art center. One explanation is that the émigré artists who had made Louisiana so vital now bypassed the Crescent City in favor of New York, Chicago, or even Atlanta. Vanguard artists struggled to gain a following, though many more traditional artists found favor with an increasingly conservative art-buying public. Art of the 1950s through the 1970s often focused on celebration of indigenous culture, best expressed in the flowering of what has been termed naïve, outsider, visionary, or folk art. Often created by self-taught African American artists such as Clementine Hunter, David Butler, and Sister Gertrude Morgan, postwar Louisiana folk art has been lauded as an authentic and spontaneous expression of the will to form peculiar to the region.

Modern and contemporary art has on occasion recaptured the prominence of its historic precedent. Acadian painter George Rodrigue has earned an international reputation for his odes to Cajun mythology, Clarence John Laughlin's surreal plantation fantasies are part of the photographic canon, and the frank, sometimes disturbing photographs of George Dureau are well known. In addition, a diverse group of contemporary sculptors, painters, printmakers, collage artists, and photographers, such as Willie Birch, John Scott, George Schmidt, Jacqueline Bishop, Gene Koss, Simon Gunning, Phil Sandusky, Dan Tague, Skylar Fein, Thomas Neff, Henry Casselli, Bruce Brice, Michael White, Douglas Bourgeois, and Simon Gunning have achieved a strong regional following, if not recognition on an international scale. The fine arts continue to thrive by degrees, owing in part to the laudable efforts of galleries across

Fig. 11.7. *Do You Know Him?*, Sister Gertrude Morgan, c. 1970.
Acrylic and felt-tip pen on paper, 11¼ × 8¼ inches.
Louisiana State Museum, Gift of The Gitter-Yelen Foundation, 1998.025.029

the state; of museums dedicated to showing living artists such as the Ogden Museum of Southern Art, the Contemporary Art Center, NOMA, the Masur Museum, and the LSU Museum of Art; countless local art festivals; and ambitious events such as the Prospect New Orleans series.

Historical analysis and collective memory tend to distort, and one suspects that contemporary artists' complaints about lack of patronage or public support were echoed by their nineteenth-century counterparts. Still, the outlook for the arts today seems almost as dire as it was in the late 1860s. With a slowly dwindling population, failing schools, declining revenues, a diminishing number of public-spirited individual and institutional patrons of largesse, political and social opposition to nonquantifiable public spending, and the ever-present specter of environmental threats, the future of the arts in Louisiana is anything but assured. But, as was demonstrated by the dozens if not hundreds of artists who chronicled the aftermath of Hurricane Katrina, challenge often invigorates and ignites epiphany. Put another way, hope for renewal springs eternal.

FURTHER READING

Bonner, Judith H., and Estill Curtis Pennington, eds. *New Encyclopedia of Southern Culture.* Volume 21: *Art and Architecture.* Chapel Hill: University of North Carolina Press, 2013.

Bruns, Mrs. Thomas Nelson Carter. *Louisiana Portraits.* New Orleans: National Society of the Colonial Dames of America in the State of Louisiana, 1975.

Cline, Isaac M. "Art and Artists in New Orleans during the Last Century." Reprint from the *Biennial Report.* New Orleans: Louisiana State Museum, 1922.

Harter, John Burton, and Mary Louise Tucker. *The Louisiana Portrait Gallery: Volume 1—To 1870.* New Orleans: Louisiana State Museum, 1979.

Holden, Jack D., H. Parrott Bacot, and Cybèle T. Gontour, eds. *Furnishing Louisiana: Creole and Acadian Furniture, 1735–1835.* New Orleans: Historic New Orleans Collection, 2010.

Houston, David. *The Art of the South: The Ogden Museum of Southern Art.* London: Scala Publishers, 2006.

Mahé, John A., and Rosanne McCaffery, eds. *Encyclopedia of New Orleans Artists, 1718–1918.* New Orleans: Historic New Orleans Collection, 1987.

McAlear, Donna. *Collection Passions: Highlights from the LSU Museum of Art Collection*. Baton Rouge: Louisiana State University Museum of Art, 2005.

Pennington, Estill Curtis. *Downriver: Currents of Style in Louisiana Painting, 1800–1950*. Gretna: Pelican Publishing Co. 1991.

Poesch, Jessie J., ed. *Printmaking in New Orleans*. New Orleans: Historic New Orleans Collection, 2006.

Smith, Margaret Denton. *Photography in New Orleans: The Early Years, 1840–1865*. Baton Rouge: LSU Press, 1982.

Wiesendanger, Martin, and Margaret Wiesendanger. *19th Century Louisiana Painters and Paintings from the Collection of W. E. Groves*. New Orleans: W. E. Groves Gallery, 1971.

Yelen, Alice Rae, ed. *Passionate Vision: Self-Taught Artists from 1940 to the Present*. New Orleans: New Orleans Museum of Art, 1994.

LSU FOOTBALL AND OTHER SPORTS IN LOUISIANA

BARRY C. COWAN

> So welcome to LSU, where the football is so good the earth moves, where the tailgate chow is so good the Food Network should own broadcast rights, and where the entire atmosphere is so special that people from the other side of the world would rather spend their days listening to a tiger's roar in Death Valley than go home to the peace and comfort of the Shire.
>
> —JIM CAPLE, *ESPN Magazine*

Sports play an incredibly large part in the lives of Louisianians. They follow the games and personalities, and reminisce about events long after they have happened. "Do you remember the game where . . ." starts many a conversation and can apply to a game, a player's feat, a coach's call, or an especially good pot of jambalaya at the tailgate party. People tailgate next to each other or have season tickets in the same section of the stadium and become lifelong friends. Sports are part of our shared history. Everyone remembers where they were on Halloween night, 1959, when LSU's Billy Cannon ran back an Ole Miss punt for a touchdown and a victory over the Rebels. We remember Doug Williams defeating John Elway in Super Bowl XXII. We remember when LSU won its first College World Series in 1991, and decided that football might not be the only sport that matters. This shared history allows us all to be part of the event, even if only as a spectator.

Louisiana has been called a sportsman's paradise, but that usually refers to hunting and fishing. Other sports are played and followed, but football truly is Louisiana's sport. Whether it is a college game on Saturday night or the pros on Sunday, few subjects, except maybe politics, are discussed more during the season or speculated about as much the rest of the year. Fall social events revolve around football schedules, especially LSU's and Southern University's, and inconsiderate (at best!) is the bride who schedules her wedding on a home-game Saturday. Since hunting and fishing are usually early morning activities, careful outdoorsmen plan their day to make it back in time to see the game.

LSU football is the 500-pound tiger prowling the living room of Louisiana sports. People have strong feelings about it: they love it, hate it, commiserate with each other over it, laugh and cry over it. Tiger Stadium is their shrine. Fans fill the stadium, and whether the Tigers are winning or not, they come back year after year hoping, and expecting, to see the next 89-yard punt return for a touchdown on Halloween night, another Earthquake Game, or a chance at the national championship. Baton Rouge becomes a quiet city after kickoff on home-game Saturdays, at least outside of Tiger Stadium. With most people attending the game or watching it at home or at a watering hole, Baton Rouge's notorious traffic is much easier to navigate, restaurants have plenty of tables available without reservations, and stores are empty of all but the most dedicated shoppers.

Intercollegiate football began in Louisiana in 1893 when LSU played Tulane in New Orleans's Sportsman's Park. The result was a 34–0 Tulane victory, but this lackluster start began the phenomenon that LSU football has become and a rivalry that lasted nearly a century. Tulane had a slight advantage, having played one game previously against the Southern Athletic Club in New Orleans. LSU's coach was Charles Coates, a newly hired chemistry professor from Johns Hopkins who had also played football there. Coates proposed the game because he thought it might be fun for the boys, and is said to have stayed up the night before pounding nails into the team's shoe soles for homemade cleats. The game against Tulane was the only one played in 1893, and it was Coates's only game as coach. Football excitement caught on quickly, and to accommodate the crowds, LSU soon built a small athletic field with bleacher seats on the

Fig. 12.1. In the 1902 season, LSU defeated Auburn 5–0 in Baton Rouge. The game was played on the athletic field south of the Pentagon Barracks on LSU's downtown campus. LSU finished the season with a 6–1 record. *LSU Photograph Collection, RG #A5000, Louisiana State University Archives, LSU Libraries, Baton Rouge, La.*

north end of the "old campus," on what is now the state capitol grounds in downtown Baton Rouge.

The sometimes bitter LSU-Tulane rivalry established bragging rights for the best team in Louisiana and, from 1933 to 1966, had Southeastern Conference championship implications. This rivalry was fueled as much by the fans as it was by the teams. Tulane fans and students painted "T.U." in green on LSU campus buildings and at one time kidnapped Mike the Tiger; Tiger fans in turn painted "LSU" in purple on Tulane's buildings. Special trains with reduced fares took fans to the games. By 1905, the desire to win was so strong that administrators of the two schools accused each other of various rules violations, including player recruitment and having "ringers" on their teams. From 1905 to 1911, the two teams refused to play each other because of these and other unresolved differences, but supporters, students, and finally administrators buried the hatchet. After the Tigers suffered a 14–0 loss in Baton Rouge in 1938, a riot between LSU and Tulane players, cheerleaders, and fans erupted on the field and spilled out into the area surrounding Tiger Stadium. Dozens were injured, and the student governments of both schools decided enough was enough. In an effort to foster better relations, students created "The Rag" in 1940. This was a trophy flag that was awarded to the winning school at a banquet after the annual game. The Rag carried the logos and colors of both schools, separated diagonally with the Louisiana seal in the center. The original Rag burned in a fire at Tulane in 1982. Tulane began to deemphasize athletics in the 1950s and left the SEC in 1966. LSU and Tulane have played each other intermittently since 1992.

By 1907, LSU football began to be noticed outside of the southern United States. The Tigers sailed from New Orleans to Cuba to play the first football game held outside of the United States on Christmas Day, 1907, against the University of Havana. LSU won 56–0 against an inexperienced team made up of some of the largest men in Cuba. The Cuban players were fortified by wine served on the sidelines. That, no doubt, partially accounted for the lopsided score. Later known variously as the Bacardi Bowl, Rhumba Bowl, and Cigar Bowl, the game was held seven times between 1907 and 1946, and pitted Cuban teams against teams from the southern United States. Tulane played in the 1910 game against the Havana Athletic Club and was defeated 11–0.

Politics, which may rival football as Louisiana's favorite sport, has always played a role at LSU on and off the football field, but Huey Long's involvement in the football team in the 1930s was unprecedented. He had allied himself with the Tigers and wanted them to be winners because he couldn't be associated with losers. He sat with the team on the sidelines, gave pep talks in the locker room, and disputed the referees. Long insisted that four injured players recuperate at the Governor's Mansion, where they ate steak, collard greens, and pineapple upside-down cake twice a day and showed Long how to diagram plays. Long accompanied the team on road games to Vanderbilt and Rice, led the band as it paraded through Nashville and Houston, and "loaned" students money for food and train fare so that they could attend the games. Long also

Fig. 12.2. In 1958, Coach Paul Dietzel (*second from right*) devised a three-squad team. Shown here are members of the White Team, who were adept at playing both offense and defense. From left to right, they are Billy Cannon, Johnny Robinson, J. W. "Red" Brodnax, Dietzel, and Warren Rabb. *Charles East Papers, Mss 3471, Louisiana and Lower Mississippi Valley Collections, LSU Libraries, Baton Rouge, La.*

co-wrote several songs about LSU, such as "Darling of LSU" and "Touchdown for LSU," with bandleader Castro Carazo. Head coach Lawrence "Biff" Jones resigned because of Long's interference. In the 1960s and early 1970s, Governor John McKeithen recruited a few players for the Tigers, but he never interfered like Long did.

LSU has had many great football teams over the years, but none are as renowned as the 1958 National Championship team. The 1958 team had a perfect 11–0 season, including the Sugar Bowl victory over Clemson that secured the Tigers' first national championship. This was also their first undefeated season since the 1908 team went 10–0. There were some close games—Florida was defeated 10–7, and the Tigers barely beat Mississippi State 7–6—and some not so close, as Tulane was crushed 62–0.

Overall, LSU outscored its opponents 282–53. Billy Cannon and center Max Fugler were named first-team All-Americans and Paul Dietzel was national coach of the year. The 1958 season is still mentioned with reverence by fans and the local press to this day. When the Tigers are having a good season, meaning no losses, people wonder if they can have that elusive perfect season again. That speculation builds until the first loss, then talk turns to firing the coach or switching quarterbacks.

Ironically, by the end of the 1957 season, Dietzel had been unable to do better than a 5–5 record. Doubts about his abilities had begun to surface, and many fans were calling for his replacement. There were some great players during those years, including fullback Jim Taylor and defensive tackle Earl Leggett, as well as some emerging talents, but the Tigers were unable to put together a winning effort. For the 1958 season, Dietzel decided to create a three-squad team: the White Team, powerful and fast players who were equally adept at offense and defense; the Go (originally Gold) Team, who were lighter and faster offensive specialists; and the Chinese Bandits, who were defensive specialists. The three-squad team allowed mass substitutions to take place as situations on the field warranted and kept fresh players on the field. The White Team was anchored by halfbacks Billy Cannon and Johnny Robinson, quarterback Warren Rabb, and fullback J. W. "Red" Brodnax. The Go Team's stars were halfback Don "Scooter" Purvis, who later became an assistant coach under Charles McClendon; ends Scotty McClain and Don Norwood; and quarterback Durel Matherne. The big men of the Chinese Bandits were cornerbacks Andy Bourgeois and Hart Bourque, ends Mel Branch and Gaynell "Gus" Kinchen, and guard Tommy Lott. The Chinese Bandits captured the fans' imagination to such an extent that today few remember that there was actually a three-squad team. For many fans, the names of the men who played on the 1958 championship team are still household words.

Over the years Tiger Stadium has hosted many games that have become legendary, but the 1988 LSU-Auburn game is one of the more unusual. LSU's 1988 season began with two wins and two losses. The Tigers had beaten Texas A&M and Tennessee, but lost to Ohio State and Florida. The next game, on October 8, was against Southeastern Conference rival Auburn, who had a 4–0 record and was ranked number four in the nation. Overall, the game was a defensive struggle, with Auburn moving the ball but getting only two field goals in the second and fourth quarters. LSU had trouble moving the ball and had not scored at all. It appeared that LSU might lose its third straight game.

With a little over six minutes left in the game, LSU had the ball and was putting together a solid drive that started on its own 25-yard line. Tommy Hodson was in at quarterback and gaining solid yardage, completing passes and gaining first downs. Auburn's defense stiffened when the Tigers reached their eleven-yard line and Hodson threw three incomplete passes. With 1:47 left in the game, on fourth down, Hodson lofted a pass to Eddie Fuller in the end zone for a touchdown. The crowd of over 79,000 erupted, causing a seismograph in the Geology Building to register earth movement. LSU won the game 7–6, handing Auburn its only SEC loss that season. People who attended the game (including the author) still remember the sudden, sharp explosion of cheers from the crowd.

The ground movement was discovered the next morning by a seismologist while performing a daily reading on the seismogram in the Geology Building. It was determined that the movement had occurred at the moment of the Hodson-to-Fuller touchdown pass. The seismogram is housed at LSU's University Archives and has been photographed by numerous sports networks around the time of the LSU-Auburn game.

Among the most iconic of LSU's star football players is Billy Cannon. A great athlete in football and track and field at Istrouma High in Baton Rouge, Cannon played halfback for the Tigers from 1957 to 1959 and won the Heisman Trophy. He is best known for his fourth-quarter 89-yard punt return for the game-winning touchdown against Ole Miss on Halloween night, 1959, in Tiger Stadium. J. C. Politz, "the voice of Tiger football," called the game on the radio, and his description of the run and highlight film are replayed every year on local news broadcasts around Halloween or before the Ole Miss game, thus immortalizing Cannon's run. Cannon's number (20) was retired after the 1959 season, and he was inducted into the College Football Hall of Fame in 2008.

Billy Cannon's Heisman played a role in helping to legitimize the fledgling American Football League as Cannon signed with the Houston Oilers in 1960. The National Football League's Los Angeles Rams

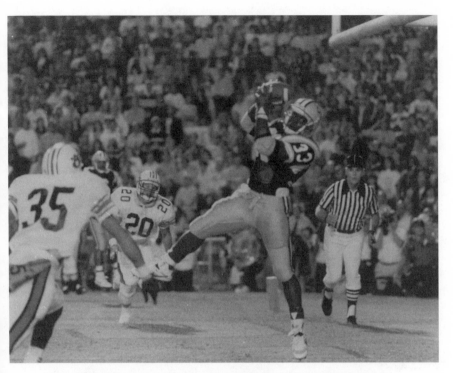

Fig. 12.3. The reception that caused an earthquake. Eddie Fuller's touchdown catch in the end zone against Auburn in 1988 came with 1:47 left in the game on fourth down, and the crowd reaction registered on the seismograph in the Geology Building. Fuller's catch paved the way for a 7–6 LSU victory.
LSU Photograph Collection, RG #A5000, Louisiana State University Archives, LSU Libraries, Baton Rouge, La.

drafted him that year, but the Oilers made a better offer. The Rams sued and lost. Cannon signed with the Oakland Raiders in 1964 and is one of a handful of players who played in the AFL the entire ten years of the league's existence. Decades later, and despite some downturns in his personal life, Cannon is still revered as a hometown hero.

Grambling has also produced star athletes over the years. Among the best known is Doug Williams, the first African American quarterback to lead a team to victory in the Super Bowl. Originally from Zachary, Louisiana, he played college ball at Grambling and was a first-round draft pick of the Tampa Bay Buccaneers in 1978. After a dispute with Tampa Bay's ownership over his salary, the lowest of any starting quarterback in the NFL, Williams left after the 1982 season for the United States Football League. In 1986, he signed with the Washington Redskins as a backup quarterback to Jay Schroeder. Schroeder was injured during the 1987 season, and Williams was chosen to start in the playoffs. He led the Redskins to a 42–10 victory in Super Bowl XXII against John Elway and the Denver Broncos and was named Super Bowl MVP. As of 2013, Williams remains the only African American quarterback to lead a team to victory in the Super Bowl. His performance in Super Bowl XXII is believed to have played a major role in opening the door for black quarterbacks in the NFL.

After leaving the NFL, Williams held coaching and scouting jobs with the U.S. Naval Academy and the Jacksonville Jaguars before becoming head coach at Morehouse College in 1997. In 1998, he became the head coach at Grambling, succeeding Eddie Robinson, who had been the Tigers' coach since 1941. Williams coached the team to three consecutive Southwestern Athletic Conference championships from 2000 to 2002. He left Grambling after the 2002 season to become an executive with the Tampa Bay Buccaneers. In 2011 he returned to Grambling as head coach.

Sports rivalries come and go. In the 1970s, the Bayou Classic between Southern University and Grambling State University eclipsed the annual LSU-Tulane game as the main in-state rivalry. Southern and Grambling had played each other in relative obscurity since 1932, but the idea for a major happening in a neutral location took shape in 1974. Held around Thanksgiving in New Orleans, the Bayou Classic is more than a football game. It is a homecoming for both schools, even though both have their own homecoming activities. The pageantry of the Battle of the Bands between the Southern Marching Band (the Human Jukebox) and Grambling's Tiger Marching Band draws almost as many spectators as the football game. There are also charitable events, a parade on Thanksgiving Day, and numerous banquets and parties. The game itself is the only one between historically black colleges to be nationally televised and to have major corporate sponsorship.

Professional sports began in Louisiana when the New Orleans Saints arrived in 1967. For most of the team's existence, it has been mediocre at best, posting its first winning season only in 1987. The Saints don't have the fan base of LSU, but their often-exasperated fans are some of the most loyal in the National Football League. They have worn bags over their heads in the lean years and called the team the Aints, but keep coming back and hoping for greatness or at least a victory. The Saints became the hope of New Orleans after Hurricane Katrina and the resulting floods devastated 80 percent of the city. The Superdome was used as a shelter of last resort and sustained heavy damage from its unintended use and from the storm. With no place to play, the Saints became a vagabond team during the 2005 season, playing "home" games in San Antonio's Alamodome and in LSU's Tiger Stadium. Major repairs and renovations to the Superdome completed in record time allowed the Saints to return to New Orleans and play at home for the 2006 season. The team posted a 10–6 record and won the NFC South divisional championship, their first postseason victory since 2000. This quick return to the city, which was still barely functioning after Katrina, and the Saints' winning record, gave the people of New Orleans and Louisiana a sense of hope and showed the rest of the country that the city was on its way back. The victory in Super Bowl XLIV over the favored Indianapolis Colts proved that New Orleans was back for good, and the CBS telecast was the most-watched program in U.S. television history.

Tailgating is essential to any sporting event in Louisiana. Few fans have a simple picnic lunch laid out on a pickup's tailgate before the game. At LSU and Southern, the party begins on Friday afternoon and into the early hours on Saturday. Motorhomes and trucks and SUVs with trailers arrive on campus filled with canopies, tables and chairs, and, most importantly, food and drink that would rival those at the best restaurants. Soon the aroma of jambalaya, alligator sauce piquante, gumbo, and the ever-popular barbecue fills the air. For those getting an early start on Saturdays, eggs, bacon, and bloody marys are served. It's no surprise that magazines like *Sports Illustrated* and *Parade* have said that food prepared by LSU tailgaters is among the best in the country. If someone wearing the opposing team's colors walks by a Tiger tailgater's site, he or she will be taunted with "Tiger bait!" but offered a hot plate and cold drink. Louisianians are rightfully proud of their culinary skill and are eager to share.

Although not as far-reaching as football, baseball in Louisiana does have a dedicated and loyal following. LSU baseball lived for many years in the shadow of Tiger football but has gradually come into its own. Both sports began at LSU in 1893 with games against Tulane—but unlike the football team, the baseball team won. The baseball team was also the first to wear purple and gold. Early teams played against professionals such as the Chicago White Sox, offering opportunities to gain experience but little chance of victory. The longest-serving baseball coach was Harry Rabenhorst, who coached from the late 1920s to the mid-1950s.

LSU baseball was not always the powerhouse that it is today. The Tigers won a handful of SEC championships between 1939 and 1975, but their seasons tended to be hit or miss: either they were a good team that contended for the conference championship, or they were mediocre. In 1975 the Tigers went for the first time to the NCAA tournament, but they were eliminated in the regionals. When Skip Bertman arrived in 1984, the team began to have consistently good seasons, and by 1986 the Tigers were contenders in the first of sixteen appearances in the College World Series. The Tigers became national champions six times between 1991 and 2009 and have created their own aura that comes close to rivaling that of the football team.

Alex Box Stadium is the home of Tiger baseball. Called Varsity Baseball Field when it was built, the original stadium opened in 1938. When LSU player Simeon Alex Box was killed in North Africa in 1942 during World War II, the name was changed to honor him. A larger, more modern facility replaced the old in 2009. Fans tailgate for the baseball games with the same enthusiasm as shown during football season. LSU has led the nation in baseball attendance since the 1990s. Because Alex Box Stadium is a more intimate place than Tiger Stadium, the opportunity for fan interaction, with one another and the team, is greater. People like the "K Lady," Anita Haywood, become widely known. Haywood has been hanging Ks (K being the symbol for strikeouts) every time an LSU pitcher strikes out an opposing batter at the stadium since the 1980s.

Basketball, especially when superstars like "Pistol" Pete Maravich and Shaquille O'Neal were on the court, has periodically captured the attention of Louisiana fans in the "P-Mac," as LSU's Pete Maravich Assembly Center is affectionately called. Women's basketball also flourished at times. Louisiana Tech's "Lady Techsters" won the 1981, 1982, and 1988 national championships, and LSU's Seimone Augustus was National Player of the Year three times. Finally, the Louisiana-themed renaming of the NBA's team in New Orleans—the Pelicans—gave basketball in the state another quick boost.

The opportunity to see professional-level sports in Louisiana—outside of football and, more recently, basketball—does not come very often for Louisianians, but when it does, they turn out for it. From 1976 to 1990, professional-level drag racing came to Louisiana in the form of the National Hot Rod Association's Cajun Nationals, where top fuel dragsters, funny cars, and pro stocks thundered down the quarter-mile tracks. The event was held at LaPlace Dragway in 1976 and from 1977 to 1990 at State Capitol Dragway in Erwinville. At the height of its popularity, the Cajun Nationals attracted 40,000 spectators over the three-day event.

The Cajun Nationals was an event that paid points toward the national championship, and the top drivers in each class passed through Louisiana. Names like Don "The Snake" Prudhomme in funny car, "Big Daddy" Don Garlits in top fuel, Bill "Grumpy" Jenkins in pro stock, and many more raced here. The local favorite was the funny car team of Paul Candies and Leonard Hughes from Houma and their driver Richard Tharp.

The event began on Friday with qualifying, semifinals took place on Saturday, and final eliminations on Sunday. The losers in the semifinal rounds load up and head to the next race, while the winners go on to the final eliminations until a winner emerges in each class, determined by the lowest elapsed times, called ET. Funny cars and top fuel dragsters, running on a volatile (if not hallucinogenic) mixture of nitromethane and methanol, stormed down the quarter-mile track in the low six-second to high five-second range in the 1970s to low fives to high fours in the 1980s. The engines produced 5000 to 6000 horsepower during these times.

Always dramatic at night, "under the lights!" as the radio commercials said, with flames shooting up from their exhaust headers, top fuel and funny cars are the stars of the show. The noise made by their supercharged ("blown" in drag racing parlance) engines is not only heard but felt. As the cars pass, your body and the grandstands vibrate, and it feels like the earth moves. By the end of the weekend, your ears are ringing and you smell like burned rubber and nitromethane with a little cigarette smoke, beer, and sweat mixed in for good measure. It all adds up to a very visceral experience. Unlike ball sports, fans can see what happens in drag racing's "locker room," the pits. Fans can see and hear a top fuel dragster being tuned and are deafened by the engine's roar; you can't go into the locker room at Tiger Stadium and watch a player's knee being taped.

Why did the Cajun Nationals come to an end? State Capitol Dragway was not updated for years and had some idiosyncrasies. An interstate natural gas pipeline ran beneath it, the runoff area at the end of the track was on leased property that was not under the racetrack owner's control, and the track had no sewer system. New tracks opened in Houston and Memphis with better pit areas and amenities for sponsors, racers, and fans, and permanent restroom facilities. Those two cities also had larger markets to draw from as professional automobile racing became increasingly commercialized by the late 1980s. Now called State Capitol Raceway, the track still hosts sportsman class events, but the big names no longer race there. LaPlace Dragway no longer exists.

Sports are a palpable part of the culture here in Louisiana. We can see, feel, hear, and taste sporting events, reminisce about them, and take pride in them. College football rivalries, the chance for a national championship, bragging rights for the best team in the state, a Super Bowl victory over a heavily favored team, and the chance to watch nationally recognized competitors give us all something to look forward to. We make plans around the various sports seasons and get tickets to bowl games and championship tournaments as soon as they become available. We love sports in Louisiana. The competition, color, spectacle, and sometimes their idiosyncrasies make it hard not to love them.

SUGGESTED READING

Aiello, Thomas. *Bayou Classic: The Grambling-Southern Football Rivalry*. Baton Rouge: LSU Press, 2010.

Cowan, Barry. *Louisiana State University*. Mount Pleasant, S.C.: Arcadia Publishing, 2013.

Finney, Peter. *The Fighting Tigers, 1893–1993: One Hundred Years of LSU Football*. Baton Rouge: LSU Press, 1993.

LSU Sports Information Office. *2012 LSU Football Media Guide*. Birmingham: EBSCO Media, 2012.

Martin, Mark E., and Barry C. Cowan. *Historic Photos of LSU Football*. Nashville: Turner Publishing, 2009.

Rabalais, Scott. *The Fighting Tigers, 1993–2008: Into a New Century of LSU Football*. Baton Rouge: LSU Press, 2008.

Ruffin, Thomas F. *Under Stately Oaks: A Pictorial History of LSU*. Baton Rouge: LSU Press, 2002.

Taylor, Herbert Warren. *Forty-Two Years on the Tiger Gridiron: A History of Football at the Louisiana State University, 1893–1935*. Baton Rouge: Claitor, 1936.

Vincent, Herb. *LSU Football Vault: The History of the Fighting Tigers*. Atlanta: Whitman Publishing, 2008.

Williams, Doug, with Bruce Hunter. *Quarterblack: Shattering the NFL Myth*. Chicago: Bonus Books, 1990.

CONTRIBUTORS

ALEX V. COOK is an author and professional-in-residence at the Manship School of Mass Communication at Louisiana State University. His book *Louisiana Saturday Night: Looking for a Good Time in South Louisiana's Juke Joints, Honky-Tonks and Dance Halls* was published in 2012 by LSU Press.

BARRY C. COWAN is an archivist in the University Archives at Louisiana State University. He is a long-time Baton Rouge resident and received bachelor of arts degrees in history and German from LSU. Cowan's published works include *Louisiana State University* (2013), *Historic Photos of LSU Football* (2009; co-authored with Mark E. Martin), and articles in KnowLA (an online encyclopedia of Louisiana) and *The New Encyclopedia of Southern Culture*. Cowan also contributed to *A Unique Slant of Light: The Bicentennial History of Art in Louisiana* (2012) and writes the "Tiger Trivia" column in *LSU Alumni Magazine*.

J. MICHAEL DESMOND, a licensed architect, teaches architectural and urban history, along with architectural and urban design, in the LSU School of Architecture. His book *The Architecture of LSU* (LSU Press, 2013) explores romantic and renaissance inspiration in the 1920s campus design of Frederick Law Olmsted Jr. and the German-American architect Theodore Link. His professional firm, Desmond-Cuddeback Architects, was responsible for the design of the award-winning Bluebonnet Nature Center in Baton Rouge.

SYLVIE DUBOIS is director of the Center for French and Francophone Studies and Gabrielle Muir Professor in the Department of French Studies at Louisiana State University. She studies language use in everyday situations, focusing particularly on bilingual and minority language contexts in Louisiana. She has written two books and published more than fifty articles. In recognition of her contributions to French scholarship, the French government named Dubois a Chevalier of the Ordre des Palmes Académiques.

AARON C. EMMITTE is a visiting assistant professor in the Department of French at Georgetown University. He specializes in the phonetics of Louisiana French.

ZACK GODSHALL is professional-in-residence in the Department of English at Louisiana State University and makes fiction and documentary films. His work has screened at the Sundance Film Festival and on the Documentary Channel.

A. RAYNIE HARLAN is a research associate at the Louisiana State University Agricultural Center. She works extensively in the Atchafalaya Basin studying trends in water quality, fish communities, and large-scale flow patterns.

DAVID P. HARLAN, a native of New Orleans, is the geographic information systems manager at the Nature Conservancy of Louisiana.

JOYCE MARIE JACKSON is director of African and African American Studies and an associate professor in the Department of Geography and Anthropology at Louisiana State University. As a folklorist and ethnomusicologist, she is currently completing a book on African American gospel quartets and an interactive DVD-ROM on the rural and coastal roots of jazz in southern Louisiana. She authored *Life in the Village: A Cultural Memory of the Fazendeville Community* (2003). Her main research interest is performance-centered studies of rituals in Africa and the African diaspora.

THOMAS A. KLINGLER is an associate professor in the Department of French and Italian at Tulane University. He specializes in the documentation and description of the French and Creole languages of Louisiana. He is the author of *If I Could Turn My Tongue Like That: The Creole Language of Pointe Coupee Parish, Louisiana* (2003) and co-editor of *Dictionary of Louisiana Creole* (1998) and *Dictionary of Louisiana French: As Spoken in Cajun, Creole, and American Indian Communities* (2010).

RICHARD ANTHONY LEWIS is curator of visual arts at the Louisiana State Museum in New Orleans. He is the author of *Robert W. Tebbs, Photographer to Architects: Louisiana Plantations in 1926* (2011).

ALECIA P. LONG is an associate professor in the Department of History at Louisiana State University. Her areas of research specialization include the history of Louisiana, especially New Orleans, and the intertwined histories of race, gender, and sexuality in New Orleans and the South. She is the author of *The Great Southern Babylon: Sex, Race, and Respectability in New Orleans, 1865–1920* (2004), which was awarded the Julia Cherry Spruill Prize; and co-editor of *Occupied Women: Gender, Military Occupation, and the American Civil War* (2009). Long is currently at work on a biography of Clay Lavergne Shaw, the only person ever charged in one of the many conspiracies alleged in the assassination of John F. Kennedy.

KENT MATHEWSON is a professor of geography in the Department of Geography and Anthropology at Louisiana State University. His research has taken him to Latin America, the Caribbean, and Oceania, where he has studied ancient and traditional agriculture. He also publishes on the history of geography and anthropology and on Louisiana's place in the Atlantic world. He is the author or editor of a number of books, including *Irrigation Horticulture in Highland Guatemala* (1984), *Re-Reading Cultural Geography* (1994); *Concepts in Human Geography* (1996); *Dangerous Harvest: Drug Plants and the Transformation of Indigenous Landscapes* (2004); and *Carl Sauer on Culture and Landscape* (2009).

RYAN ORGERA graduated from the Department of Geography and Anthropology at Louisiana State University with a Ph.D. in geography, specializing in culture and the environment. He is currently a project manager and adjunct professor at Monmouth University in New Jersey.

WAYNE PARENT is the Russell B. Long Professor of Political Science in the Department of Political Science at Louisiana State University. He is the author of *Inside the Carnival: Unmasking Louisiana Politics* (2004), as well as dozens of published articles and chapters, and is co-editor of *Blacks and the American Political System* (1995). He also frequently comments about Louisiana politics to the national, state, and local press.

MICHAEL PASQUIER is an associate professor of religious studies and history at Louisiana State University. He is the author of *Fathers on the Frontier: French Missionaries and the Roman Catholic Priesthood in the United States* (2010) and editor of *Gods of the Mississippi* (2013). His work on the history of religion in the United States has been supported by the American Academy of Arts and

Sciences, the National Endowment for the Humanities, and the National Endowment for the Arts.

MAGGIE HEYN RICHARDSON is an award-winning freelance journalist whose work has appeared in *Eating Well* and on public radio program *On Point*, and is featured regularly in the *Baton Rouge Business Report* and *225* magazine. Richardson's book on Louisiana foodways will be released by LSU Press in 2015.

KAREN WILLIAMS is an instructor of English at Louisiana State University, specializing in rhetoric, American cultural history, contemporary literary theory, and carnival. Her published works include short stories in *Microcosm* and *Louisiana Literature*, as well as an article, "St. Expedito's Role in South Louisiana Catholicism," in *Louisiana Folklore Miscellany*. Her many presentations at scholarly conferences include research on the Federal Writers' Project in Louisiana, the songs of the Mardi Gras Indians, the differentiation between Creole and Acadian in Kate Chopin, and ex-slave narratives in Louisiana. Born and raised in St. Helena Parish, she finds no end to the uniqueness of her native state.

INDEX

Academy of the Sacred Heart, 204

Acadia, 51

Acadia Parish, 51

Acadiana/Acadian Triangle, 50–54, 86–87, 88, 89, 130, 166, 170, 171; as epicenter of Cajun culture, 87

Acadians, 10, 22, 39, 51, 53, 62, 68, 86, 88, 116, 143; folklore of, 97–99; in New Orleans, 64. *See also* Cajuns

Adams, John Quincy, 25, 46–47

Adams-Onis Treaty (1821), 47, 49

African Americans, 27, 41, 49, 57, 82, 141, 153; art of, 222; and labor systems, 57; and right to vote, 142–43, 150; role of music in culture of, 57, 59–60

Africans, 38

Age of Immigration (1880–1920), 11–12

agriculture, 3–4; early farmers in Louisiana, 7

Alaux, Alexandre, 219

Albrizio, Conrad, 221

Alex Box Stadium, 236

Alexandria, La., 45

All Saints (Osbey), 115

All the King's Men (Warren), 31, 72, 111–12

alligators, 5, 15

Almonester, Don Andrés, 69

Amans, Jacques, 215

Anderson, Sherwood, 221

Angola Prison, 160

Antrobus, John, 217

architecture, 36, 181–82, 221; Art Deco style, 195–96; Beaux Arts classicism, 194; building ensembles, 203–4; church design, 200–201; colonial and eclectic periods, 194–95; contemporary, 204–7, 209; effect of Public Works Administration projects on, 196; Federal style, 186; French Creole buildings, 183; Gothic Revival style, 191, 193; Greek Revival style, 186–89, 191; high-rises, 198; log cabins, 184; lumber mills, 198; Native American mound sites, 182–83; plantation houses, 185–86, 187–88; post–World War II, 199–204; raised cottages, 183; Romanesque Revival style, 193–94; sugar refineries, 198. *See also* Louisiana State University (LSU); Shushan Airport (New Orleans)

Army Corps of Engineers, 28

Arnold, Edward Everard, 220

Arroyo Hondo, 46

Artists Association of New Orleans, 218

arts, the, 210–12; and age of partisanship, 215–18; art criticism, 212–13; artists' earnings, 214; early national period, 212–15; folk art, 222; "French Quarter School," 220–21; and Hurricane Katrina, 224; "la petite renaissance,"

Bonaparte, Napoleon, 22–23

Bosque, Suzette, 24

Bossier City, La., 45

Bourbon Democrats, 26, 27

Bourgeois, Andy, 231

Bourgeois, Beau, 137

Bourgeois, Donald, 136–37

Bourgeois, Douglas, 222

Bourgeois, Lester, 136

Bourgeois, Valerie Jean-Baptiste, 136

Bourque, Darrell, 114

Bourque, Hart, 231

Bouteux, Jean Baptiste Michel Le, 182–83

Box, Simeon Alex, 236

BP oil spill, 32, 148, 149, 154

Brain, Jeffrey, 74

Brammer, Robert, 217

Branch, Mel, 231

Breaux, Chick, 136–37

Breaux, Cleoma, 160

Br'er Rabbit, 97

Brewster, Edmund, 212–13

Brice, Bruce, 222

Bringer, Emanuel Marius Pons, 188

Brodnax, J. W. ("Red"), 231

Broussard, Grace, 174

Broussard, Van, 174

Broutin, François, 184

Brown, James, 195

Buck, William Henry, 218, 219

Buddhists, 73, 102

Burton, James, 167

Bush, George H. W., 150

Bush, George W., 148, 150, 151

Butler, David, 222

Butler, Robert Owen, 102–3

Cabildo, the, 22

Cable, George Washington, 103

Caddo Parish, 44; courthouse of, 195

Caddo tribe, 37, 56

Cahokia, Ill., 182

Cajun Music Pioneer (Falcon), 160

Cajun Nationals, 237–38

Cajuns, 10, 14, 51–52, 131; Cajun Renaissance, 92–93, 94; Cajun Vernacular
English (CVE), 91–95; cultures of,
50–51; documented history of, 87–88;
folklore of, 97–99; language of (Cajun
French), 85, 86–89, 90; music of,
53, 89, 93; representation of, in film,
175–76

Calcasieu Parish Courthouse, 194

Calcasieu River, 46

Caldwell Parish Courthouse, 196

Cameron Parish, 86

Canary Islands, 9–10

Canary Islanders (Isleños), 52, 97; cultural
celebration of, 85

Cane River, 40, 90, 185, 207

Cane River Creole National Historical
Park, 185

Cannon, Billy, 226, 231, 232–33

Canova, Dominique, 217

Caple, Jim, 226

Carazo, Castro, 230

Cash, Johnny, 195

Casselli, Henry, 222

Catholicism. *See under* religion

Cavelier, René-Robert, sieur de LaSalle, 19

Challoner, William Lindsey, 220

Charles, Bobby, 172–73

Charles III of Spain, 52

Charrier, Leonard, 73–74

Chenier, Clifton, 53, 162

"Chicken Strut" (the Meters), 167–68

Chinese Bandits (LSU), 231

Chitimacha tribe, 9, 51, 62; war with the
French, 62–63

Choctaw tribe, 9, 41, 56, 61, 63, 135; Jena
Choctaw, 45

Chopin, Kate, 96, 103, 115–18

El Camino Real, 46

Elway, John, 226, 234

Eskew + Dumez + Ripple architectural
firm, 205

Europeans, 36; exploration of Louisiana
region by, 38–39; German immigrants,
51; intermarriage with Native Americans, 48; Italian farmers, 59; Italians
and Hungarians in Baton Rouge, 55;
persistence of old-country traditions in
Louisiana, 59–60; reliance on Native
Americans, 38; Spanish colonists, 48,
52; synthesis and influence of, in Louisiana, 51. *See also* French Louisiana

Evans, Harold, 54

Evans, James Guy, 220

Evans, Thomas, 54

Evergreen Plantation, 187

Falcon, Joe, 160

Faulkner, William, 221

Fein, Skylar, 222

Felicianas, 57

films/cinema. *See* authenticity, in films

fire ants, 6

First Acadian Coast, 51

fishing, 4, 10, 13, 38, 41, 50, 52, 62, 84, 94,
116, 126, 131, 227

Flagfin shiner, 15

Flaherty, Robert, 177

Fleischbein, Franz Joseph, 215, 217

flooding, 5, 28–29; Great Flood (1929), 29

Florida Parishes, 12, 54, 55, 57, 59, 68, 118,
120, 201

Florien Free State festival, 50

Folse, Chef John, 134

Fontenette, Gustave, 54

food/culinary culture, 36, 126–28; boudin,
136–37; coffee, 129; crawfish, 128, 129;
Creole cream cheese, 133–34; effect of
hurricanes on, 132–33; eggplant, 129;
filé, 135–36; food festivals, 131; gumbo,

134–35; "Holy Trinity," 129; hot peppers, 129; influence of immigrants on,
131; king cakes, 128; local fruits, 128;
and natural assets of Louisiana, 131;
okra, 129; outdoor cooking/grilling,
129; oysters, 128, 129; po'boys, 129;
regional food identities, 130; religious
and secular holiday cuisine, 128, 129;
seasonal eating, 128–29; shrimp, 128;
snowball stands, 128. See also *New
Orleans Times-Picayune*, food recipes in

football. *See* Grambling State University;
Louisiana State University (LSU); New
Orleans Saints; Southern University;
Tulane University

Fort Polk, 49

Fort St. Louis, 19

Fortier, Alcée, 97

Foster, Gov. Mike, 148

Fran, Carol, 173–74

France, 20, 21, 22, 68, 98, 215; colonists
from, 38–39, 63–64, 65; medieval
France, 53; transfer of Louisiana territories to Spain, 9

Frank, Keith, 158–60

Franklin, Aretha, 195

free blacks (*gens de couleur libres*), 10–11,
40–41, 66

French and Indian War, 21

French Canadians, 63–64

French Louisiana, 63–64

Freret, William, 191

Friedlander, Lee, 75

Fuller, Eddie, 232

Gaines, Ernest, 96, 109–11

Gallier, James, 189, 191

Gallier Hall, 189, 191

Garbeille, Philippe, 220

Garlits, Don ("Big Daddy"), 237

Garner, Larry, 59

Gathering of Old Men, A (Gaines), 109

Iberville Parish Courthouse, 196
"I'm a King Bee" (Slim Harpo), 163
"I'm Leaving It All Up to You" (Dale and
    Grace), 174
Indian Angels, 56
Interview with the Vampire (Rice), 108
Isleños. *See* Canary Islanders (Isleños)
Israelite Baptist Church, 80–82

Jackson, Andrew, 24–25, 204
Jackson Barracks, 204
Jackson Parish Courthouse, 196
Jackson Square, 203
Jai été au bal (film), 176
Jarmusch, Jim, 175
Jarvis, John Wesley, 214
jazz. *See under* music
Jefferson, Thomas, 23
Jenkins, Bill, 237
Jenkins, Louis ("Woody"), 150–51
Jews, 69, 73, 181
Jindal, Gov. Bobby, 148
Jocque, Beau, 162
Johnson, Lyndon B., 31, 150
Johnson, William Gary ("Bunk"), 54
Johnston, Frances Benjamin, 221
Johnston, J. Bennett, 143
Joliet, Louis, 19
Jones, Lawrence ("Biff"), 230
Jouett, Matthew Harris, 214

Kazan, Elia, 174–75
Kelley, Arthur ("Guitar"), 59
Kennedy, John F., 150, 174
Kershaw, Doug, 161–62
Key, Lionel, 135–36
Key, V. O., 139; view of Louisiana politics,
    146
Kinchen, Gaynell ("Gus"), 231
King, B. B., 195
King, Martin Luther, Jr., 80
Kingsley, Karen, 187, 191

Kniffen, Fred, 56
Koasati tribe. *See* Coushatta (Koasati)
    tribe
Koch, Richard, 221
Komunyakaa, Yusef, 113
Koss, Gene, 222
kudzu, 6
Kukla, John, 23

L. B. Landry High School, 205
LaCour House, 183
Lafayette, La., 50, 131, 160, 173, 176
Lafayette Square, 189, 191
Lafever, Minard, 188
Lafitte, Jean, 46, 69
Lafourche Parish, 87
Lake Charles, La., 50
Lakefront Airport. *See* Shushan Airport
    (New Orleans)
Lamoisse, Elizabeth, 220
Landrieu, Mary, 148, 149, 150–51, 152
Landrieu, Mitch, 149
Landry, Pierre Joseph, 220
Lane, Mills, 188
Lane, Pinkie Gordon, 114
languages, 84–85; Cajun French, 86–89;
    Cajun Vernacular English (CVE),
    91–95; Creole French, 89–91; Native
    American languages, 85; and private
    bilingual schools, 88; Sicilian and
    Italian, 85. *See also under* Muskogean
    tribe
Latin America, 12
Latrobe, Benjamin Henry, 187
Laughlin, Clarence John, 218, 222
Laura Plantation, 97
Law, Frederick, 218
Law, John, 20
Lawrence, John, 201
Ledbetter, Huddie ("Leadbelly"), 44, 195
Leesville, La., 49
Lehr, Dick, 198

Le Moyne, Jean-Baptiste, sieur de Bienville, 20, 63
Le Moyne, Pierre, sieur d'Iberville, 20, 63
Lesson before Dying, A (Gaines), 109–11
"Let's Make a Record" (Morgan), 164–65
levees, 5, 8, 10, 52, 59, 132; "levees-only"
policy, 28
Lewis, Jerry Lee, 44
Liebling, A. J., 142
Lightnin' Slim, 59, 163
Lilienthal, Theodore, 218
Lion, Jules, 217–18
literary carnival, 96, 123; carnival figures,
103–8; categories of, 99–102; concerning or set in New Orleans, 103–8;
and folklore, 96–99; and image of the
southern belle, 100; mixing of cultures
in, 102–3; nonfiction, 111–13; poetry
and the carnival philosophy, 113–15;
universal appeal of Louisiana literature, 108–11; writing from local color,
115–18, 120–23
Livingston, Robert, 23
Lomax, Alan, 44
Lomax, John, 44
Long, Earl, 31, 139, 145, 154; politics of, in
civil rights era, 142–43
Long, Huey Pierce, 72–73, 111–12, 139–40,
145, 150, 154; assassination of, 29–30;
economic populism of, 141–42; involvement in LSU football, 229–30;
personal Bible of, 78–80; Share Our
Wealth agenda of, 29; success as politician, 140–41. *See also* Longism
Long, Russell, 140
Longism, 139–42, 149; perpetuation of,
after Long's assassination, 30
"Longites" and "Anti-Longs," 149
Los Adaes, 46, 130
Lott, Tommy, 231
Louisiana: antebellum economic development in, 11; cultural creativity in, 33;
ethnic diversity in, 11–12, 41, 43, 153;
historical overview of, 18–34; linguistic
differences from rest of United States,
24; natural riches of, 13–15; north-
south divide in, 4–5; political and
commercial interests of, 25–26; racial
diversity of, 24; regional identity of, 12;
settlement patterns and regionalization
in, 5–12; Sicilians in, 60; southern-tier
parishes of, 4; Spanish tenure/coloniza-
tion in, 8, 9. *See also* French Louisiana;
Louisiana cultural regions
Louisiana cultural regions, 39–40; Florida
Parishes, Mississippi River Road, and
eastern Acadiana, 54–60; Greater New
Orleans area, 60–69; Red River Val-
ley and Neutral Strip, 45–50; upper
Louisiana delta and north-central hill
country, 40–44; western Acadiana/
Cajun country, 50–54
Louisiana Cypress Lumber Company, 198
Louisiana Hayride radio program, 43,
170–71, 195
Louisiana Hayride scandals, 30
"Louisiana Man" (Kershaw), 161
Louisiana pancake batfish, 15
Louisiana Power and Light (Dufresne), 101–2
Louisiana prairie, 50
Louisiana Purchase (1803), 10, 23, 61,
64, 91, 118, 185; exclusion of "Neutral
Ground" in treaty, 45–46
Louisiana Scandals, 30
Louisiana Sports Hall of Fame and North-
west Louisiana History Museum, 207
Louisiana State Capitol, 191, 196, 206
Louisiana State Exhibit Building, 195
Louisiana State Museum, 189, 220
Louisiana State University (LSU)
—architecture, 202–3; Laboratory for
Creative Arts and Technologies, 206;
LSU Museum of Art, 206, 224; LSU
School of Art Gallery, 206; LSU Union

Building, 202; Parade Grounds, 202;
University Laboratory School, 203
—baseball program, 226, 236
—football program, 227–34; famous
Cannon run, 226, 232; Earthquake
Game, 227, 231–32, 233; games against
University of Havana, 229; Huey Long's
involvement in, 229–30; LSU-Tulane
rivalry, 228–29; Mike the Tiger mascot,
226, 228; 1958 National Championship
team, 230–31; origins of, 227–28; "the
Rag," 229. *See also* Tiger Stadium
Louisiana Story (film), 177
Lurie, John, 175
Lux, Rudolf, 214

Magnolia Mound Plantation, 185
Mahalia Jackson School, 199
Mallard, Prudent, 214
Mangelsdorf, Hans, 221
Manouvrier, Jules, 214
Manship Theater (Baton Rouge), 206
Maravich, "Pistol" Pete, 236
Mardi Gras, 53–54; *chansons de Mardi
Gras,* 53; *courir de Mardi Gras,* 53;
Mardi Gras Indians, 66, 68, 105–6
Marquette, Jacques, 19
Marretta, Sam, 60
Martin, Carol. *See* Fran, Carol
Matherne, Durel, 231
Mauthe, Jamie, 134
Mauthe, Kenny, 134
McCain, John, 151
McClain, Scotty, 231
McClendon, Charles, 231
McCracken, James, 214
McCracken, William, 214
McCrady, John, 222
McKeithen, John, 230
Meeker, Joseph Rusling, 219
Melungeons, 48, 70n4
Meters, the, 167–68

Meucci, Antonio, 212
Meucci, Nina, 212
Mexicans, 10
Michot, Louis, 160
Miller, J. D., 163, 166
Miller Memorial Library, 200
Millet, Clarence, 221
Minden, La., 184
Minden Lumber Company, 198
Mississippi Embayment, 3
Mississippi River, 2, 18, 57; flooding of,
28–29; "German coast" of, 9; loess
landscapes of, 4
Modern Baptists (Wilcox), 117–18
Moissenet, Felix, 218
Molinary, Andres, 218, 219
Monroe, James, 23
Monroe, La., 43
Montel, Sam, 174
Moore, James. *See* Slim Harpo (James
Moore)
Morgan, Gertrude, 164–65, 222
Morgan City, La., 50, 52
Moviegoer, The (Percy), 108–9
Mr. Quintron, 165–66
Mugnier, George François, 218
Müller, Robby, 175
Murrell, John, 46
music, 37, 158–75; blues, 59; brass bands,
59–60; Cajun music, 53, 89, 93, 94,
176; *chansons de mardi Gras,* 53; coun-
try music, 44; jazz, 37, 54, 60, 66, 158;
lining-out songs, 43; Mississippi Delta
blues, 44; musical genres in Acadiana,
53–54; narrative songs (*décimas*), 52,
97; rock and roll, 44; rockabilly, 44;
sacred harp tradition, 43; secular music, 43; songs of Mardi Gras Indians,
105–6; zydeco, 27, 53, 159, 160, 162–63,
176. *See also under* African Americans
Muskogean tribe, 56
Muslims, 73